MAKING THE MOST
OF *MICROSOFT OFFICE*

Making the Most of *Microsoft Office*

SHARON YODER
University of Oregon

IRENE SMITH
University of Oregon

PEARSON

Boston ■ New York ■ San Francisco
Mexico City ■ Montreal ■ Toronto ■ London ■ Madrid ■ Munich ■ Paris
Hong Kong ■ Singapore ■ Tokyo ■ Cape Town ■ Sydney

Series Editor: Arnis E. Burvikovs
Editorial Assistant: Christine Lyons
Marketing Manager: Tara Whorf
Editorial-Production Service: Omegatype Typography, Inc.
Manufacturing Buyer: Andrew Turso
Composition and Prepress Buyer: Linda Cox
Cover Administrator: Kristina Mose-Libon
Electronic Composition: Omegatype Typography, Inc.

For related titles and support materials, visit our online catalog at www.ablongman.com.

Between the time Website information is gathered and published, some sites may have closed. Also, the transcription of URLs can result in typographical errors. The publisher would appreciate notification where these errors occur so that they may be corrected in subsequent editions.

Many of the designations used by manufacturers and sellers to distinguish their products are claimed as trademarks. Where those designations appear in this book, and Allyn and Bacon was aware of a trademark claim, the designations have been printed in initial or all caps.

Library of Congress Cataloging-in-Publication Data

Yoder, Sharon.
    Making the most of Microsoft Office / Sharon Yoder, Irene Smith.
       p.   cm.
    Includes index.
    ISBN 0-205-37601-0
    1. Microsoft Office.   2. Business—Computer programs.   I. Smith, Irene Elizabeth.   II. Title.

    HF5548.4.M525 Y63 2003
    005.369—dc21

                                                                    2002038321

Printed in the United States of America

10   9   8   7   6   5   4   3   2   1   08   07   06   05   04   03

To our "610" students whom we shall miss:

> *For their tolerance of draft copies of this book,*

> *For their feedback on the contents, and*

> *For their many questions that enriched the content of this book.*

CONTENTS

PREFACE

This book is designed to help you become a productive user of *Microsoft Office. Office* is a collection of software tools that allows you to do word processing, use simple graphics, create databases, design spreadsheets, and create presentations. The collection of software tools is designed to help you solve problems, accomplish both simple and complex tasks, and increase your personal productivity.

There are many versions of *Office*—some that run under the *Windows* operating system and some that run on the Macintosh—and each newer version of *Office* adds more features. However, many of the features of the software are the same in each and every version. This book focuses on the *Office 2000* software that runs on machines that use *Windows.* And, despite the focus on the *Windows* version, most of the information contained in this book also applies to the Macintosh versions.

Despite our focus on *Office 2000,* much of what is included in this book will even be useful to those who are using some other version of the *Microsoft Office* software. *Office* has emerged as a collection of software including *Microsoft Office, Microsoft Excel, Microsoft PowerPoint,* and most recently *Microsoft Access. Microsoft Access* is a database program included with the *Windows*-based version and does not appear in any Macintosh version of *Office.* The Macintosh version presently includes *Entourage,* a telecommunications application, which will not be covered in this book. It is impossible for one book to cover every feature of *Office.* This book attempts to help you develop the basic skills so that you can continue to learn as you make use of the power of *Office.*

WHAT YOU SHOULD KNOW TO BEGIN

Although you are not expected to know anything about *Office* to begin using this book, you *do* need to know how to open computer applications, open documents, and use a mouse. You should be able to use pull-down menus to make choices. That is, you need to be familiar with either the *Windows* environment on a PC or the Mac OS environment on a Macintosh. Because there is a version of *Office* that will run within Mac *OS X,* if you are using that operating system, you need to be familiar with navigating this new and somewhat different Macintosh environment.

This book also assumes that you have some familiarity with using a computer to create a text document. For example, you should understand how a word processing application could be used to create a simple document such as a letter or a memo.

If you are already past the basics of *Office,* this book includes enough information to lift your skill level even higher. As you learn about such features as stylesheets and templates, you will move beyond the level of simply entering text, pictures, and numbers. You will soon be combining the options the software provides to enhance your communication, regardless of the purpose of your document.

SOFTWARE VERSIONS

The instructions that come with your version of *Microsoft Office* explain what system requirements are needed for your computer to use *Office*. The instructions also tell you how to install the software on your computer.

One of *Office*'s strengths is that it is very similar on the two different types of computer systems. This provides flexibility in sharing files with other users. Files easily move between the Macintosh and the *Windows* operating systems. The major components for word processing, working with spreadsheets, and doing presentations are similar in interface and operation. The database application is included only in the *Windows* version, and the telecommunications package is included only in the Macintosh version.

Your computer may have a version different from *Microsoft Office 2000*, but your version will include many of the same features and you can use this book to help you master the steps we introduce. Keep in mind, however, the appearance of the screen may differ somewhat from the earlier versions, and the same feature may be located in a different menu. Even if you do not yet have *Office 2000*, this book can still provide you with the information and guidance that allows you to increase your ability to use your software effectively.

Understanding the conventions used throughout the book will help you to easily follow and understand the material. For example, when you are asked to access an item from the application menu bar, you will find both the menu name and the item name given in boldface text. The names of commercially available products appear in italics. Each chapter contains a short summary to provide you an easy way to check your understanding of the information it contained. The table of contents and index are extensive to help you quickly locate specific information or topics.

Notes about technical aspects of *Office* will be shown in a sans serif typeface and will begin with the words *Technical Note*.

Technical Note: Technical notes will be shown like this. These notes will discuss technical details of interest to more advanced users or will address potential problems that may occur when using *Office*.

This technical note style is also used to indicate specific and significant material relevant to only the Macintosh environment or to only the *Windows* environment.

In addition, you will find entries flagged with a short vertical line to the left. These entries represent important ideas to keep in mind as you develop your skills. The entries might ask you to recall a previously introduced concept or help you isolate a special concept that you need to keep in mind as you work.

This style of text will indicate a rule or special guideline that you should remember to apply as you move toward word processing and ensuring that your documents are created to optimize communication with your readers.

Microsoft Office looks much the same on the Macintosh as it does in *Windows.* However, any significant difference between version *2000* for *Windows* and other recent versions of *Office* will be noted in the text and illustrated with a screen shot where appropriate. Your mastery of one version will easily allow you to be productive if you are required to work on a different platform.

WHAT VERSION OF *OFFICE* DO I HAVE?

Remember, this book is primarily based on version *Office 2000* for *Windows.* However, you can apply much of the information to all versions of the software. Before you proceed, it is important to determine which version is on your machine so that you will be prepared to look for similarities and differences.

If you are a *Windows* user, the version number appears on the screen when you open the software. You can also see this screen by choosing **About** from the **Help** menu.

If you are running *Office* on a Macintosh operation system older than *OS X,* the version number appears on the screen when you open the software. If you have the application open, you can also go to the **Apple Menu** and choose **About.** Information about the *Office* application appears. If you are using Macintosh *Office* in *OS X,* you can choose **About** from the menu to the right of the Apple menu.

WHO SHOULD USE THIS BOOK?

The book is designed for anyone who wants to use a computer to increase personal productivity. In addition to learning how to use the variety of tools and applications in *Office,* we hope readers will increase their overall computer skills and improve their understanding of how to create documents that effectively communicate to their readers. Included in the text is information that applies to almost any computer application as well as suggestions for producing well-designed documents.

The material covered in this book is of value to students as well as their teachers. It will be useful to those who use the computer at school, at home, or in the office. This book encourages you to go beyond the "get the job done however you can" approach to "use the software to efficiently get the job done." Once you have skills in using the powerful features that are included in the software, you will save both time and energy. Although you will need time to replace old habits with new ones, you will soon find yourself saving time and energy and producing quality documents that more effectively meet your needs.

The style of the book encourages experimentation and exploration. Many books that teach about software are based on one or more projects that readers complete while working through the book. In this book, chapters are largely independent of each other. Readers are encouraged to apply the concepts and skills to personal or professional work. Think in terms of the tasks you already do and use this information to help you develop new and better ways to complete your work.

Microsoft Office is a collection of well-established and powerful computer applications. This book covers the word processing and drawing features of *Word,* the presentation possibilities of *PowerPoint,* the spreadsheet tools of *Excel,* and the database options of *Access.* Although *Access* is discussed only for users working within the *Windows* operating system, Macintosh users could easily adapt the concepts in the database chapters to the database application of their choice. Not every feature of each environment is included in detail. However, at the completion of this book, you will have made progress toward becoming a power user of computer technology and will be ready to pursue further exploration on your own with complete comfort and confidence.

At the end of each chapter, a summary reinforces the new concepts presented in the chapter. In addition, some tips and extensions may be included to help you to move beyond the basics given in the chapter. The summary is helpful in doing a quick review of what you have learned or for reminding yourself of a particular concept.

NATIONAL EDUCATIONAL TECHNOLOGY STANDARDS

There are emerging standards in technology for both students and teachers. The student standards are organized into several age-appropriate sets. The teacher standards are written into groupings that provide some direction to teacher preparation programs and staff development for teachers already in classrooms.

The technology standards for students are presented in six broad categories.

1. Basic operations and concepts
2. Social, ethical, and human issues
3. Technology productivity tools
4. Teaching communications tools
5. Technology research tools
6. Technology problem-solving and decision-making tools

Within these broad categories, the National Educational Technology Standards (NETS) define performance indicators for determining student competency levels. These indicators occur at four specific grade ranges—PreK–2, 3–5, 6–8, and 9–12. A complete discussion of these standards can be located at the International Society for Technology in Education (ISTE) Web site, www.iste.org.

The NETS for teachers were developed by ISTE primarily to guide the decisions being made in teacher preparation curriculum but are also applicable to teachers in the field. The standards for teachers include six broad categories.

1. Technology operations and concepts
2. Planning and designing learning environments and experiences
3. Teaching, learning, and curriculum
4. Assessment and evaluation
5. Productivity and professional practice
6. Social, ethical, legal, and human issues

The specifics used to evaluate progression in each area are presented in detail at www.iste.org.

This book will allow you to gain mastery of skills required to meet many of these standards. Students working through the examples and following the instructions will find it a great way to build competency in using technology. Teachers can follow the examples and know that they are mastering skills and concepts at their required level. In addition, teachers will gain skills enabling them to model correct technology usage and to prepare students more effectively.

HOW TO USE THIS BOOK

Perhaps the best way to use this book is to work through it from beginning to end. However, if you are an experienced computer user, you may simply need to skim each chapter, paying special attention to features unique to this version of *Office*.

If you have only limited experience with integrated packages but are quite experienced in using your computer, you can skim the first chapter and be successful in working through the other chapters in any order you wish.

Remember that you will be learning to word process—leaving your typing habits behind. You will learn (1) to publish your documents rather than just enter text and (2) when and how to use a database or spreadsheet. In other words, you will gain the skills and confidence to approach many tasks made easier with your computer tools.

As you will likely notice, there are several formatting conventions discussed that are not adhered to in this text. When this occurs, a navigational icon like the one here appears in the margin. This signals you to check out the Appendix on p. 243 so you can see examples of the formatting used in a perfectly prepared document.

Good luck and enjoy your exploration of the power provided by *Office*.

ABOUT THE AUTHORS

Dr. Sharon Yoder has taught mathematics and computer science at the junior high and high school level for fifteen years. Her most recent public school experience was as a secondary computer science teacher and computer coordinator involved in developing system-wide computer curriculum and planning teacher in-service training.

In addition, she has taught mathematics, computer science, and computer education at a number of universities in northeastern Ohio, including Kent State University, the University of Akron, and Cleveland State University. After a year as an education specialist for Logo Computer Systems, Inc., she returned to teaching. For the last fifteen years, Sharon has taught a variety of computer education courses at the University of Oregon. At present, she focuses her time on teaching technology courses for the Technology Specialization of the Elementary Education Program at the University of Oregon.

Dr. Yoder is a frequent presenter and conductor of technology workshops at regional and national technology-in-education conferences. She has been involved in a number of book publishing projects, including a number of books about using *MicroWorlds* and *MicroWorlds Pro*. She has also written books about *HyperStudio* and *Grade Machine* (from Misty City) as well as a number of books on desktop publishing and hypermedia design.

Dr. Irene Smith has been a high school and junior high educator for twenty years. She has taught academic mathematics programs, coached a number of varsity sports, and served as a counselor in the public school system in British Columbia. After earning her Ph.D. from the University of Oregon, she spent six years working with the International Society for Technology in Education's (ISTE) Intel project *The Journey Inside: The Computer*. She conducted training workshops, developed training material, and edited *The Journey Inside* newsletter. She was also a consultant and instructor for ISTE's distance education program.

Dr. Smith is a frequent presenter and conductor of technology workshops at regional and national technology-in-education conferences. She is also involved in a number of publishing projects including *Getting Started with HyperStudio, Learning Stagecast Creator, The Beginner's Guide to Grade Machine,* and others.

Currently Dr. Smith teaches technology courses at the University of Oregon in the fifth-year technology specialization for students receiving their master's degree in elementary education.

CHAPTER ONE

Word Processing: Getting Started with *Microsoft Office*

Microsoft Office is a collection of well-established and powerful computer applications. In this chapter you will begin to examine word processing in *Word*. Please note that word processing involves a great deal more than simply entering text into a document. Beginners will want to work step-by-step through the various examples. Those experienced with word processing should at least skim the chapter and read the summaries.

As you work through the concepts presented in the next sections, keep in mind that these skills will allow you to meet many of the National Educational Technology Standards (NETS) for Students and Teachers. The preface provided a brief introduction to both sets of standards and complete details can be found at www.iste.org.

WINDOWS USERS

Depending on how you have your computer set up, *Microsoft Word* will most likely appear in the **Start** menu under **Programs.** [Figure 1.1]

FIGURE 1.1

If you are unable to see *Microsoft Word* on the **Start** menu, you can use **Search** from the **Start** menu to locate it. However, if the programs that are included in *Office* are missing from the Start menu, it is best to reinstall it just in case the installation is incomplete.

And Then You See . . .

You briefly see a splash screen that identifies the version of *Microsoft Word* you are using. Then a new, blank word processing document appears. [Figure 1.2]

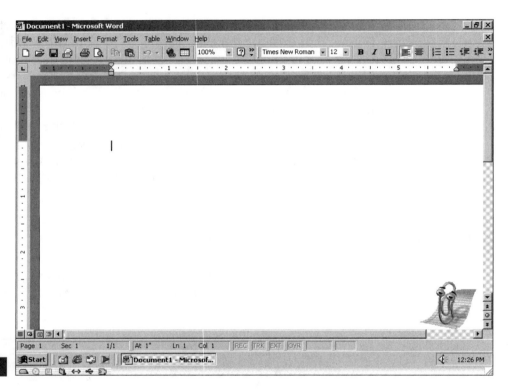

FIGURE 1.2

You can also choose **New** from the **File** menu and select **Word Processing** from the drop-down menu that appears.

Technical Note: In some versions of *Word* you see a window labeled Project Gallery. This window lets you choose from various types of documents, including a new blank document.

MACINTOSH USERS

Your first task is to locate and open the *Microsoft Word* application. Open the hard drive of your computer and locate the folder labeled *Microsoft Office*—most likely found in the Applications folder. Most versions of *Office* have a number at the end of the folder name. So, you might see *Microsoft Office 98* or *Microsoft Office 2001*.

Double-click on the folder to open it. You see a list of applications and other folders. For example, *Office 2001* looks like Figure 1.3.

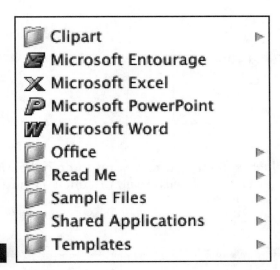

FIGURE 1.3

If necessary, you can use the **Find** feature found in the **File** menu of your Macintosh.

Macintosh Users—*OS X*

If you are using Macintosh *OS X* or above, a display like that shown in Figure 1.4 will appear. Notice that the appearance of menus and screens is somewhat different. To open *Microsoft Office*, locate Office in the Applications folder. Double-click to open it.

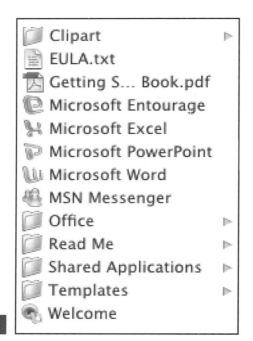

FIGURE 1.4

While the *Office* folder is open, you may want to drag the *Microsoft Word* application icon to the Dock so it will be easy to launch the next time you use the computer. [Figure 1.5]

FIGURE 1.5

Once you launch the *Word* application, you will have a new document window open, ready for you to begin working.

THE OFFICE ASSISTANT

You may also see a small character on your screen. For example, you might see a smiling paperclip on your *Windows* screen or a little computer on your Macintosh screen. [Figure 1.6]

FIGURE 1.6

These icons provide access to immediate help if you are having problems. However, some people find them annoying. You can make them disappear by going to the **Help** menu and choosing **Hide the Office Assistant.**

THE WORLD OF *WORD*

Take a few minutes to examine your computer screen carefully. At the top of the document, you see the document name. Below the document name are the menus used in *Word*, and below the menus are the Toolbars. The Toolbars visible can be changed by going to the **View** menu and choosing **Toolbars.** There are also rulers at the top and left side of the document. [Figure 1.7]

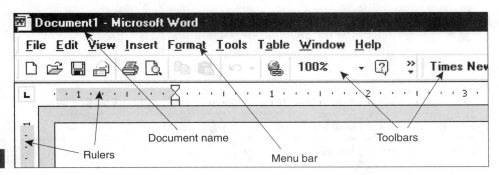

FIGURE 1.7

If you are using a Macintosh version of *Word,* the document name appears just above the top ruler.

At the bottom of the screen, you see the Office Assistant and the ruler. At the bottom of the page is the Status bar. The Status bar gives you information about your document, helping you determine the cursor location within the document. [Figure 1.8]

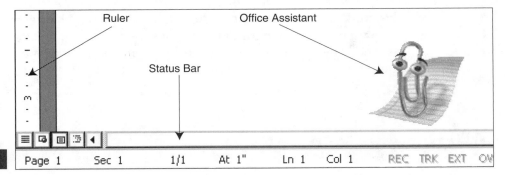

FIGURE 1.8

Technical Note: The amount of the document and number of buttons at the top that you see depend on the size of the screen you are using. If part of the document is cut off, use the scroll bars at the bottom and the side of the document to change the displayed portion of the document. Also, because the items that appear can be customized by the user, you may see slightly different options.

Before you begin to enter text, note that there is a small vertical line, called the *insertion point,* at the top left corner of the work area. The insertion point indicates where text will be entered when you begin to use your keyboard. Note that this insertion point is about one inch from the side and the top of the document. This is because your new document most likely has margins set at 1 inch.

Next, enter a few words. You may notice small, light dots between the words you have entered. If you do not see these small dots, go to the **Tools** menu and choose **Options.** Click on the View tab. In the section labeled Formatting marks, check the All box.

If you are using Macintosh, your choice is slightly different. If you are using *OS X* or above, choose **Preferences** from the **Word** menu. If your Macintosh operating system is any other version, move to the **Edit** menu and select **Preferences.** In the dialog box that appears, select the View tab, and in the section for nonprinting characters, select All. [Figure 1.9]

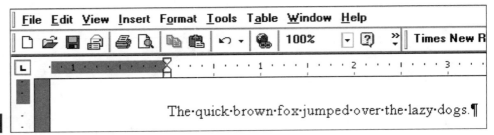

FIGURE 1.9

The small dots you see are not periods. They are symbols that represent spaces. These marks are placed there when you press the spacebar. You also see a paragraph marker (¶) at the end of the text. Each time you press Enter (or Return on a Macintosh), the paragraph marker appears indicating that you are starting a new paragraph.

If you have never done word processing with these normally invisible keystrokes showing, you may find them distracting. However, you will soon find them invaluable for determining whether your file is formatted as you intend. The Show/Hide ¶ button found in the toolbar lets you turn these marks on and off easily. [Figure 1.10]

FIGURE 1.10

If you do not see this icon on your toolbar, first go to the **View** menu and select **Toolbars.** Be sure the Standard toolbar is checked. If you still do not see the button, click on the arrows at the end of the Standard toolbar. [Figure 1.11]

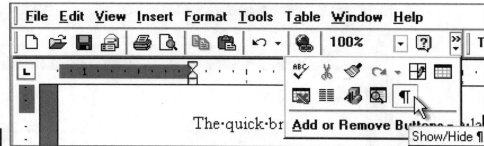

FIGURE 1.11

It is possible that your software has been customized and someone has removed this button. Check your Help feature if you want to reset the button to appear on the Standard toolbar.

The examples in this book will generally be shown with these formatting marks showing. Remember, if you want *Word* to open with these marks showing, check the All box in the View tab of the **Options** choice on the **Tools** menu. [Figure 1.12]

Formatting marks

☐ <u>T</u>ab characters   ☐ Hi<u>d</u>den text
☐ <u>S</u>paces   ☐ Optional h<u>y</u>phens
☐ Paragraph m<u>a</u>rks   ☑ A<u>l</u>l

FIGURE 1.12

On the Macintosh, the **View** choice is found under the **Preferences** menu and instead of Formatting marks, the section is called Nonprinting characters.

These settings will now automatically be on whenever you create a new document. This feature can still be toggled on and off as you work by using the Show/Hide ¶ button on the toolbar.

WORKING WITH TEXT

Now that you have opened *Microsoft Word,* created a word processing document, and examined the screen, you are ready to explore word processing in more detail.

Entering Text

To begin to explore word processing, you need to enter some text. The content of the text you enter is unimportant. You are simply going to learn to manipulate that text in various ways.

Enter at least two paragraphs of text. Use enough sentences in your paragraph to make use of your word processor's ability to automatically move text to the next line when needed. This feature is called *word wrap.* [Figure 1.13]

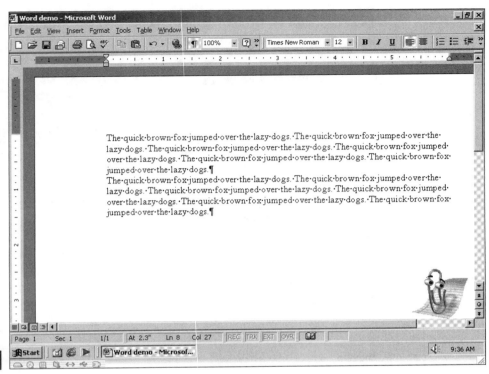

FIGURE 1.13

Even if you have never used a typewriter, you may have been taught "typewriter rules" for entering text. The guidelines for using a typewriter are embedded deeply in our educational system, but the word processor is far more powerful than a typewriter. In progressing through this chapter, you will learn to use "word processor rules" to enter text.

Notice how the words wrap to the next line when you create a paragraph. Historically, a typewriter was not able to automatically wrap the text to begin the next line. So, simply enter the sentences you want in one paragraph and use the Return or Enter key *only* when you want to start a new paragraph. This is the *first word processing rule* you must learn.

> *When using a computer, pressing Enter (PC) or Return (Macintosh) creates a new paragraph.*

Note that this means that your word processor considers just a few words on a line—such as a title—to be a paragraph.

The *second rule* you need to remember is

> *Put only one space after punctuation before you begin a new sentence.*

Yes, your typing teacher taught you to put two spaces after the punctuation mark. But you are now using a word processor, not a typewriter. The word processor recognizes that you have entered punctuation marks followed by a space. It then automatically puts slightly more than one space into the text. If you use two space characters, your word processor places almost three space characters between your sentences, resulting in a text appearance that is difficult to read.

Modifying Text

One of the advantages of using a word processor instead of a typewriter or pencil and paper is the ease of inserting additional text, deleting text, and changing text. In this section, you will examine ways *Word* helps you revise the text you have written.

- **To insert text.** Use the mouse to place the I-beam pointer where you want the new text to appear, click your mouse button, and begin entering text where the insertion point appears. [Figure 1.14]

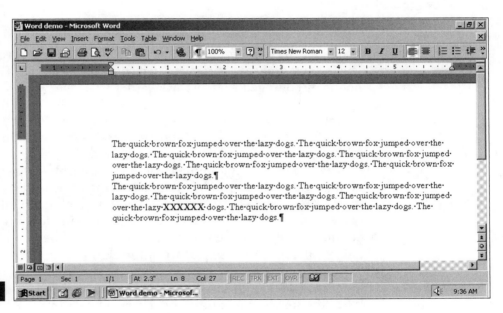

FIGURE 1.14

- **To enter a new paragraph.** Use the mouse to place the I-beam pointer and click to place the insertion point after the last word in the previous paragraph. Press Return or Enter and begin entering text in your new paragraph. If you need to create two paragraphs from text that is already in the document as a single paragraph, place the insertion point where you want to split the text and press Return or Enter.
- **To delete text.** Place the I-beam pointer after the characters you want to delete and click the mouse to display the insertion point. Press the Delete key on the Macintosh or the Backspace key on the PC until the characters are removed.
- **To duplicate text.** To duplicate text that you have already entered, select the text by positioning the I-beam pointer at the beginning of the text you want to duplicate. Click the mouse button and hold it down. Drag

the mouse until the desired text is highlighted. Release the mouse button. This is called *click and drag.* [Figure 1.15]

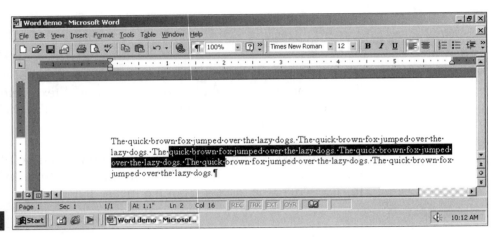

FIGURE 1.15

The block of color around the text indicates that it is selected. Learning to click and drag takes practice, so if you have never done this before, do not be discouraged if it feels awkward.

Once the text is selected, choose **Copy** from the **Edit** menu. This moves a *copy* of your text to a location in the memory of your computer called the *Clipboard.* The Clipboard contains the last item copied or cut from the document as you continue working.

Place the I-beam pointer where you want the copy of your text to appear and click to show the insertion point. Choose **Paste** from the **Edit** menu. These steps result in a document that contains the chosen text twice—once in the original position and once in the pasted position.

- **To move text.** To move text from one place in the document to a different position, choose **Cut** from the **Edit** menu. Using **Cut** removes the text from the original position. At this moment, the text is no longer in the document. Instead, it is held on the Clipboard. After you **Paste** the text into position, the text reappears in the document but is now where you chose to paste it. The copy you placed on the Clipboard remains there until you **Copy** or **Cut** again or until you close the *Word* application.

It is easy to make mistakes when using **Cut, Copy,** and **Paste.** Take a look at the **Edit** menu after you have done a **Cut.** You see that there is an **Undo** choice at the top of the menu. Choosing this option immediately lets you step back to where you were before the last action was taken. Try it!

Shortcut keystrokes for many *Word* menu choices are found on the right-hand side of the pull-down menus. **Cut, Copy, Paste,** and **Undo** are used often enough that you will probably want to memorize the keystroke shortcuts for the commands. The menu on the left is from the PC version of *Word.* The menu on the right is from the Macintosh *OS X* version of *Word.* [Figure 1.16]

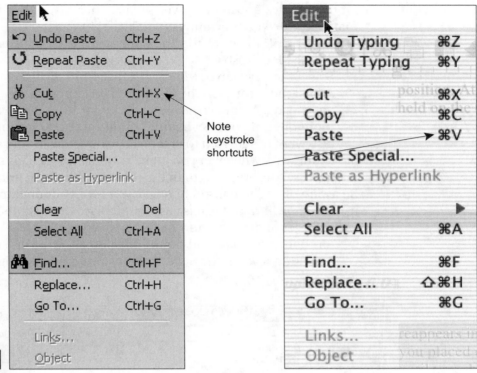

FIGURE 1.16

Saving Your Work

Saving your work regularly and in an organized manner is important. In *Word* you save by choosing **Save As** or **Save** from the **File** menu. If you do not save regularly, you can easily lose a lot of work if there is a power failure, something goes wrong with your computer, or you make a serious error. It is important to develop good habits for saving your work regardless of the software you are using.

Saving Guidelines.   Here is a list of *very important* rules to follow to protect you from losing work. Mark this page in your book so that you can constantly remind yourself of these rules. Better yet, make a copy of these guidelines and put them next to your computer.

- Use **Save As** if you want to *change the name* of the document or if you want to *specify where* the document will be saved. Otherwise, use **Save** to update the version of the document that you have previously saved.
- Be sure to use *meaningful names* for your documents. Carefully named documents make your work easier to locate. Good naming also avoids having to open a document to see what is in it.
- If possible, use only letters and numbers in the names of your documents (except for extensions that begin with a period, such as ".doc" for *Word*).

- *Word* provides an **AutoRecover** feature that saves your changes automatically into your currently open file.
    1. Select **Options** from the **Tools** menu on the PC; select **Preferences** on the Macintosh.
    2. Select the **Save** tab or the **Save** choice from the list.
    3. Adjust the settings in the dialog box that appears.
    4. Set to save AutoRecover information at least every ten minutes—more often if your keyboarding skills are still developing. You may also want to set *Word* to create a backup copy of your work.
- Save your work whenever you make *major changes*. This may make saving necessary more often than the recommended ten minutes.
- Be aware of and in control of *where you save* your document. If you are using a large hard drive, it is easy to misplace documents. Pay attention to the folder or directory in which you save your work.

    In both *Windows* and on the Macintosh, you can see the path to your document when the **Save As** dialog box appears. [Figure 1.17]

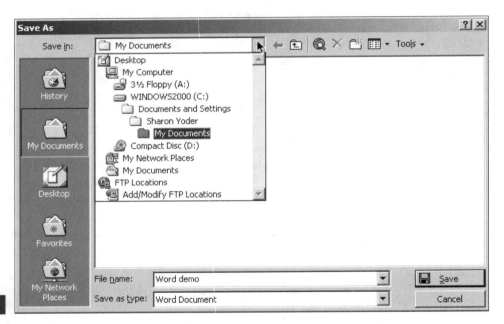

FIGURE 1.17

- Make sure you use *incremental saving* all the time. This technique is discussed in the next section.

Now, cover up the preceding list and see if these keywords remind you of the guidelines that you should follow when saving:

- **Save** versus **Save As**
- Meaningful names
- Letters and numbers
- Ten minutes
- Major changes

- Save where
- Incremental saving

Incremental Saving—A "Lifesaving" Technique.   When creating and modifying documents on a computer, most people resave their document using the same name—over and over and over. This means you are continually adding to or changing the same file. This is a dangerous practice. If a disk fails, if the computer "crashes" during a save, or if your file gets corrupted for some other reason, the problem is more than just a loss of your recent changes. It is possible to lose your entire document.

Leaving yourself vulnerable to disaster is easily avoided by using *incremental saving*. Incremental saving simply means changing the name of your document each time you make a major change. This name change ensures that you are creating a completely new file each time you do a major save of your work. [Figure 1.18]

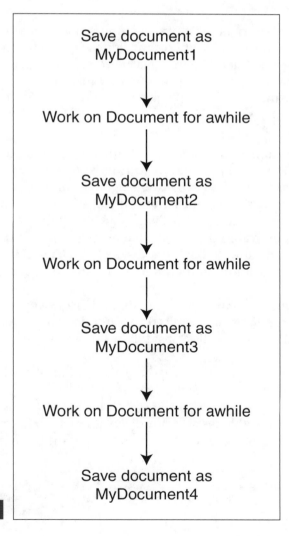

FIGURE 1.18

Possible naming schemes might be:

Sample11, Sample12, Sample13, Sample14
Sample1a, Sample1b, Sample1c, Sample1d
Sample4–15–1, Sample4–15–2, Sample4–16–3, Sample4–16–4
SampleA, SampleB, SampleC, SampleD

Notice that the naming scheme is based on a minor element that changes rather than a major name change. You should be able to easily recognize the order of your saves and be able to tell which version is the newest merely by looking at the name. Whatever system you choose, use it consistently and frequently.

Incremental saving is intended to make your life easier. When you use incremental saving, if you cannot open your most recent document, then you can step back one copy. You may lose your latest modifications, but at least you avoid the greater disaster of losing *all* of your work.

Of course as you work, you can throw away the oldest versions of your document. Make sure, however, that you keep at least three or four versions at any one time.

Saving seems so trivial to many beginners that it is often overlooked. However, it is one of the most important things you do when using a computer. Developing good habits now will save you hours and hours of work in the future. No matter how experienced computer users are, everyone loses documents from time to time. Having an earlier version for reference is essential.

Creating Backup Copies.   When you are finished working for the day, it is important to create backup copies of your most recent two or three incremental saves. Make a *backup copy* by saving a second copy of the file to a totally new storage location. For example, if you are working on a hard drive, also save your work on a removable disk—such as a floppy or Zip disk. If you are saving to a removable disk, consider putting your work on a second one—just in case. Be sure to label the disks clearly. If you have access to a server or a storage location on the Internet, be sure that you save a copy of your work there.

Creating a single backup copy is not difficult. However, making a second copy to a removable disk can be a bit tricky. How do you create a copy of your work on a second removable disk? Just follow these steps:

1. Save your document on the hard drive of the computer on which you are working. (Pay attention to where you save it.)
2. Close *Word*.
3. Insert your removable disk (floppy disk, SuperDisk, Zip disk, etc.).
4. Locate the icon representing your document on the hard drive. [Figure 1.19]

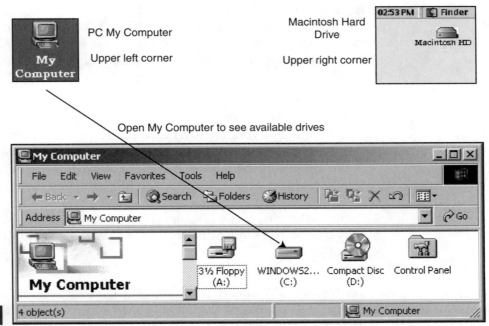

PC My Computer

Upper left corner

Macintosh Hard Drive

Upper right corner

Open My Computer to see available drives

FIGURE 1.19

Note that if you are using Macintosh *OS X*, the icon for the hard drive looks different but is in the same location.

5. Double-click on the hard drive icon to open the hard drive. Locate your saved document.
6. Click and drag your document icon to your removable disk.
7. After the copying is complete, eject your removable disk.
8. Repeat steps 3 through 6 to create a second backup copy.
9. If you are not using your own machine, it is good manners to put your original document in the Recycle Bin (*Windows*) or Trash (Macintosh) and then empty the Trash/Recycle Bin to remove your documents from the computer. [Figure 1.20]

FIGURE 1.20

If you are using *OS X* on the Macintosh, then the Trash is on the Dock, usually at the bottom of the screen.

Moving Files among Machines.   In today's rapidly changing world of technology, users often exchange files with others. The *Word* application is almost identical on the *Windows*-based and Macintosh computers. Any file created on one platform can be easily moved to the other. Here are the steps you need:

Windows *to Macintosh*

1. Create and save your file to a PC-formatted disk as you always do.
2. Move to the Macintosh (or give the disk to the person using the Macintosh) and insert the PC disk containing the file into the Macintosh. (All modern Macintosh computers read PC-formatted disks.)
3. Open *Word.*
4. Choose **Open** from the **File** menu.
5. Navigate to the floppy disk and select the file you want. Voilà! You are ready to work.

Macintosh to Windows

1. Insert a PC-formatted disk into your Macintosh. (PCs do not generally read Macintosh disks.)
2. Save your document as usual, but be sure the name has the ".doc" extension on the end of the name you have chosen, for example, Sample.doc. (The .doc is the way *Windows* recognizes *Word* files.) To be safe, limit the name of the file to eight characters.
3. Take your disk to a PC (or give the disk to the person using the PC) and insert it. Then open *Word.*
4. Choose **Open** from the **File** menu.
5. Navigate to the floppy disk and select the file you want. Voilà! You are ready to work.

Macintosh users: You can save yourself some time by routinely adding the ".doc" extension to your files. If you are using *Office 2001* or *Office X,* there is a checkbox in the **Save As** dialog box that will cause the extension to be added automatically.

The other convenient method for moving files from one computer to another is using a *server.* A server is simply a computer to which many people can connect. If you are exchanging files using a server, it is best to use extremely short and simple names. Some server software has limitations requiring you to follow special conventions.

- Use only eight characters for the name.
- Use only letters and numbers in the name.
- Do not put spaces in the name.
- Macintosh users need to add the appropriate extension to the name (.doc for *Word*) if your software does not do it automatically.

Make using these naming conventions a habit. This will save you and the people sharing your documents a lot of frustration and time.

It may seem as though the steps covered regarding incremental saving, creating a backup, and naming conventions are basic and obvious. However, making it a habit to use these steps will ensure your work is always kept organized and without error. Viewed from the perspective of the National Educational Technology Standards (NETS) for Students and those for Teachers, these steps will help you master the correct way to increase productivity, become more proficient with correct terminology, and ensure ease in collaborating with others (see NETS at www.iste.org for details).

FORMATTING TEXT

In the first part of this chapter, you learned that one of the advantages of using a word processor to produce a text document is the ease of making changes and corrections. Another way in which using a word processor is particularly powerful is the ability to change the appearance of the text. This section covers techniques for modifying the appearance of text to create a document that communicates effectively.

Microcomputers spawned the desktop publishing industry. Now anyone can use a desktop computer to publish documents of his or her choice. Yet, the powerful computer tools we have on our desktops do not automatically create well-designed documents. Before the computer revolution of the mid-1980s, the publication of documents was in the hands of professionals who had a lot of knowledge about type, document layout and design, and color. The techniques discussed in this section will help you develop some of the skills that have historically been in the hands of professional printers and publishers for designing documents that communicate effectively.

Both students and teachers benefit from learning to create well-designed documents. The better designed a handout for a class, the more effective the lesson will be. Students who learn to create effective documents can communicate better with both their peers and their teachers.

Also, if you carefully read the NETS for Students and Teachers, you will be aware that increasing communication through the appropriate use of technology is a priority. The many features of the *Office* software allow you to produce documents that accomplish maximum communication with minimum effort. Each of the steps presented that teaches how to use the power of word processing can help you become more competent in using technology efficiently and effectively.

Setting Document Margins

There are two ways to control the margins in your document: you can change the margins in the entire document, or you can change them in a particular paragraph or paragraphs.

The document margins are defined as the areas in the document into which you cannot enter text. To change these settings, choose **Page Setup** from the **File** menu. Enter the margin settings you want to use. [Figure 1.21] (On the Macintosh, choose **Document** from the **Format** menu.)

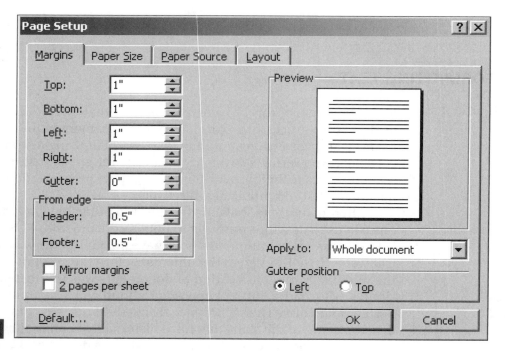

FIGURE 1.21

> *Remember—changing the numbers in the Margins setting changes the margins for the* entire *document.*

Setting Paragraph Margins

Sometimes you want different formatting for individual paragraphs in your document. For example, you might want to indent a paragraph that contains a long quotation, or you might want a poem with short lines moved toward the center of the page. Because this formatting affects only one or two paragraphs in the document, you change the paragraph margins, *not* the document margins.

For making changes at a paragraph level, you need to use the first-line indent and the left- and right-margin markers. [Figure 1.22]

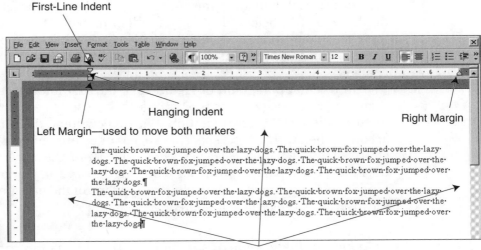

First-Line Indent

Hanging Indent

Right Margin

Left Margin—used to move both markers

Document Margins

FIGURE 1.22

Notice the white space around the text that represents the document margins set at 1 inch.

Creating a Block Indent. Next, examine the symbols that appear on the ruler. Notice that on the left end of the ruler there are more symbols than on the right end. The left- and right-margin markers control the amount that a particular paragraph is indented from the document margins.

In Figure 1.23, the first paragraph represents the standard formatting for body text in most documents and the second paragraph represents a lengthy quotation. Notice the margin settings that establish the correct formatting of the second paragraph as a quotation. The left and right margins for the paragraph are each moved in one-quarter inch from the margin line—matching exactly the indent applied to the first line in the standard body text paragraph. This left and right indent style of formatting is called a *block indent.* (The sample document on p. 243 shows an example of block indent.) [Figure 1.23]

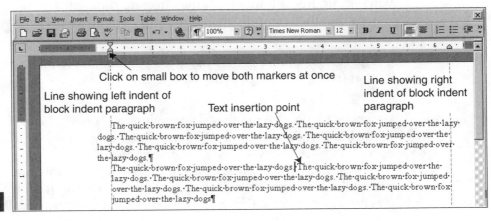

Click on small box to move both markers at once

Line showing right indent of block indent paragraph

Line showing left indent of block indent paragraph

Text insertion point

FIGURE 1.23

Be aware that to move the entire set of markers on the left, you can click on the small box below the hanging-indent marker. This holds the markers together so they move as a single unit. Also notice that to set paragraph margins, your insertion point must be placed in the paragraph you want to change.

In the first paragraph of Figure 1.23, the first line was indented more than the rest of the paragraph. This indent was used to determine the placement of the text in our quotation. With typewriters, the indent would be accomplished with several spacebar spaces or by pressing the Tab key—usually set at one-half inch. However, when using *Word*, the correct way to indent the first line of a paragraph is to use the *first-line indent* marker. Click on the top triangle and drag it to the right. The first line of the paragraph containing the insertion point is now indented.

> *To indent the first line of a paragraph, use the margin controls rather than the spacebar or Tab key.*

How far should you indent the first line of a paragraph? If you learned to indent paragraphs one-half inch, then you learned typing rules. When working on a word processor, you generally use *proportional type*. In proportional type, each letter takes up only the width that it needs—unlike older typewriters on which every letter took up the same amount of space.

How do you tell monospaced type from proportional type? Here is an easy test. [Figure 1.24]

Monospaced Type: MMMMMMMMMM
                         IIIIIIIIII

Proportional Type: MMMMMMMMMM
                         IIIIIIIIII

In monospaced type, the *M*s and *I*s take up the same amount of space, whereas in proportional type, they take up different amounts of space. This means that the amount you indent must depend on the type you are using.

> *The rule of thumb is that you should indent about two or three characters in the typeface you are using.*

For most 12-point type, this is approximately one-quarter inch. Look back at the block indent style. It is indented one-quarter inch. (The sample document on p. 243 shows a paragraph indent.)

Note that once you set up the formatting for any paragraph, the next paragraph will automatically have the same formatting style. Simply put the text insertion point at the end of the paragraph and press the Return or Enter key. Your second paragraph then has the same formatting rules applied as your first paragraph.

Creating a Hanging Indent.   You have seen that the first-line indent marker allows you to control the position of the first line of any paragraph. This first-line indent marker and the hanging-indent marker allow you to create a formatting style called a *hanging indent.* Hanging indents are used for such things as numbered and bulleted lists. To create a hanging indent, reverse the positions of the first-line indent marker and the hanging-indent marker from the preceding example. (The sample document on p. 243 shows both bulleted and numbered lists.)

See Appendix Example

> **Technical Note:**   To create bullets, using Alt + 0149 (on the numeric keypad) will create a bullet in *Windows.* Press Option + 8 on the Macintosh. Your copy of *Word* may be set to automatically add bullets to a line. In order to maintain control of your formatting, you must change several settings. Choose **Autocorrect** from the **Tools** menu. Choose both the Autoformat As You Type tab and the Autoformat tab and deselect the settings for Automatic bulleted lists.

Because the document settings determine the left edge of the document, you generally do not want to drag the first-line indent marker outside the margins. Instead, you need to first drag the hanging-indent marker to the right of the margin and then move the first-line indent marker into position if needed. [Figure 1.25]

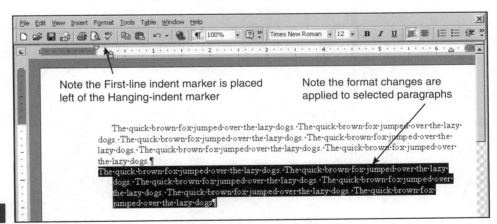

Note the First-line indent marker is placed left of the Hanging-indent marker

Note the format changes are applied to selected paragraphs

FIGURE 1.25

Here are the steps for creating a hanging indent. Notice that a hanging-indent format is used in the following list.

1. Click on the small box at the bottom of the left-margin controls, and move the entire set of symbols to the right as far as you want the lines of the paragraph *other than* the first line to begin—often that will be about one-quarter inch.

2. Click on the top triangle—the first-line indent marker—and drag it to the left. The position of the text in the selected paragraph(s) changes so that the first line of text now starts to the left of the remaining lines of text in the paragraph. Note that the hanging-indent marker indicates where all of the lines but the first one are indented.

3. After the number and period are entered, use a *Tab keystroke* before you begin to enter text. This uses the automatic tab setting that is set when the left-margin control is placed and will align the first line of text with those below.

Note that you should still use word processing rules: your first-line indent should be two or three characters to the left of the rest of the paragraph.

It is important to understand that the margins and first-line indent on the ruler apply to *paragraphs*, not documents. In making adjustments, notice that the changes are in effect for only the paragraph that contained your insertion point. Click in one of the paragraphs you have entered and then click in another. You see the margin markers move to match the formatting in the paragraph.

Automatic Bullets and Numbered Lists.   *Word* provides settings that will automatically create bulleted lists and numbered lists. When you begin to create hanging indents, you may find that your copy of *Word* is set to automatically create bulleted or numbered lists. In this book we encourage you to create your own formatting because sometimes the automatic formatting in *Word* can be hard to control. In addition, many of the built-in settings follow typing rules rather than word processing rules. At least for awhile, we suggest you turn off these settings.

Choose **AutoCorrect** from the **Tools** menu. Click on both the AutoFormat tab and the AutoFormat As You Type tab. Remove any checkmarks in the items, as shown in Figure 1.26.

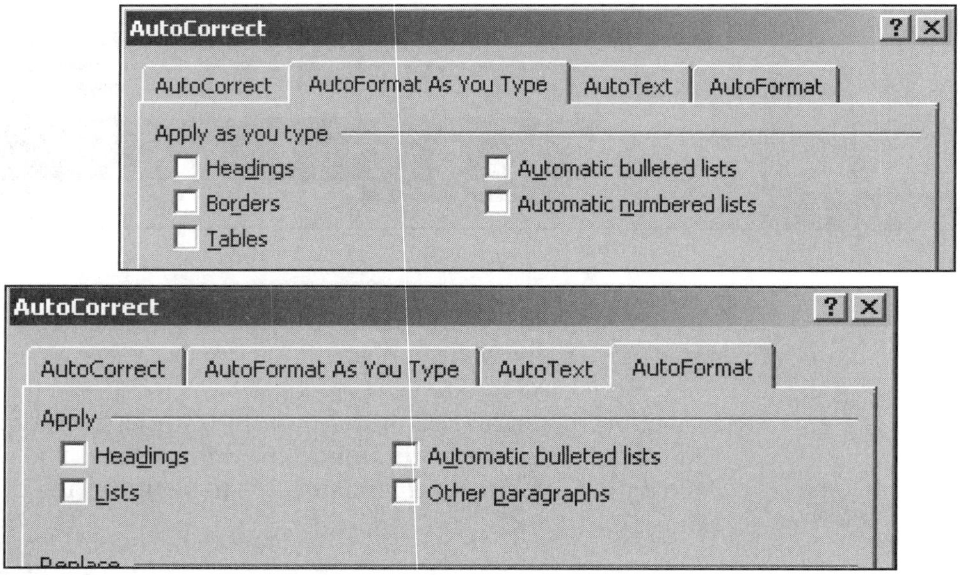

FIGURE 1.26

If you decide you want to experiment with automatic bullets or numbered lists, you can turn these settings on at a later time. In addition, you will find some options for types of automatic bullets in the Format menu.

Formatting Multiple Paragraphs.   There are various ways to change several paragraphs at one time rather than making adjustments on only one paragraph.

- Choose **Select All** from the **Edit** menu if you want to format the entire document the same way.
- Select text using the Shift-click method. Click at the beginning of the text you want to change. Hold down the Shift key. Click at the end of the text you want to change. All of the text between the two clicks is highlighted.
- Click and drag across the text you want to change.

With more than one paragraph selected, any changes you make will affect them all. In the next chapter, you will be introduced to styles—an even more powerful method of applying formatting choices.

Modifying Line Spacing and Alignment from the Ruler

In addition to changing document and paragraph margins, you can change the amount of space between the lines in a paragraph. You may see icons on the toolbar for changing the spacing. [Figure 1.27]

FIGURE 1.27

If these buttons do not appear in your version of *Word*, you can add the buttons to the toolbar. Click on the arrows at the end of the Formatting toolbar, then select Add or Remove Buttons. [Figure 1.28]

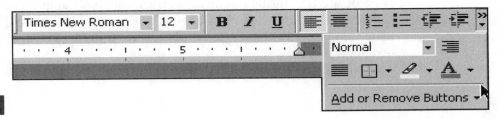

FIGURE 1.28

Finally, select the buttons you want to add. They look a bit different in the list of buttons that drops down. [Figure 1.29]

To use the line spacing feature, put your insertion point in the paragraph you want to change. Click on one of the buttons to change the line spacing. You see the line spacing change. Experiment with all of the buttons for changing the spacing.

Mostly likely you have been taught to double-space documents such as school papers. Once again, you need to update your knowledge of text formatting. No doubt you have been told to double-space papers "because they are more readable." Wrong. Research has shown that single-spacing is easier to read for comprehension and understanding. So your next word processing rule is:

Single-space your work to make it more readable.

You may also want to change the way the text is placed relative to the margins—called *alignment*. To change the alignment of the text, use the Alignment buttons on the Formatting toolbar—or on the Formatting palette if you are using a Macintosh. [Figure 1.30]

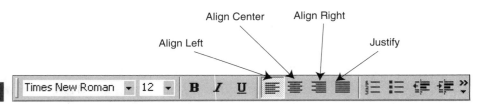

FIGURE   1.30

Left-aligned text is very reader friendly. With left-aligned text, the left edge of the text forms a straight vertical line. Left alignment is sometimes called *ragged right*—the right edge is not planned to create a straight edge. (The sample document on p. 243 shows an example of flush left, ragged right text alignment.)

Note the vertical edges of the text as shown in Figure 1.31.

Align Center   The quick brown fox jumped over the lazy dogs. The quick brown fox jumped over the lazy dogs. The quick brown fox jumped over the lazy dogs. The quick brown fox jumped over the lazy dogs.

Align Right   The quick brown fox jumped over the lazy dogs. The quick brown fox jumped over the lazy dogs. The quick brown fox jumped over the lazy dogs. The quick brown fox jumped over the lazy dogs.The quick brown fox jumped over the lazy dogs.The quick brown fox jumped over the lazy dogs.

Justify   The quick brown fox jumped over the lazy dogs. The quick brown fox jumped over the lazy dogs. The quick brown fox jumped over the lazy dogs. The quick brown fox jumped over the lazy dogs.

FIGURE 1.31

Left alignment is the most common alignment of text. Often titles are centered, but centering text is overused. Justified alignment is used in such documents as textbooks, formal legal documents, and newspapers.

Beware of using justified alignment. In Figure 1.31, the text is nicely spaced and the edges are straight. The alignment is accomplished by having the computer spread the text to completely use the line length. This forced spacing sometimes creates *white rivers* in the text, making it harder to read than other alignments. Note the extra wide space between some of the words. [Figure 1.32]

The quick brown fox jumped over the lazy dogs and ran quickly around the cranberry bush to hide. The quick brown fox jumped over the lazy dogs and ran quickly around the cranberry bush to hide. The quick brown fox jumped over the lazy dogs and ran quickly around the cranberry bush to hide. The quick brown fox

FIGURE 1.32

Thus, you have another rule of thumb to remember.

Left alignment makes your text more readable.

Be careful when you wish to use center alignment for such items as titles. If you set a first-line indent and then center text, it will be centered between the first-line indent marker and the right-margin marker rather than between the margins. [Figure 1.33]

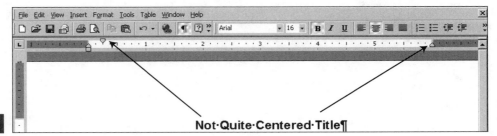

FIGURE 1.33

The first-line indent marker must be moved back to the left margin for the text to center correctly.

If you are using a newer version of *Word* on the Macintosh, these icons are found on the Formatting palette. In fact, most of the formatting that you need to do in *Word* is located in this palette on the Macintosh. Use the disclosure triangles to open the palette and display the options. [Figure 1.34]

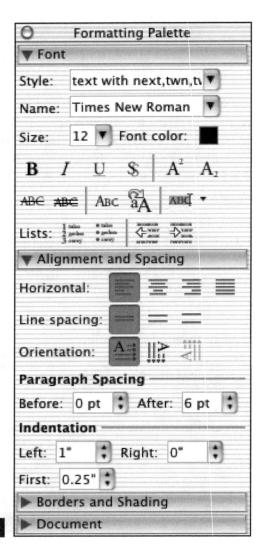

FIGURE 1.34

Other Ways to Modify Line Spacing and Alignment

Although *Word* makes it easy to change line spacing, in published documents you seldom see anything but single-spacing. Of all your options, research indicates this spacing is easiest to read. Keep in mind that the term *readability* describes text that is easily and comfortably read for comprehension. Researchers have determined that single-spacing provides the greatest readability factor for spacing between lines.

However, their research has also found that readability increases by placing a different amount of space between paragraphs than there is between the lines of text. This additional space after paragraphs is not accomplished by the traditional typing method of adding a blank line. A blank line is more space between paragraphs than is helpful to the reader. Modern word processors allow you to format text in a flexible, professional manner, producing documents that are attractive and comfortable to read.

To explore text spacing between paragraphs, choose **Paragraph** from the **Format** menu. You see a dialog box something like the one in Figure 1.35.

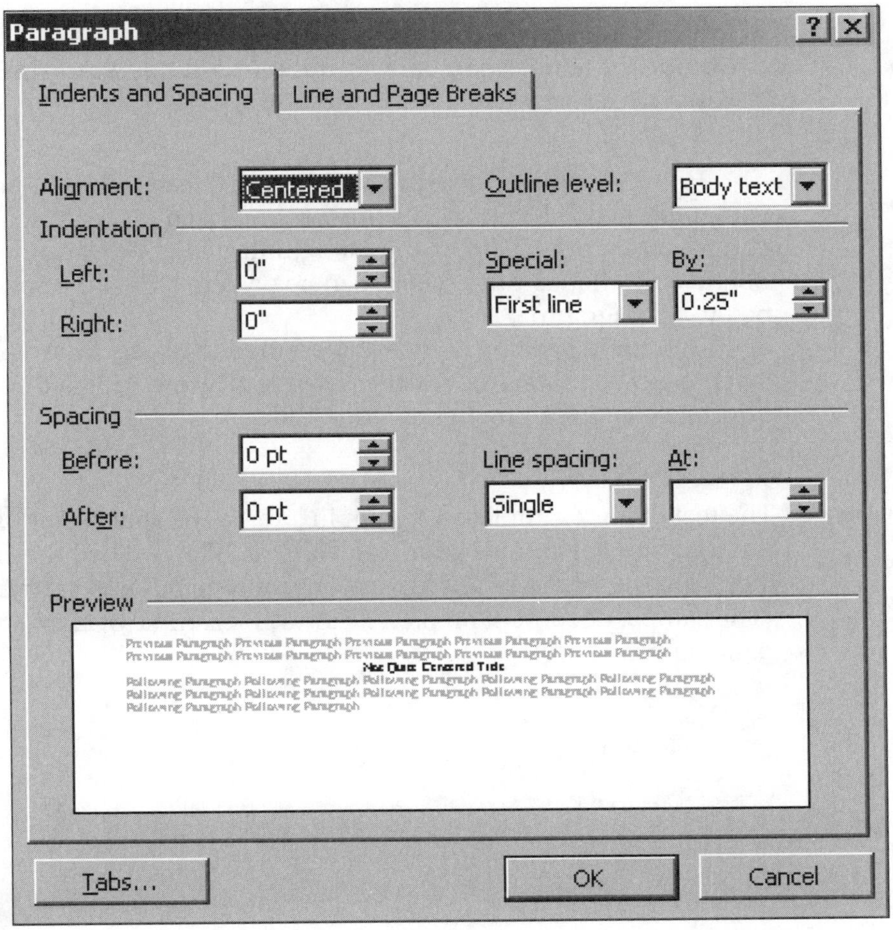

FIGURE 1.35

On newer Macintosh versions of *Word,* some of this information is also visible in the Formatting palette.

The left side of this dialog box lets you check (or set) the measurements that you are using for your left and right paragraph indents, as well as your first-line indent and hanging-indent markers. Note that the right indent and the left indent are measured from the margins; the first-line indent is measured from the left indent setting.

On the right side of the dialog box, you see the current line spacing. You can also set the line spacing from this dialog box. Thus, you can use this dialog box to set paragraph margins and line spacing instead of using the buttons on the toolbar.

When using a traditional typewriter, the only way to put more space between paragraphs than between each line of text is to press the Return key an extra time (a carriage return). This places a blank line between paragraphs. To get more space between paragraphs when using a word processor, many people use the same method—press the Return or Enter key an extra time. However, the spacing resulting from using "double Returns" does not produce very attractive text, is a waste of keystrokes, and research shows is needlessly difficult to read. Thus, you have the next word processing rule for entering text.

> *Do not space between paragraphs with double Returns/Enter keystrokes.*

How do you get the extra spacing you need between paragraphs? The Paragraph dialog box provides the tool you need to create spacing of the size you require. Look again at the Paragraph dialog box and note the Spacing Before and After settings. These can be used to adjust the spacing above and below a paragraph.

Generally, spacing of type is measured in *points.* However, you can easily change the units used for these settings by entering a different abbreviation, such as "in" for inches. [Figure 1.36]

The text in our example is 12 point in size, so the space after has been set at 6 points. For a beginner, a good guideline to follow is "half the size of the typeface." You will learn to adjust this setting for specific tasks as your skills increase. (The sample document on p. 243 shows an example of extra spacing between paragraphs.)

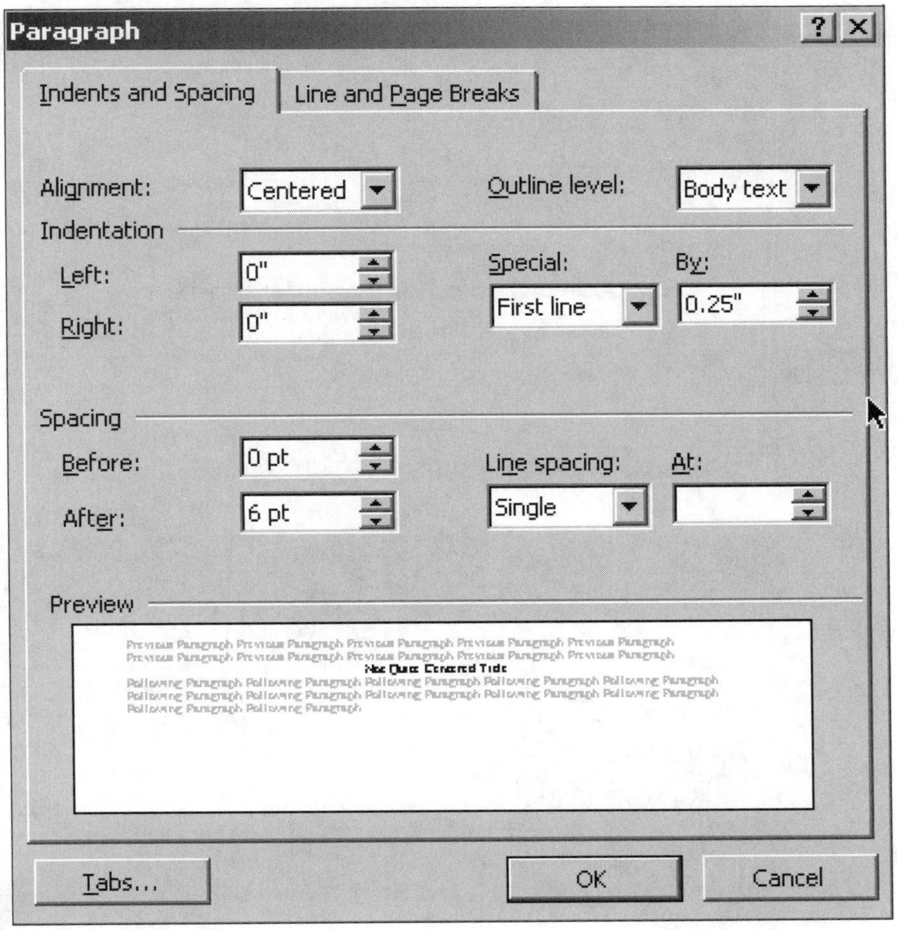

FIGURE 1.36

> *Set the spacing between paragraphs to about one-half the point size of the typeface you are using.*

You may be wondering about the *point* measurement. This is not a common measurement except when dealing with type. To translate between inches and points, there are 72 points in one inch—12-point type is one-sixth of an inch high.

When you are inserting headings or subheadings into text, using Space Before as well as Space After creates a more readable document. A heading should be close to the following paragraph, but farther from the paragraph before it. This is called the *proximity principle*—always keep physically close together items that go together logically. [Figure 1.37]

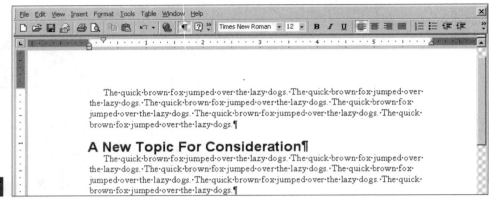

FIGURE 1.37

The heading has the settings shown in Figure 1.38.

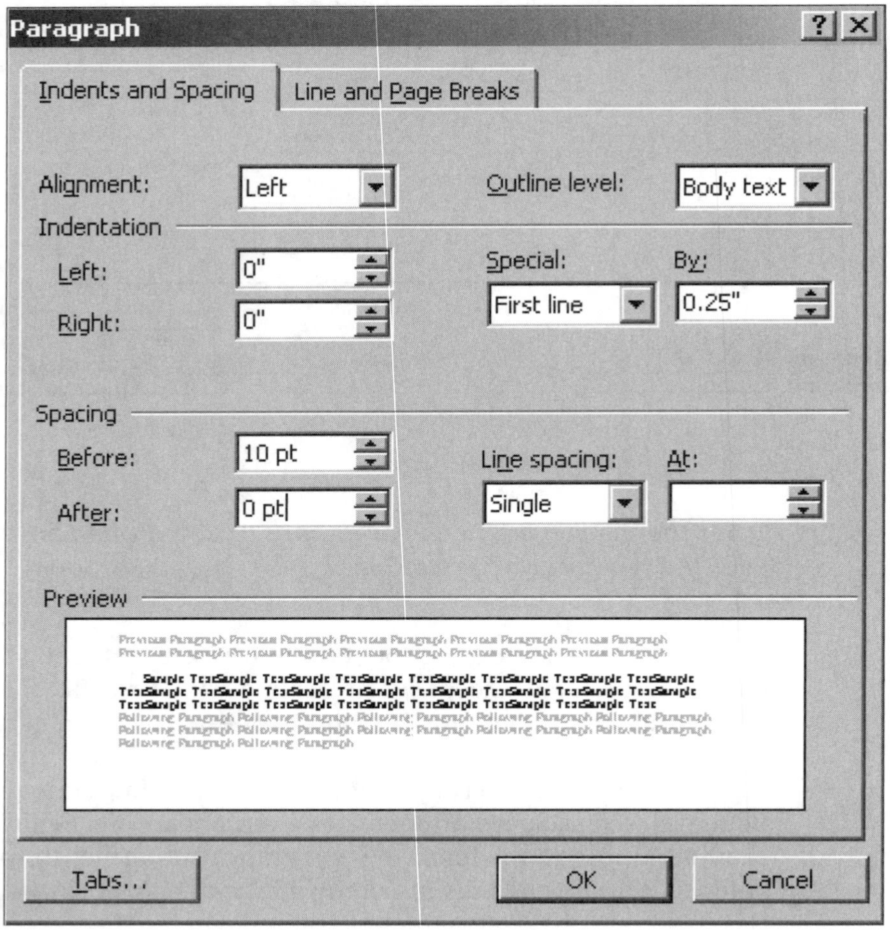

FIGURE 1.38

Keep in mind that these settings cause the space after the first paragraph to be added to the 10 points above the heading, creating quite a large space.

Just as you can change margin settings from the Paragraph dialog box, you can also change the alignment of your text from the Paragraph dialog box. Using such features as the Paragraph dialog box seems to require an extra step as you are formatting your text. It is very tempting to simply not use this feature. However, if you ignore capabilities such as this one, you will spend more time formatting your text in the long run. A well-formatted word processing document should not contain unneeded Return characters. Instead, paragraph spacing should be used to insert space above and below blocks of text.

Consider the sample in Figure 1.39—it was formatted incorrectly using tabs and extra returns instead of a hanging indent and space after.

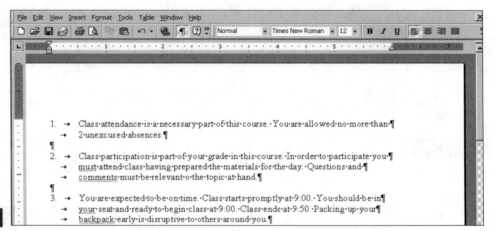

FIGURE 1.39

The next image is the same text with the typeface changed. Notice that the formatting no longer works as intended. One often needs to change the size of text or even the choice of typeface. (The word "typeface" refers to the design for the set of text characters.) In many situations, your typeface choice may get changed even if you do not intend to change it. This is particularly common when you are sharing files with others. [Figure 1.40]

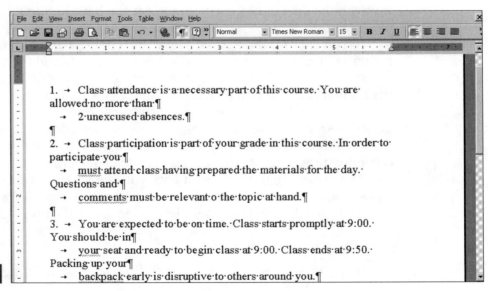

FIGURE 1.40

Once you learn to use the correct approach to your formatting, you will have no need to concern yourself with such possibilities. Not only will the problem never occur, saving you the time of fixing such problem, but you will save time in the initial steps of formatting as well.

The next image shows the correct way to format a numbered list. Note the tab used after the number, the margin settings, and the spacing between items accomplished with using Space After. [Figure 1.41]

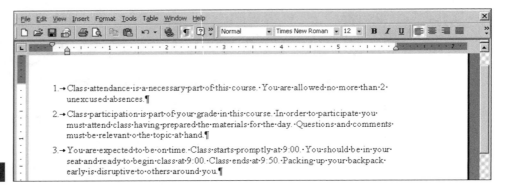

FIGURE 1.41

You can change the typeface or type size in this sample and the formatting will still be correct.

Changing the Appearance of Characters in the Text

Today most software allows you to select from a large number of typefaces. In fact, the enormous number of typefaces available today is totally overwhelming. Historically, type was created using blocks of lead. A single typeface filled a large box because a different lead block had to be created for every letter. But with the advent of the computer, we can have hundreds of typefaces at our fingertips.

If you click on the **Format** menu and choose **Font,** you see the characteristics of text that you can modify: **Font, Size, Style** and **Color.** (In the Macintosh version, the **Font** menu shows only a list of typefaces, so learn to use the **Format** menu option to access all the settings at once.)

Note that the word *font* is technically incorrect. When you select a kind of type—Arial or Bookman or Times—you are selecting a typeface. The term *font* includes the kind of typeface + the size + the style/color. Even so, most computer programs use the word *font* instead of *typeface.*

When you open the **Font** menu, you see a list of available typefaces, styles, sizes, and more. The entries in the list of typefaces will vary according to what is installed on the computer you are using. [Figure 1.42]

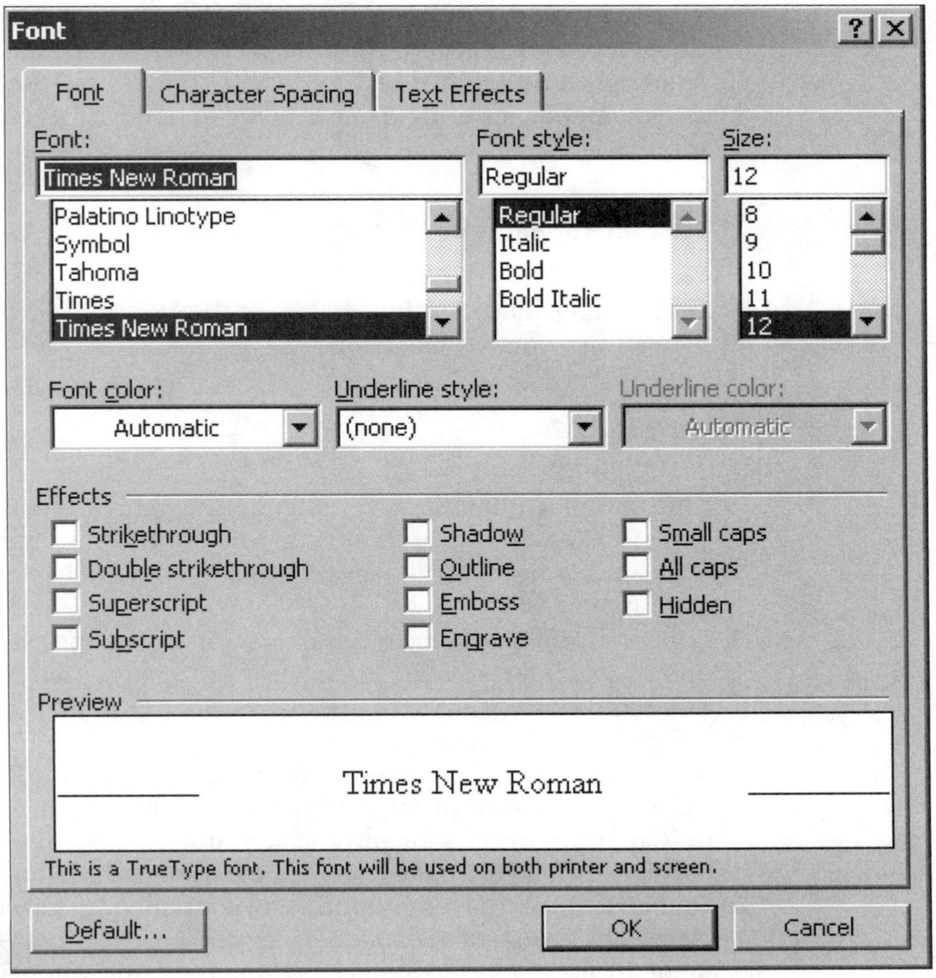

Font

| Font | Character Spacing | Text Effects |

Font:
Times New Roman

Palatino Linotype
Symbol
Tahoma
Times
Times New Roman

Font style:
Regular

Regular
Italic
Bold
Bold Italic

Size:
12

8
9
10
11
12

Font color: Automatic   **Underline style:** (none)   **Underline color:** Automatic

Effects

☐ Strikethrough   ☐ Shadow   ☐ Small caps
☐ Double strikethrough   ☐ Outline   ☐ All caps
☐ Superscript   ☐ Emboss   ☐ Hidden
☐ Subscript   ☐ Engrave

Preview

Times New Roman

This is a TrueType font. This font will be used on both printer and screen.

Default...   OK   Cancel

FIGURE 1.42

This dialog box lets you choose all of the properties of type that you want to apply. All of these setting taken together produce the font of your choice.

An important fact to remember is that the typefaces that you see on the Font menu are stored in the System folder of the computer you are using. They are *not* part of *Word*. Repeat: Typefaces are *not* part of *Word*. Thus, if you use a particular typeface and then move to a computer on which that typeface is not installed, the formatting and appearance of your document will change. Typefaces can be moved from one computer to another, but remember that they are copyrighted materials, just like computer programs.

Here are suggestions for correctly using some of the available choices for your text.

- **Underline.** This choice produces text with a thin line under the text. It is another holdover from typing rules. Because old typewriters could not produce italic text, typists used underlining as a substitute. When the document was sent to a printing house for publishing, the typesetter changed all underlined text to italic. However, you are now the writer *and* the publisher, and no one is going to remove this incorrect text formatting for you.

> *Avoid underlining text—it is difficult to read.*

Underlining places a line that cuts through the parts of the letters extending below the line of text.

> <u>Some ugly underlining—g and y cut off</u>

This makes reading the text difficult. Avoid the use of this text style. If you are required to place a line under your text, use a graphic element called a *rule* and place it to avoid touching the text itself.

- **Superscript.** This choice raises characters above the normal line of text and makes them smaller. Superscripts are often used to indicate footnotes and also appear in mathematics. For example, $x^3 + 3x^2 - 12x = 35$.
- **Subscript.** This choice produces characters that are placed below the normal line of text. Subscripts are often used in chemical formulas: H_2O.
- **Color.** Remember that when you print your document, color will appear only if you have a color printer. If you print on a printer that prints grayscale, then colored text will appear as a shade of gray.
- **Typeface.** Resist the temptation to fill your documents with lots of typefaces. Limit yourself to two typefaces per page. If you have a long document, use only two typefaces throughout the entire document. In addition, be sure you use readable type. Save the fun and fancy typeface for a few words on a poster or a greeting card.

Yes, another rule to think about as you word process.

> *Use at most two typefaces per page.*

Type and Readability

The most readable kind of type is *serif* type. The type in the paragraph you are reading is serif type. *Serifs* are small lines that complete the strokes making up the letters. These serifs are generally perpendicular to the main strokes. Serifs make reading easier because they help move your eye along the line of text. With practice you can learn to recognize serif type. Look carefully at the top line of text in Figure 1.43. Note the little lines on the tops and bases of letters.

Note some of the serifs in the Times New Roman typeface

Sample Serif Type

Note the lack of serifs in the Arial typeface

FIGURE 1.43

Sample Sans Serif Type

Now look at the second line in Figure 1.43. The second line is a typeface that is sans serif—meaning "without serifs." The general rule of thumb is to use sans serif type for headings and titles and serif type for any larger blocks of type. Because you want to limit your type to two typefaces per page, in general you use one sans serif typeface for titles and headings and one serif typeface for the body text. (The sample document on p. 243 shows sans serif type for headings and serif type for the body of the text.)

See Appendix Example

> *Use sans serif type for headings and titles and use serif for large blocks of text to improve readability.*

Because you generally enter more than a few words when using a word processor, it is a good idea to set up your word processor so that it automatically uses a serif typeface when you open a new document.

1. First, close all of your documents so that the Preferences settings you change are set for all documents instead of just the current document.
2. Select **Font** from the **Format** menu.
3. Adjust the typeface, size, and style that you want to be your default font.
4. Click on the Default button found at the bottom of the dialog box. [Figure 1.44]

FIGURE 1.44

Common serif typefaces that are easy to read include Bookman, New Century Schoolbook, Palatino, Times, Times New Roman, and Lucida Bright. For *body text*—a term meaning the main part of your document—you generally choose a size between 9 and 14 points.

Other Settings.   There are other characteristics that you can set so that when you open a new *Word* document, it will be set up the way you want. Recall that you used a Formatting toolbar button to make the invisible characters appear. On the PC, choose **Options** from the **Tools** menu. Check All in the Formatting Marks part of the dialog box. [Figure 1.45]

On the Macintosh, Open the **Preferences** menu. Check All in the Nonprinting Characters part of the dialog box.

Next, open the **AutoFormat** dialog box from the **Format** menu. Click on Options, then click on the AutoFormat tab. Be sure Smart Quotes is checked. Smart quotes are "curly"—unlike the foot (') and inch (") marks that are used on traditional typewriters in place of real quotation marks. [Figure 1.46]

You also need to make sure these settings are the way you want them in the AutoFormat As You Type tab.

Use smart quotes except *when you actually want feet or inch marks.*

Consider the other settings available in this list of options. The final option automatically creates a link if you enter a recognizable Web address in your document. If you click on it, the link tries to take you directly to the Web site. You may find this frustrating when editing your document. You may also choose to maintain control of when bold and italic appear and always use the menus or your styles to apply the attribute. The symbol substitution for the em dash is also something you may not want. Changing these settings to suit your own work style will help to increase your level of comfort and increase your production rate.

Using Tabs

Tabs are convenient but often overused. In addition, the built-in settings in most software encourage you to continue using them incorrectly. You have seen that you do not use tabs to indent or outdent the first line of paragraphs. However, you *do* use tabs to line up information.

On a traditional typewriter based on monospaced type, every letter takes up the same amount of space. When using your word processor, you have access to proportional type and each character may take up a different amount of space. Using the spacebar to format your text into columns simply does not work. In addition, the same letter may take up different amounts of space in different typefaces. This makes aligning text with the spacebar almost impossible.

Use tabs rather than spaces to line up information into columns.

To format text correctly, you need to learn to control your tab settings options. At first, working with tabs can be confusing. Your text may seem to "jump around" and be completely out of control. However, the flexibility and control the tabs provide make the time spent mastering their use well worth the effort. There are at least four types of tab settings available in *Word*. There is a small box to the left of the ruler at the top of your document. [Figure 1.47]

FIGURE 1.47

Each time you click in this tiny box, you see a different tab symbol.

Look closely at these icons. They are designed to help you remember what kind of tab you are using. [Figure 1.48]

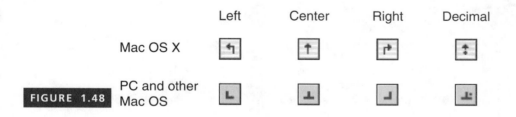

FIGURE 1.48

Check your version of *Word* to see what the symbols in your version look like.

To add a tab to your document, click in the small square to the left of the ruler until the symbol for the kind of tab you want to use appears. Then click on the ruler at the location you want to place the tab. To make use of a tab when entering text, press the Tab key. If you have the formatting marks show-ing, you see a small arrow representing the tab keystroke and the insertion point moves directly to a position corresponding to the position of the tab. [Figure 1.49]

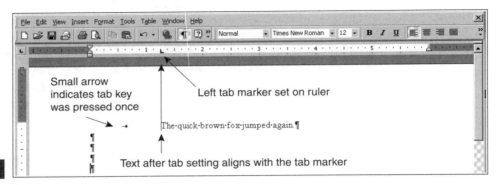

FIGURE 1.49

If you wish to change the position of the tab slightly, click and drag it right or left. If you decide to remove the tab completely, click and drag the icon off the ruler. The tab setting disappears.

The other tabs work in much the same way (see Table 1.1). Note that the text aligns according to the placement of the tab and the relationship of the type of tab to the text.

TABLE 1.1

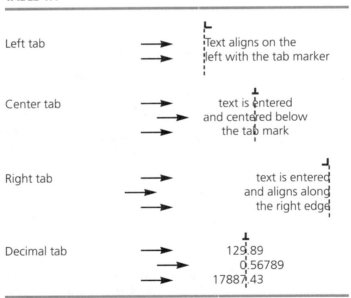

You need to keep in mind a number of points when working with tabs.

- When you set a tab, it applies only to the selected paragraph(s).
- When you open a new *Word* document, tabs are preset every half inch. (The typewriter strikes again.)

- Preset tabs do not show on the ruler.
- The first tab that you set "removes" the preset tabs to the *left* of the new tab.
- A tab is automatically set at the hanging indent marker when you create a hanging indent.

SAVING AND PRINTING

Earlier in this chapter you learned about saving and, in particular, about incremental saving. Hopefully by the time you read this section, you have already saved your work more than once. If not, then you need to reread that earlier section—particularly the guidelines for incremental saving. Just a reminder—you use **Save As** from the **File** menu to change the name of a file.

Printing from *Word* is straightforward, as long as your computer is correctly connected to a printer. Select **Print** from the **File** menu. A dialog box appears. The options available in this dialog box depend on the printer for which your computer is configured and whether you are using a PC or a Macintosh. If you have problems with printing, consult the manuals that came with your computer and printer, or ask someone who is familiar with your type of computer and printer to assist.

SUMMARY AND TIPS

At the end of each chapter of this book, a summary provides a list of reminders of the main ideas covered in the chapter. In addition, other helpful ideas may be included. For example, this chapter has an introduction to shortcut keys.

You Are Smarter Than Your Computer

For most people, learning to use a new piece of technology can be a frustrating experience. Whether it is using a complex sound system, programming a VCR, or setting a clock radio, all of us have experiences that make us feel stupid. However, it is important to understand that you are not dumb. The problem is not with you—it is with the designers of the technology. Not enough attention gets paid to the user interface—the way in which you, the user, interact with the technology. Look around you to find examples of poorly designed interfaces everywhere—in light switches, door handles, kitchen appliances, and graphic calculators.

Computers are particularly frustrating. Even finding the "on" switch can be difficult. The designers of the computer cases are often so caught up in the "beauty" of their products that they forget the computer uses.

However, once the computer is "up and running," the frustration turns from the hardware to the software—the programs that control the computer itself and that allow users to perform a variety of tasks. Some software is well designed and easy to learn and use; other software is confusing and frustrating. Again, the fault lies with the designers of the computer software, not with you. If you can remember that problems you have with the computer are often problems with the user interface and not with you, you have made a major step toward power computing without the frustration of feeling helpless.

Unfortunately, no matter how well the hardware and software are designed, computers are so complex that things can—and do—go wrong. You, the intelligent computer user, can do some things to protect yourself against computer problems and save yourself a great deal of frustration.

Control Those Files

Perhaps the single most important thing to learn as a beginner is to manage the files you are using. Work at getting a clear understanding of where your files are being stored when you save. Both *Windows* and the Macintosh operating system come with tutorials that will help you understand these concepts. Taking the time now to understand file management will pay off richly in the future.

Once you understand where your files are, the next step is to develop a system for saving files, as discussed earlier in this chapter. Too many beginners simply save their files over and over using the same name. This practice will sooner or later lead to disaster. The first thing you should do when you sit down to work on a previously created file is to save it under a new name. Then, if you have a "computer problem" with the new file, the original file is still there to fall back on. You can always delete really old files—something else you should understand how to do.

Save your work frequently—at least every ten minutes and certainly after every major change. If you work for a long time, change the name of the file again. With this method of saving, you produce an "electronic trail" of work that you can return to if need be.

Backup and Backup Again

Finally, learn to backup regularly. Leave yourself time at the end of every computing session. Be sure you save your file on two different disks. Remember the discussion earlier in this chapter about keeping backup copies? It is important to create a backup copy at the end of every working session.

Keep in mind that disks are mechanical in nature and they can and do fail. This is particularly true of disks that you carry around with you. The longer you carry them around, the more vulnerable they become. Magnetism, heat, or dirt can damage the information stored on your disks. Even putting a backpack down on top of the television can cause the disks inside to become damaged from the magnetism produced by the television set.

So, although your experiences with computing will probably not be completely without frustration, you can save yourself grief by understanding where and how your files are saved, developing a naming scheme for saving, and backing up everything you do. Even the most skilled computer users need to take these steps to protect themselves.

Designers do work hard to produce an intuitive and comfortable interface. However, creating one product that meets each person's definition of those terms is impossible. Relax. Make notes of the problem and your steps in finding a solution. This reflection on your learning will shorten the time needed to solve similar problems and also help you avoid new ones. Before long, you will be spending less and less time searching for answers to problems that, as a beginner, never seemed to end.

KEYSTROKE AND MOUSE SHORTCUTS

Some people prefer using keystrokes rather than the mouse to perform tasks on a computer. If you are a "keyboard person," you will find an extensive list of shortcuts in the Help menus in *Office*.

Table 1.2 lists essential keyboard shortcuts that everyone should learn because they save so much time.

TABLE 1.2

ACTION	*WINDOWS*	MACINTOSH
Cut	Ctrl + X	⌘ + X
Copy	Ctrl + C	⌘ + C
Paste	Ctrl + V	⌘ + V
Save	Ctrl + S	⌘ + S

Toolbar Buttons

Table 1.3 gives the function of some of the buttons on the default toolbars.

TABLE 1.3

DESCRIPTION	PC	MAC	DESCRIPTION	PC	MAC
New Document			New Folder		
Save			Print		
Cut			Copy		
Paste			Show/Hide nonprinting/ formatting characters		

Take a few moments to explore the other buttons on the toolbar. If you hold the mouse over a button—do not click—a small tab will appear that describes the function of the button. Also, you may have noticed that as you activate buttons in *Office 2000,* the toolbar changes slightly.

Customizing Toolbars

If you want to add or remove buttons from the toolbar or create your own custom toolbar, choose **Customize** from the **Tools** menu. Clicking on Commands shows you choices for buttons that you can add to toolbars. Make use of the built-in Help feature if you have difficulties.

BEYOND THE TYPEWRITER— WORD PROCESSING RULES

Throughout this chapter you have seen a number of rules to use when entering text. Here is a list of the rules and a couple of new ones based on what you have just learned.

1. Press the Enter key (*Windows*) or Return (Macintosh) to start a new paragraph.
2. Use only one space after punctuation—including commas, colons, and semicolons. (The two-spaces-after-periods rule is a typewriter rule. The word processor inserts the correct amount of space for printing when you enter punctuation with *one* space.)
3. Indent a paragraph the width of two or three characters in the typeface you are using. (In general, the "half inch" or "5 space" rule used for typing is too big.)
4. Use the first-line indent marker—not tabs—to indent the first line of a paragraph.
5. Do not use double Returns for spacing between paragraphs. Instead, use Paragraph spacing, Before and After.
6. Never use underline text style. Use italic style instead. (Underlining is the typewriter's substitute for italics.)
7. Use only two typefaces per page. More typefaces can make your page hard to read.
8. Sans serif type—such as the type used for headings in this book—should be used for headings and titles.
9. Serif type is more readable and should be used for body text. (Serifs are the small "ornaments" on the ends of letters, such as the ones in this type.)
10. Body text—the main blocks of text to be read—should be between 9 and 14 points. Only headings and titles should be larger.
11. Use smart quotes instead of foot and inch marks—unless it is foot and inch marks you need.
12. Do not control text position using the spacebar. Instead, use alignment, margins, and if necessary, tabs, to add spacing to your document.
13. Set your tabs to control the placement of text rather than using preset ones.

Indeed, these rules are a change from what you probably learned in the past. However, the time spent relearning is well worth it. You will produce more professional-looking documents, and better than that, your computer work will be much faster and easier.

Power Word Processing in *Microsoft Word*

In the previous chapter, you learned—or reviewed—the basics of word processing with *Word*. In addition, you learned a bit about using word processing rules instead of using typewriter rules on the computer.

In this chapter you will learn to use some of the more advanced features of *Word*. This material is the key to becoming an efficient and effective user of your word processor. Some of the topics presented are easy to use. Others are more difficult and take time to master; however, taking the time *now* will save you many hours later.

EXTENDING THE WORD PROCESSOR

If word processing is new to you, this next section should be approached in several sessions. There are a lot of new ideas introduced. You may want to skim this chapter for now, then return to it later when you have had more experience. If you are a more advanced user, you may be surprised at what you gain from this chapter. There is always more to learn about how *Word* can help you to be a more efficient computer user.

Many people assume that because today's students have "grown up with" computers that they are efficient and effective users. A more accurate assessment is that most of today's students have no fear of computer technology. They point and click and keyboard as if they are experts. In fact, most students do not have even the basic word processor skills covered in Chapter 1.

To meet the technology standards in the category of mastering technology productivity tools, both students and teachers need instruction. Learning the powerful tools embedded in modern word processors is not automatic. It takes practice and instruction. The details of how to use some of the powerful features of *Word* effectively are in this book, but it also takes discipline and practice to make these details part of your day-to-day work.

Using Tab Leaders

In the previous chapter you learned to set the four kinds of tabs by clicking and dragging the appropriate tab icon to the ruler. You can also set tabs by choosing **Tab** from the **Format** menu (or double-click on a tab you have already set). This dialog box shown in Figure 2.1 appears.

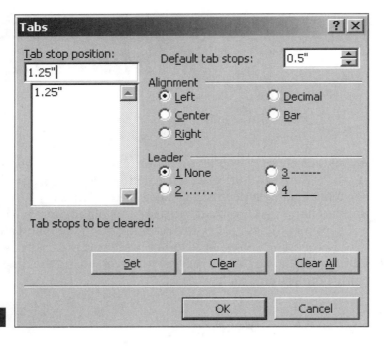

FIGURE 2.1

On the right side of this dialog box, there are several choices under **Leader.** These are choices for creating tab leaders—characters that fill the empty space before a tab. Some examples of how tab leaders can be used are shown in Figure 2.2.

Name: _____	Date: _____	
Chapter 1 _____	12	_____ .1
Chapter 2 _____	27	_____ .2

FIGURE 2.2

Many people create these effects by pressing the underline, hyphen, or period key over and over. This creates the same problem that occurs if you try to space proportional type with the spacebar—text will not line up exactly. In addition, if you decide to make a typeface change, the appearance of your document is often "very messed up," as our students say. Learning to use tabs and tab leaders correctly can save you many hours of formatting—and reformatting.

Examine Figure 2.3, which shows one right tab with a solid tab leader.

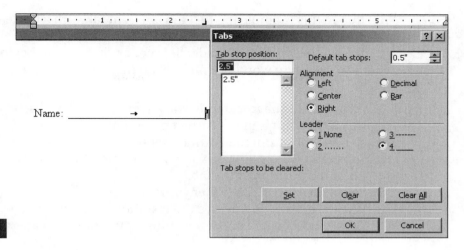

FIGURE 2.3

The image shows the settings in the Tab window, as well as the corresponding appearance of the ruler and the appearance of the text with the settings applied. Try reproducing this tab—or one like it—to be sure you understand how to create this kind of tab leader.

Use tab leaders to repeat characters between text and the tab setting rather than hyphens, periods, or other symbols.

The next example shows two different tabs. The first tab placed on the ruler is a right tab, the second one placed on the ruler is a left tab. Again, you can see the tab settings, the ruler settings, and the results when applied to the text. [Figure 2.4]

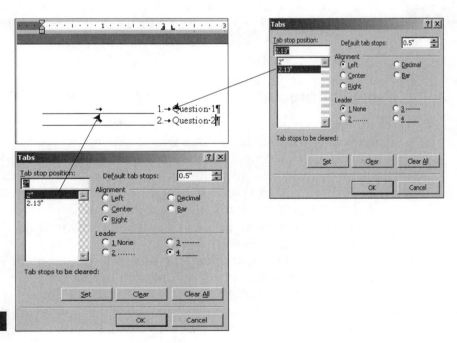

FIGURE 2.4

Note that in this example the first tab is a right tab with a tab leader. The second tab is a left tab with no tab leader.

To set a tab with a tab leader, it is generally easier to begin with the Tab window rather than working from the tab marker on the ruler.

1. If you already have text into which you want to set tabs, be sure that your insertion point is in the correct paragraph.
2. Choose **Tabs** from the **Format** menu.
3. Select the type of tab you want: Left, Center, Right, or Decimal.
4. Enter the position of the tab.
5. Select the kind of tab leader you want to use.
6. If your settings do not give the text the appearance you want, open the Tabs window again and adjust the settings until you are satisfied.

If you have other tabs in the *same* paragraph, repeat steps 2 through 5. Also note that for any tab that is already set, you can double-click on the tab icon to open the tab window if you decide to add a leader.

Keep in mind that setting tabs both with and without tab leaders takes practice. Because the preset tabs (at every half inch) are invisible, it can be confusing when setting tabs at other places on the ruler. It helps greatly to remember that all the preset tabs to the left of the first tab you set disappear. Thus, even though you have set a tab at, say, 3 inches, you still have preset invisible tabs to the right of the tab you set. [Figure 2.5]

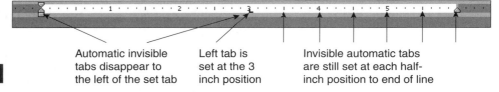

FIGURE 2.5

Automatic invisible tabs disappear to the left of the set tab

Left tab is set at the 3 inch position

Invisible automatic tabs are still set at each half-inch position to end of line

Using Footnotes

Footnotes provide references to material in the text of your document. *Word* allows you to insert footnotes into your document without having to manually check their placement or their numbers. Footnotes can be created to appear at the bottom of the same page as the footnote number or at the end of the document. If you place them at the bottom of the page, the reader can immediately read them within the context they are used. If you place them at the end of the document, they can be placed in an appendix and the reader can refer to them as they wish.

To insert a footnote, place the insertion point where you want the footnote number and select **Footnote** from the **Insert** menu. Our example sets the dialog box to place the footnotes at the bottom of the page. [Figure 2.6]

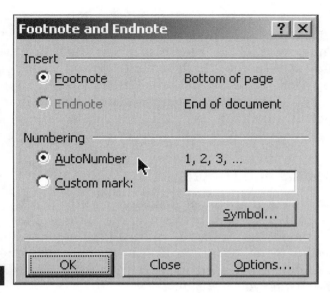

FIGURE 2.6

The Options button provides a variety of settings for footnotes. If you have your footnotes set to go at the bottom of the page and have AutoNumber selected, *Word* places the footnotes as follows.

Once you click on OK, a number immediately appears at the location of the insertion point *and* the insertion point is moved to the bottom of the page, where the footnote number also appears. [Figure 2.7]

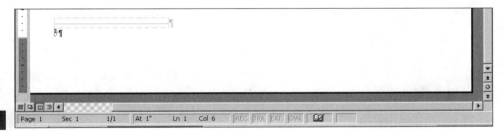

FIGURE 2.7

You are then ready to enter the text you wish to include in the footnote before moving your text insertion pointer back into the body of the document. [Figure 2.8]

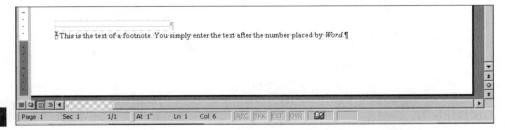

FIGURE 2.8

Footnotes are automatically sequentially numbered. If you add a foot-note that appears in the text after the first one, it will be labeled with the next sequential number. If you add a footnote in front of the first, all the footnotes in the document are automatically renumbered and repositioned to appear correctly in the footnote list. To delete a footnote, locate the appropriate foot-note number within the body of your page and delete the number. This step removes the corresponding text at the bottom of the page automatically. Footnotes will renumber if you still have others in the document.

Using Headers and Footers

Headers and footers are elements that are repeated on each page of a docu-ment. For example, the page numbers at the bottom of the page of many books are in the *footers*. At the top of each page of many books you see a header that contains either the title of the book or the title of the chapter. This book contains different headers on the left and right pages; the right header indicates the chapter you are reading.

To insert a header or footer, select **Header and Footer** from the **View** menu. The page of your document dims and the cursor moves to the area reserved for the header. You enter text or graphics in this rectangle in the same way that you enter text in the body of the document. You also see a tool-bar for working with headers and footers. [Figure 2.9]

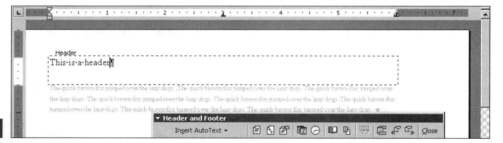

FIGURE 2.9

Remember, whatever you put in a header or footer appears on every page of your document. It is *not* appropriate to put a title in your header. However, you might put your name so that it appears automatically on every page of your document. Or, you might put the name of a multipage worksheet or the date an assignment is due. Because information in the headers and footers appears on every page, it can help you and your students keep track of all the pages of handouts or other documents you use.

To return to the body of your document, click the Close button on the toolbar. If you want to remove a header or footer, again access **Header and Footer** from the **View** menu and delete the text you entered. Once the content is removed, the reserved area is not visible.

To speed up your work, you can simply double-click in the header or footer area to work with headers or footers. To move back to the document area, you can double-click in the document area. Notice also that when you are working in the Header and Footer view, the special toolbar available pro-vides navigation and formatting shortcuts. [Figure 2.10]

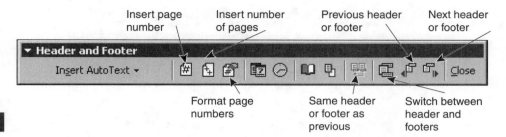

FIGURE 2.10

The value of these options will become clearer after we have addressed the issue of sections later in this chapter.

Often, you do not want the header or footer to appear on the first page of your document. Frequently, you use the first page of a document as a title page and this is more effective without the elements you would probably place in the header and footer. To accomplish this distinction, go to **Page Setup** on the **File** menu and select the Layout tab. In the dialog window that appears are some special settings for headers and footers. [Figure 2.11]

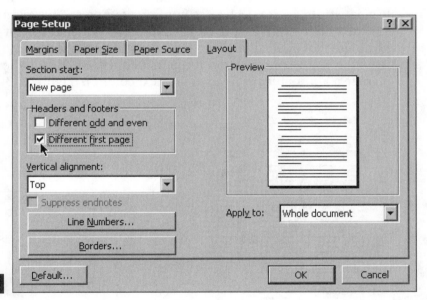

FIGURE 2.11

Technical Note: Macintosh users will find this option by choosing **Document** on the **Format** menu and selecting the Layout tab.

Selecting Different first page keeps the headers and footers from appearing on your first page.

Creating and Using Columns

Documents such as newsletters and books are often printed with text in more than one column. You can create columns in *Word* by choosing **Columns** from the **Format** menu. [Figure 2.12]

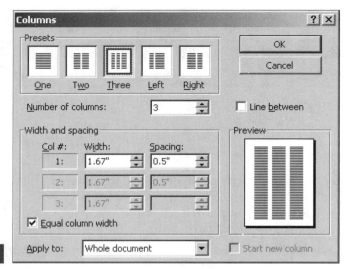

FIGURE 2.12

You can click on one of the icons to choose a column setup or you can use the settings at the bottom of the dialog box to set up your columns. You can easily create from one to twelve columns on your page. This feature can make a class newsletter both easy to create and professional in appearance.

Note that the text on a page moves into the first column. There will only be text in the second column if the first column is filled. When a column is filled, text automatically *flows* to the next column. [Figure 2.13]

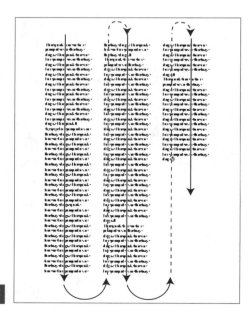

FIGURE 2.13

Experiment with the column settings on a page of text so that you understand how text flows from one column to the next.

Sometimes you want text to go only partway down the first column and then begin appearing in the second column. To accomplish this, choose

Break from the **Insert** menu. By selecting Column break, you force the text to move to the next column regardless of how much text is placed in the column. [Figure 2.14]

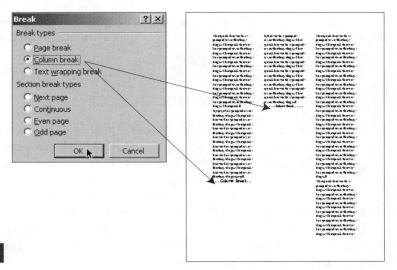

FIGURE 2.14

If you have the formatting/non-printing symbols visible you see the words "Column Break" appear where you made the insertion. Insert your column breaks as they are needed, or enter all your text and then adjust the placement of the text with column breaks.

Columns can also be adjusted for column width and space between columns. If you choose **Columns** from the **Format** menu, you can modify column sizes and spaces easily. If you want more than three columns, then you must choose Number of columns in the dialog box below the icons and enter a value. Then you can adjust the width and the spacing between columns for each column. [Figure 2.15]

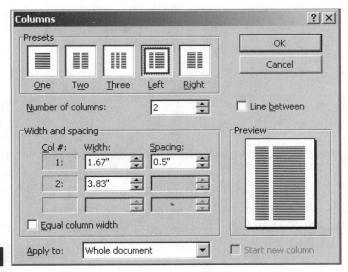

FIGURE 2.15

The column feature in *Word* is incredibly flexible. In addition, the software lets you work directly from the ruler to make adjustments to the settings. To change the spacing between columns, try clicking in the ruler on the shaded bars that indicate the space set between your columns. You can increase or decrease the size of the bar and note a corresponding change in the width of your columns. In the beginning, you will find dealing directly with the dialog box easier, but as you move to using the bars, your work speed will increase.

Customizing Documents That Use Columns

There are many more ways to use a word processor than writing papers or memos. You can create newsletters, brochures, business cards, flash cards, and much more. You can create documents for your own day-to-day use or as part of classroom projects.

One type of publication to create is a brochure. Creating a brochure not only gives you practice in learning to use your word processor more effectively but also gives teachers and students practice in using technology as a communications tool. Both of these are categories in the NETS technology standards for students, developed by ISTE.

In the preceding section you saw how to change the widths of your columns or the space between the columns. For example, suppose you want to create a trifold brochure, which requires turning the page sideways and folding it into thirds. [Figure 2.16]

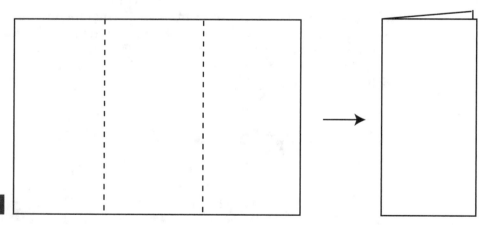

FIGURE 2.16

The following steps can be used to create a trifold brochure.

- Set up your page to be horizontal—called *landscape*. The normal orientation of the page is called *portrait*. To change to landscape orientation, select **Page Setup** in the **File** menu. On the PC, choose the Paper Size tab. [Figure 2.17]

PC

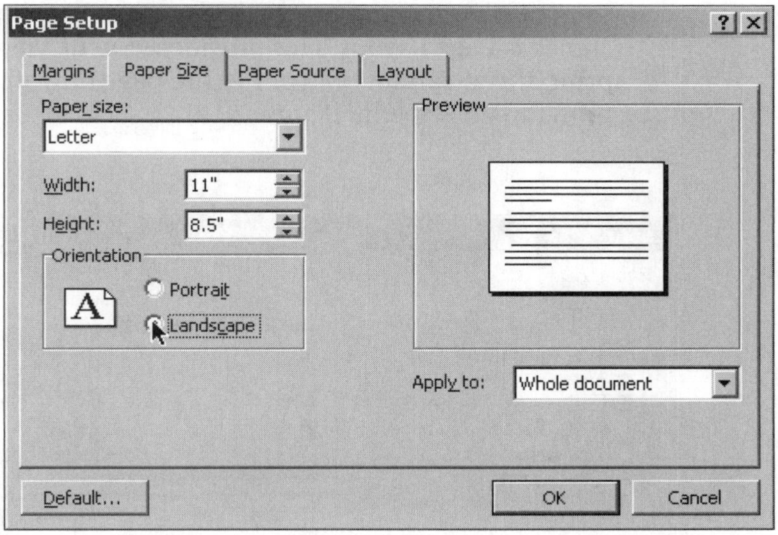

FIGURE 2.17

On the Macintosh, shown here in *OS X,* click the appropriate icon. [Figure 2.18]

MAC

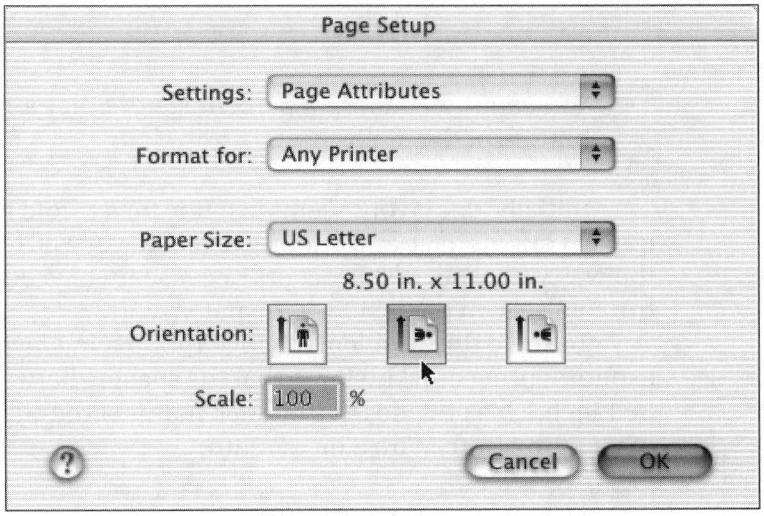

FIGURE 2.18

Note that you may see some differences in your print dialog box depending on your printer, your version of *Office,* and the operating system you are using.

- Next, set all four of the margins at 0.5 inch. On the PC, click on the Margins tab in the Page Setup dialog box. On the Macintosh, choose **Document** from the **Format** menu.
- Choose **Columns** from the **Format** menu and click on the appropriate icon to create three columns.

- Select **Print Layout** from the **View** menu. On the Macintosh, the menu choice is **Page Layout.** This provides you the view of your page as it will print. If you cannot see your entire page on your screen, choose **Zoom** from the **View** menu. [Figure 2.19]

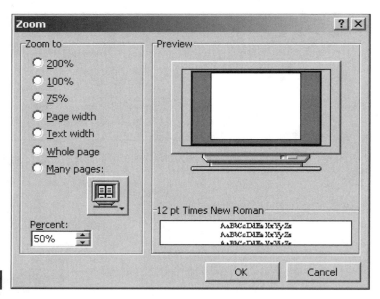

FIGURE 2.19

You can then choose a percentage or enter a number in the box at the bottom of the dialog box.

Initially, this layout seems just fine for a trifold brochure. However, if you put text on this page and attempt to fold it, you will find the page does not fold the way you expect. This occurs because there is not enough space between the columns on the inside of the paper.

To solve this problem, change the spacing *between* the columns. Some experimenting quickly shows that the spacing between the columns needs to be 1 inch. This provides the 0.5-inch margin around the content of each panel of your brochure. With a bit of math:

- 11-inch paper is used in landscape view.
- Left margin = 0.5 inch; Margin between column one and two = 1 inch; Margin between column two and three = 1 inch; Right margin = 0.5 inch.
- Add the margins: 0.5 + 1 + 1 + 0.5 = 3 inches.
- Subtract the margins from the page width: 11 − 3 = 8 inches.
- Divide by the number of columns: 8/3 = 2.667 inches for each column.

To adjust the columns, choose **Columns** from the **Format** menu. Be sure to check Equal column width. Enter the computed values. [Figure 2.20]

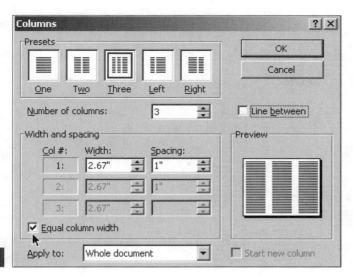

FIGURE 2.20

The completed document, ready for text and graphics, has wider space between columns so that it will fold correctly. If you put text into this document format, you can see the narrow margins and the wide column spacing. [Figure 2.21]

FIGURE 2.21

With this setup, each folded portion will have a margin of 0.5 inch, which is the size of your initial document's outside margins setting.

Another type of document that makes use of columns is a newsletter or flyer. For such a document, you use portrait orientation and most likely 1-inch outside margins. For this document, your spacing between columns should be less than the outside margins. [Figure 2.22]

FIGURE 2.22

The above document establishes a three-column grid. Here, *Word* has been left to establish the columns with the default settings of 0.5 inch between columns, the document has been set with 1.0 inch outside margins, and the remaining space has been evenly divided to form three equal columns. All pages in the newsletter should follow this same design grid.

However, to vary the appearance in the document, you might choose to have one wide column and one narrow column. That is, you "merge" two columns to create one. To maintain consistency to the grid you established, the space between the two columns is also merged into the new "wide" column. Here, the wide column appears on the left, although you can also place the wide column on the right side of the page. [Figure 2.23]

FIGURE 2.23

To set up this new page for a newsletter with two columns of different widths by using a three-column grid, again start by doing a little math:

- 8.5-inch paper width is used for portrait orientation.
- Both outside margins are set at 1 inch.
- Total outside margins: 1 + 1 = 2 inches.
- Space between columns is 0.5 inch (default value).
- This leaves 5.5 inches to be divided into three equal columns of 1.83 inches that establish your design grid.
- Space for narrow column: 1.83 inches.
- Space for wide column is 1.83 inches + 1.83 inches + 0.5 inch = 4.16 inches. (The merging of two of the original columns and the space between them.)

Technical Note: With calculations such as these, there is often a round-off value involved. When you actually let the computer create the two unequal columns following your grid, the numbers in the grid may be slightly different than your original calculation. In our example, the 1.83 inches is not an exact value since we rounded and ignored part of the number. The computer is using this when it creates a large column of 4.17 inches rather than our value of 4.16 inches.

To achieve these settings in the Columns dialog box, be sure to deselect the Equal column width setting before you begin to enter values. These settings maintain the original 3-column design grid, but provide some variation and interest to the layout of your document. You can use these two different layouts within the same document, resulting in a more interesting and flexible appearance for your newsletter elements.

If you have one of the most recent versions of *Office*, you may have a choice that will automatically set the two unequal columns for you. Choose **Columns** from the **Format** menu. [Figure 2.24]

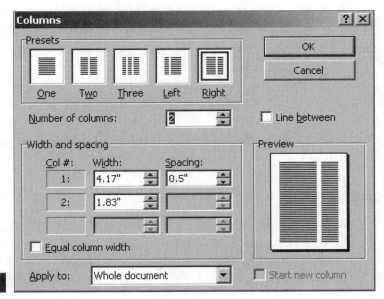

FIGURE 2.24

Note, however, that you can manually set any combination of column settings rather than using the choices among the icons in the dialog box. Use the numbers that you need as illustrated earlier.

Again, you are ready to add text and graphics. Note that even though the columns are unequal, the original three-column design grid for the document has been maintained. Be sure to use the full width of both columns when you place the elements of your newsletter into the document. Resist the temptation to use only part of the wide column. Maintaining a consistent grid is one way to ensure you produce professional-looking documents.

The three-column layout provides many choices for producing newsletters. Your pages can be three narrow columns, a narrow column followed by the wide column, or the wide column followed by the narrow one. You may decide to ignore the default setting that *Word* suggests as spacing between columns and enter your own value. For example, the 0.5 inch used here may be slightly larger than needed to create the space between columns.

If you want column settings different from those available at the top of the Columns dialog box, you can adjust the settings to suit your needs. Of course you can set up more complex grids. For example, if *Office* is set up for five columns, you could divide your document into two columns as shown in Figure 2.25.

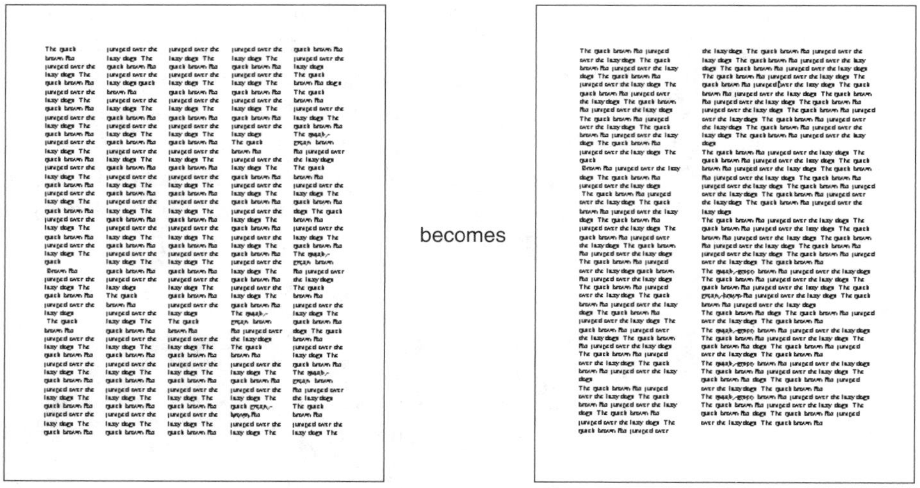

FIGURE 2.25

You can use this five-column design grid for creating a variety of layouts for your document.

Using Sections

As the documents you create become more complex, you may have need for several different formatting choices within the same document. In our example of a newsletter, for instance, you might choose to create a six-page newsletter and have four pages of three equal columns and two pages with two columns—one wide and one narrow—as previously shown. This is easily accomplished, because *Word* contains the tools to let you create documents divided into parts that have different characteristics—for example, three columns on one page and two columns on the next. These parts of a document are referred to as sections. Learning to use sections correctly can save you a lot of time by putting more than one layout in a single document.

Go to the **Insert** menu and select **Break;** you see four choices for starting a new section. [Figure 2.26]

FIGURE 2.26

Figures 2.27 and 2.28 are examples of how you might use sections in your own documents. You can have a section start on a new page.

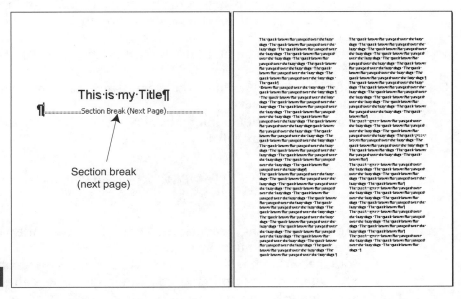

FIGURE 2.27

Or, you can start a section on a new line to vary the organization within the page.

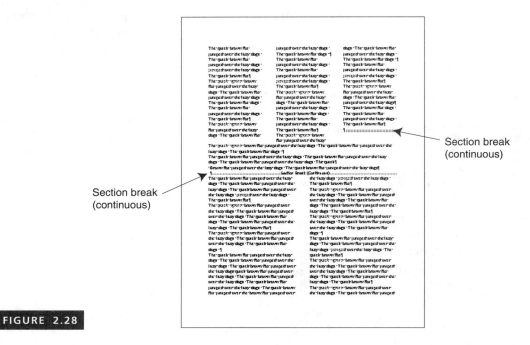

Section break
(continuous)

Section break
(continuous)

FIGURE 2.28

Sections give you a great deal of power when formatting long or complex documents.

To adjust section settings:

1. Place the pointer at the location in the document where you want the section break to appear and then click the mouse button.
2. From the **Insert** menu, choose **Break** and then select the type of break you want.
3. Move the mouse pointer into the section that you want to adjust. Click *anywhere* in that section.
4. Choose the formatting you want, such as centering, number of columns, or typeface.
5. Move your insertion point to the next section you wish to format.
6. Repeat steps 2 through 4.

Here are some ways that using sections can make managing documents easier.

■ To omit numbering, headers, and footers from your title page, select Different first page in the Layout tab of the **Page Setup** dialog box accessed from the **File** menu. Macintosh users, go to **Format/Document** to locate the Layout tab. Your other option would be to place the title page in a separate section and format the section without headers and footers.

- Formal publications often start new chapters on odd numbered pages. Start a new section for each chapter and set it to start on an odd page. If students are making their own books, they should learn to use sections to make their books more polished and professional.
- To change the headers and/or footers for different parts of your document, insert section breaks, place the cursor in the area you want to format, and adjust the header and footer settings. If you are creating a series of worksheets, you can put them in the same document and use section breaks to insert identifying information in each header. Editing headers and footers in different sections is made easier with the navigation tools included in the toolbar that was introduced earlier.
- To number the first part of your document with Roman numerals and the second part with Arabic numerals, insert a section break after making sure the cursor is in the page you want to work with. Then choose **Page Number** from the **Insert** menu to format the numbers for each section. [Figure 2.29]

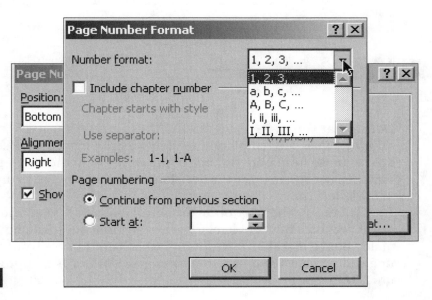

FIGURE 2.29

Often novice users think that they must create multiple documents to put together a complex document such as this book or a set of instructional materials. With sections, however, a wide variety of layouts are possible in the same document.

TOOLS TO EMPOWER

So far in this book we have focused on the word processing environment per se. *Word* has many powerful tools, many of which go beyond the scope of this book. In this section you will get a brief exposure to some of these tools. Eventually you will want to explore some of these tools in more depth. The Help facility in *Office* is a good way to explore the many features available.

Find and Replace

One of the most powerful functions of computer software is the ability to perform repetitious tasks. One such task is locating specific information in a document and then, perhaps, changing that information.

By selecting **Find** or **Replace** from the **Edit** menu, a dialog box with several tabs appears. Click on the Replace tab. If you want to replace every occurrence of *cat* in your document with *dog* the dialog box shown in Figure 2.30 appears.

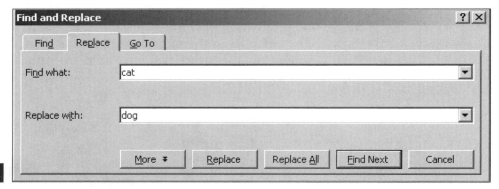

FIGURE 2.30

Notice that you have to be careful. Unless you want to change *catalog* to *dogalog,* avoid the temptation to simply click Replace All. Because you are able to move from one instance of the word *cat* to the next—by clicking on Find Next—you can make the decision to replace or not each time *Word* stops at the letters *cat.*

There is a different option to control the replacement problem of *cat* to *dog* that avoids this problem. Click on the More button at the bottom of the dialog box to reveal further options. Check Find whole word only. This setting will prevent *Word* from replacing parts of words inappropriately. [Figure 2.31]

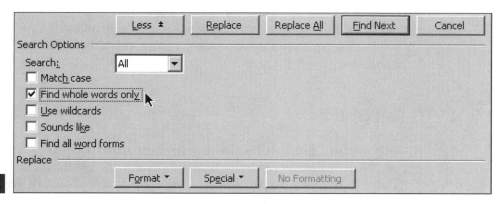

FIGURE 2.31

Then, instead of having to approve each replacement, you can use the Replace All button.

While Find and Replace is extremely powerful, it can also be dangerous. It is always a good idea to save your work before doing a find and replace. Then, if you discover an error, you can open your most recently saved document and try again.

You can also use the Find and Replace feature to locate special characters such as spaces, tabs, or returns. For example, perhaps you learned to put two spaces after periods and are having a hard time changing to word processing rules. You can search your document for every period followed by two spaces and replace them with a period and a single space.

To find and replace characters such as end of paragraph marks and tabs, you use special codes. Expand the Find and Replace dialog box by clicking on the More button on a PC or on the disclosure triangle if you are using a Macintosh. Click on the Special button at the bottom of the expanded dialog box. [Figure 2.32]

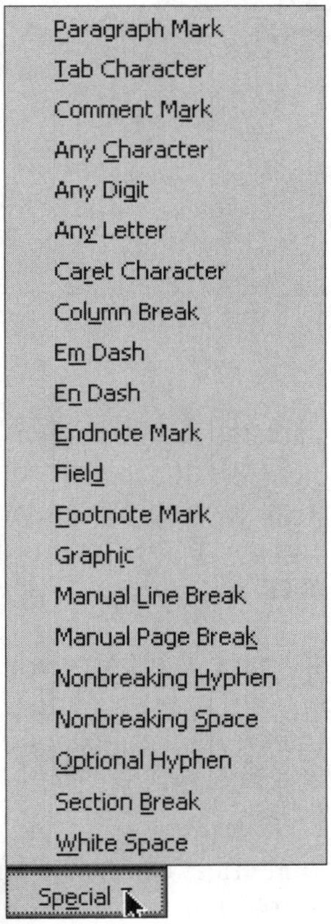

Paragraph Mark
Tab Character
Comment Mark
Any Character
Any Digit
Any Letter
Caret Character
Column Break
Em Dash
En Dash
Endnote Mark
Field
Footnote Mark
Graphic
Manual Line Break
Manual Page Break
Nonbreaking Hyphen
Nonbreaking Space
Optional Hyphen
Section Break
White Space
Special

FIGURE 2.32

Choices from this menu will insert codes into the Find and Replace boxes. For example, if you choose tab, you see ^t; if you choose paragraph remark, you see ^p.

Checking Spelling

As computers have become more and more a part of our lives, the ability to spell check a document is an expected feature in most software. In *Word,* select **Tools** and then choose **Spelling and Grammar.** *Word* will check your grammar, but for now, we will only look at spelling. When you first choose **Spelling and Grammar,** you can remove the check at the bottom of the dialog box so that *Word* does not check grammar. [Figure 2.33]

FIGURE 2.33

There are many options that you can set for spell checking. Click on the Options button, then adjust the settings to suit your needs. For example, most versions of *Word* are set to check spelling and grammar as you enter text. Some people find this annoying and prefer to turn it off. Spend some time examining these options. If you need more details, use *Office* Help to learn about the available choices.

Students should be taught to spell check every document before they turn it in. Using a spell checker, however, takes practice, and students need to learn both the benefits and the limitations of spell checkers. Here are several things to keep in mind when using a spell checker.

- A word being questioned by the spell checker may or may not be misspelled. The final decision is still yours. For example, the spell checker may not recognize a person's name or the name of a place or a product.
- Words that you use frequently can be added to a personal dictionary. You can also have *Word* automatically correct your most common misspellings. Be careful. If you "teach" *Word* to spell a word incorrectly, it will happily accept the spelling every time you make the same mistake.

■ The spell checker is unable to determine if you have used words such as *there* and *their* correctly. The spell checker does not flag these words if you have them spelled correctly but used them incorrectly. Ensuring correct usage of words is still your responsibility. Using the spell checker does not remove the need for you to carefully read and edit your work before you consider yourself finished.

Inserting Date, Time, and Page Number

Word allows you to insert dates, times, and page numbers that automatically change as you revise and reuse the document. For example, if you select **Date and Time** from the **Insert** menu, you see a dialog box that provides a wide choice of date and time formats. [Figure 2.34]

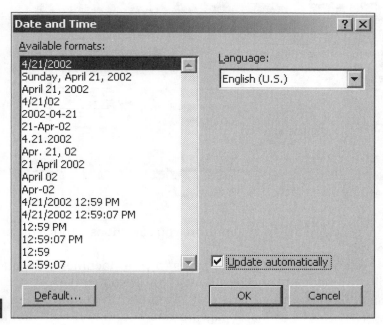

FIGURE 2.34

If you check Update automatically, each time you open the document the current date and/or time will appear. If you leave this box unchecked, then the current date and/or time are entered but they do not automatically change to reflect the new date and time when the document is reopened. For example, suppose you choose **Date and Time** from the **Insert** menu. You do so at 2:05 P.M. on Sunday, February 9, 2003, in the format of 02/09/03 2:05 P.M. and you then open the same document on the morning of February 12. The entry will read 02/12/03 11:22 A.M.

The software is making use of the built-in clock in your computer and inserting the date or time at the location of the insertion point. Using **Insert/Date and Time** tells *Word* to always refer to the computer before displaying these elements. If you have checked Update automatically, the entry will automatically update each time you open the document. This also means that if the clock on your computer is set incorrectly, then the date and time will be incorrect in your document. Check the Date/Time Control Panel on your computer to correct the settings if necessary.

As you gain skills with *Word,* remember that you are also moving closer to a goal of meeting the NETS technology standards developed by ISTE. Understanding features of your computer such as how the built-in clock interacts with other software is part of the category of standards that addresses understanding basic operations and concepts.

If you choose **Page Numbers** from the **Insert** menu, you see a dialog box letting you make decisions for positioning and formatting your page number. [Figure 2.35]

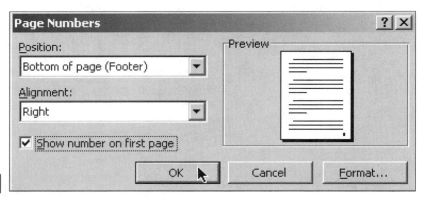

FIGURE 2.35

If you click on the Format button, you can choose from a list of page number options.

If you later add several pages to your document, the additional pages will automatically number themselves. If you go back and remove the first page, the remaining pages will automatically renumber. In general, use a header or footer to insert page numbers so that they are not affected by the other text on the page. You will find a button on the toolbar provided for working with headers and footers that will give you a shortcut to insert the numbers.

Saving Templates

Sometimes you create a document that contains elements you want to use again and again. For example, it might be a document that you use each time you create a lesson plan, or a document that includes items you would include on most worksheets you create. [Figure 2.36]

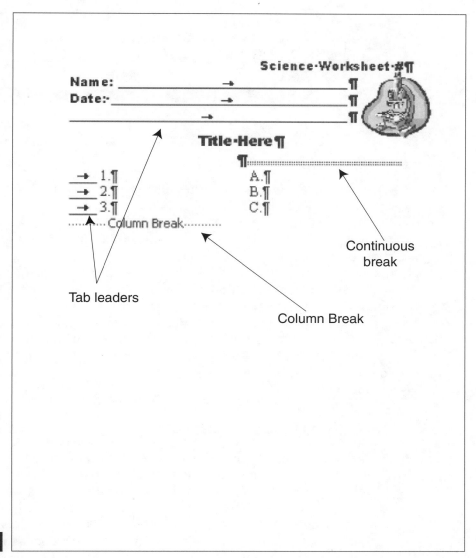

FIGURE 2.36

Notice that creating a worksheet can make use of several of the new skills you have learned in this chapter—tab leaders, column breaks, and section breaks.

Each time you want to create another worksheet, you can save a great deal of time by opening this same document. The formatting is already in place and you only have to update the content. However, the best way to accomplish this reusing of your work is to save the original worksheet document as a *template*. When you open a template document, a copy of the document is opened and the original is left unchanged.

Any document can be saved as a template. Simply choose **Save As** from the **File** menu. Choose Document Template from the drop-down menu. [Figure 2.37]

When you save a document as a template it is automatically put in the special Template folder found in the *Office* folder.

When you choose **New Document** from the **File** menu, your newly saved template appears as one of your choices. (If you are using a Macintosh, choose **Project Gallery/My Templates.**) Each time you start a new document from a document such as the worksheet template above, the new document starts with the name **Untitled.** All the elements at the top of the template document appear in the new, untitled document.

A template document can include many elements beyond those illustrated here. Later in this chapter will be an introduction to styles and stylesheets. Using styles, you can create templates that exactly meet your personal and professional needs. Such documents can save an enormous amount of time.

Documents in Other Formats

Word runs on both Macintosh computers and on computers running *Windows.* Documents created on one type of computer can easily be moved to the other. Two "tricks" can help you move documents back and forth.

- If you are saving a *Word* document on a Macintosh, add .doc to the end of the name. This is the *extension* that *Windows* needs to recognize the document as a *Word* document. Better yet, if your Macintosh version of *Word* includes the option Append File Extension, check this box in your Save As dialog box.
- If you are opening a *Word* file that was created on a computer using a different operating system from your own, do not double-click on the document icon to open it. Instead, first open *Word* and then choose **Open** from the **File** menu. Locate the document on your hard drive and let the software open the document for you.

Usually, *Word* documents are saved as a standard *Word* format or the special *Word* template format. However, *Word* comes with a wide variety of *translators* that allow *Word* to open and save documents in other formats. To open other types of documents, you must tell *Word* to look for documents other than those it created. For example, if you wanted to open a file sent to you as an *AppleWorks* file or a *WordPerfect* file, you need to direct *Word* to look for files other than *Word* files. In the **Open** dialog box, a drop-down menu has a number of options, including All Files, that lets you go beyond just *Word* files.

In addition to actually opening a file from a different application, *Word* allows you to insert a great many other types of files into a *Word* document. For example, if you received a photograph from a friend that was saved as a JPEG or JPG file, *Word* is able to place the file as an image inside a *Word* document. Once you have inserted the photograph, you will be able to view, print, and save the image as a *Word* document exactly as if you had started with *Office.*

In addition to opening files from other applications, *Office* includes translators allowing you to save *Word* documents in a variety of formats. If you choose **Save As** from the **File** menu, you can select a format from the drop-down menu below File Format in the Save dialog box.

Other Useful Features

- **Thesaurus.** The Thesaurus in *Word* is much like a paper thesaurus. It is helpful in finding synonyms when you are composing text. Choose **Tools→Language→Thesaurus.** On the Macintosh, choose **Thesaurus** from **Tools.**
- **Hyphenation.** One of the main reasons for hyphenation is to improve the appearance of your document. Without Auto-Hyphenate activated, the standard word wrap is applied. Unless the entire word fits on a line, the word is moved to start the next line of text. In *Office 2000,* choose **Tools→Language→Hyphenation.** If you have a Macintosh version of the software, **Hyphenation** is found on the **Tools** menu.
- **Word Count.** This feature allows you to count the contents in a selected portion or the entire document. You get a count of characters, words, lines, paragraphs, pages, and sections. Select **Word Count** from **Tools.** To obtain a count for only part of your document, highlight a portion of the text before you select **Word Count.**

CUSTOMIZING YOUR SCREEN

Office offers a variety of choices for the way a document appears on the screen. This section examines a number of these options. Keep in mind these settings can be changed in most *Office* applications, not just *Word.*

- **Rulers.** If you choose **Rulers** from the **View** menu, you can hide or show the rulers in your document. You can also change the units used on the ruler. Choose **Options** on the **Tools** menu. Click on the General tab and change the units. (On the Macintosh, choose **Preferences** and click on the General tab.)
- **Zoom.** If you choose **Zoom** from the **View** menu, you can set the magnification at which you view your document. Note that you can enter the percentage you want at the bottom of the dialog box if the size you prefer is not on the list. [Figure 2.38]

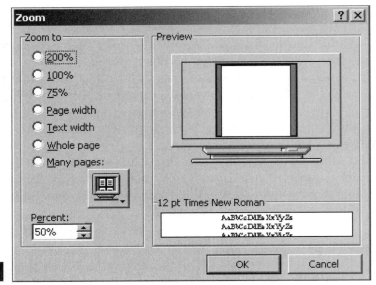

FIGURE 2.38

This extremely valuable feature lets you size documents down so that you can see multiple pages. It lets you enlarge documents so that you can see each detail.

■ **Layouts.** The **View** menu allows you to change the way in which you see a document. **Normal** shows you the text and images in your document. **Print Layout** (**Page Layout** on the Macintosh) lets you see the margins and headers and footers of the page.

■ **Split Box.** When documents get large and complex, it is sometimes useful to be able to view different parts of the document at the same time. The Split Box feature lets you subdivide a document horizontally. [Figure 2.39]

FIGURE 2.39

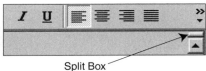

Split Box

To remove a split, double-click on the small rectangle in the scroll bar.

STYLES AND STYLESHEETS

Word, like most other modern productivity software, has a feature called *styles.* For most users, stylesheets are the most powerful—but least used—capability of *Word* and similar software. *Word* has two different kinds of styles.

■ **Character.** Used to format groups of characters.
■ **Paragraph.** Used to format entire paragraphs.

This book will not cover every possible use of styles, but once you master the basic ideas, you should be able to apply styles to your own work.

The next section covers paragraph styles. But before we explore how to *create* styles, let's explore the concept of styles. So . . . what is a style? Look at the heading in Figure 2.40.

FIGURE 2.40

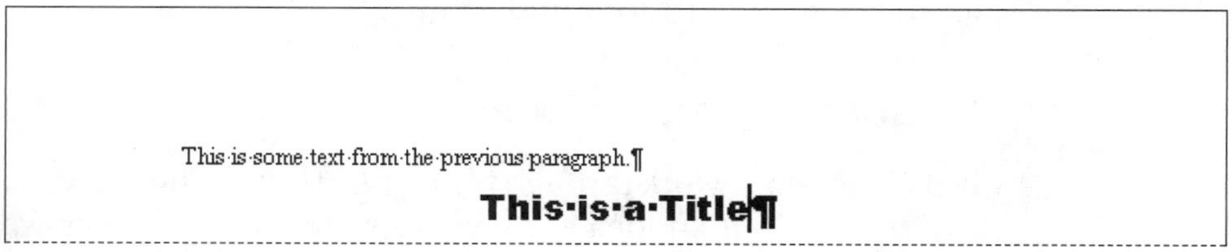

This·is·some·text·from·the·previous·paragraph.¶

This·is·a·Title¶

The words in the title—*This is a Title*—have the following attributes:

- Typeface = Arial Black
- Type size = 18 point
- Left margin = 0 inches
- Space before = 6 points
- Space after = 2 points
- Paragraph alignment = centered
- Line spacing = single-spaced

This is a considerable list of attributes, and it takes a lot of mouse clicks and menu choices to apply all of these properties. This set of attributes can be named as a paragraph style and used again and again, taking only one step to apply the complete set of attributes.

The text that precedes the sample title has an entirely different set of attributes.

Is it necessary to set each attribute in each paragraph each time you want to format text to look a particular way? No. Fortunately, *Word* provides the power of styles to make your work easier.

Word lets you give a *name* to an entire list of formatting decisions. This list of formatting rules is called a *style*. To give another paragraph this exact set of attributes, you merely *apply* the style. Suppose the preceding list of attributes is given the name "side heading 18." In one simple step you can use this name to apply *all* of the formatting attributes to any paragraph in your document. Further, the style can be stored for later use and even moved from one document to another.

Most documents contain text using different sets of formatting attributes. Look again at the text in this book. You should be able to identify several different types of formatting. Can you locate paragraphs in this book that could be given the following style names?

- **Body text.** (Hint: used for most of the text paragraphs.)
- **Continued.** (Hint: text without a first-line indent for such instances as after a graphic.)

- **Bulleted list.** (Hint: used for the text you are now reading.)
- **Picture.** (Hint: used to position pictures.)

How did you do? Did you find at least one example of each? Can you find still other types of paragraph formatting? There are many different styles in this particular document. Whether you have just a few styles or many styles, taken together the set of styles in a document is called its *stylesheet*. The stylesheet for this book is quite long and complex.

Creating Styles: An Example

If at all possible, work through the steps in this section as you are sitting at the computer to get an idea of how styles are created. For now, do not be concerned with understanding the technical concepts behind styles. Instead, focus on learning how to produce your own styles. Later, more details will be given. Focus on mastering the basic steps, and adding to your skills with stylesheets becomes relatively easy.

Creating a Base Style.   Styles work best if related styles are "tied together" or "associated" in your stylesheet by using a *base style*. A base style usually includes many of the common attributes you want in your text.

Follow these steps to create your base style. To begin, open a new word processing document. For now, leave the document without any text.

1. Choose **Style** from the **Format** menu. This shows the Style window that is used to design or modify styles. [Figure 2.41]

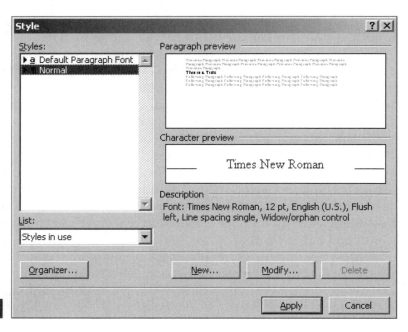

FIGURE 2.41

2. Click on the **New** button in the Style window. The New Style dialog box appears. Modify it to look like Figure 2.42.

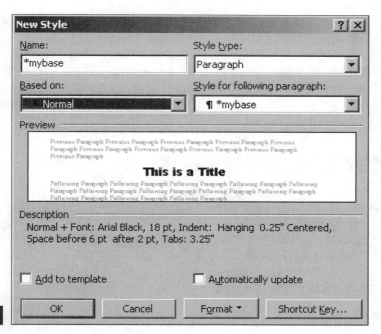

FIGURE 2.42

- In the Style type list, select Paragraph—most of the styles you use will be paragraph styles.
- Give your style a name—it is best to use lowercase letters and to identify base styles with a special character, such as the asterisk shown above.
- Click on the drop-down menu below Based on and select Normal. Click OK. The style name that you just created is now listed in the drop-down style menu found on the Formatting toolbar. If this toolbar is not visible, use **Toolbars** in the **View** menu and select Formatting from the list. [Figure 2.43]

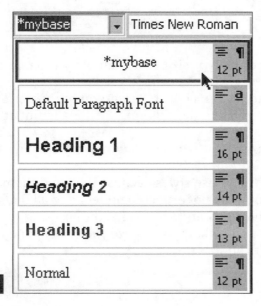

FIGURE 2.43

This menu is also found on the Formatting palette in recent Macintosh versions of *Word*.

3. Next, you need to select the attributes that will define your style, *mybase*. Choose **Style** from the **Format** menu. Click on *mybase* and then click the Modify button.

4. Click on the Format button at the bottom of the dialog box. [Figure 2.44]

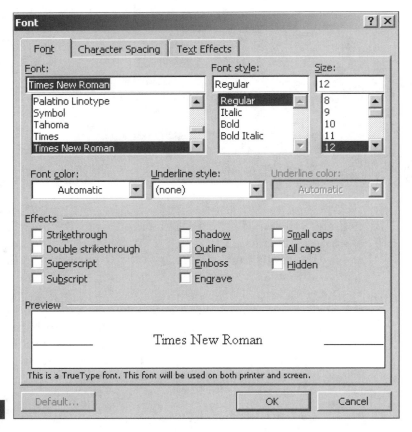

FIGURE 2.44

Choose a typeface and type size. This example uses 12-point Times New Roman.

5. From the Format button, choose **Paragraph** and enter *6 points* in the After box under spacing. In addition, set the alignment to left before closing this dialog box.

6. Click on **Close** in the Style window. Your new style is now defined.

Many people refuse to use styles because they find them hard to learn and understand. For now, do not expect to understand all that is happening. Continue to follow the steps and you will soon be using them efficiently. Later, you will reach a point where you realize you understand the concept of styles without any extra effort.

Styles may take time to learn, but once you have mastered the skills they will save you a great deal of time and effort. Not only will your skills be of value inside *Word,* there are many other applications that include this same concept, although the specific steps may differ. Your mastery in this setting will allow you to easily make use of styles in other applications.

Creating a Text Style.   When you create a base style, you usually include attributes that are to be used in much of the text in your document. This base style is merely used to save time in defining and modifying the styles you apply to your text. It does not get applied directly. For the other styles in your document, simply add or subtract attributes from your "base" style.

You are now ready to create a style for your regular formatting—formatting such as the paragraph you are reading. This kind of paragraph is usually referred to as *body text.* With one exception, the steps used to create your own style for body text are the same as those you completed earlier.

In our example we will create a style called *mytext.*

1. Choose **Style** from the **Format** menu to display the Style window.
2. Click on the **New** button in the Style window. Modify the New Style dialog box as shown in Figure 2.45.

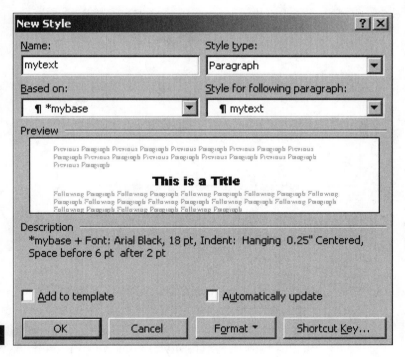

FIGURE 2.45

Make sure you use the drop-down menu to change the Based on style to your base style. Be sure you select "paragraph" for the Style type.

3. You are ready to add any necessary formatting to *mytext*. In our case, the set of properties for **mybase* and *mytext* are much the same. You may want to make other changes in your body text style.

4. For example, you might want to add a first-line indent. Choose Paragraph from the Format button. Adjust the formatting to create a first-line indent of about two or three characters—usually close to the 0.25 inch setting shown—and click OK. [Figure 2.46]

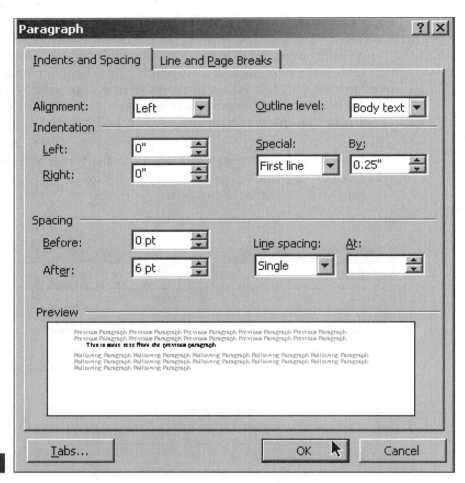

FIGURE 2.46

5. Click on **OK** in the Paragraph dialog box and then **OK** in the New Style dialog box. The style *mytext* now appears in the styles list.

Keep in mind that the style *mytext* has *all* of the characteristics of the base style called **mybase*—except ones that you changed. In the above example, we changed only the first-line indent. All of the other attributes—6 points after text, typeface, and so on—are part of both styles.

Creating a Heading Style.   Next, create a style for a centered heading. You use a heading style less frequently than the *mytext* style, and it will be considerably different than *mytext*. Also, this style will have fewer attributes in common with your base style.

To create your heading style, follow these steps:

1. Choose **Style** from the **Format** menu to display the Style window.
2. Click on the **New** button in the Style window. Modify the New Style dialog box as shown. [Figure 2.47]

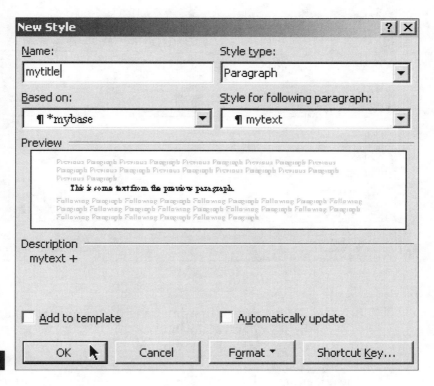

FIGURE 2.47

Be sure you remember to use Based on. You may also want to set the style for following paragraph to *mytext,* because in general the next formatting after a title will be your body text.

3. Now you are ready to add any necessary formatting to *myheading*. Make changes such as these:
   - Use the Format button and select the Font option. Choose a sans serif typeface, such as Arial or Helvetica.
   - In the same dialog box, choose a larger point size such as 18 or 24, add Bold style if you wish, and click OK.
4. Again, use the Format button; this time, select Paragraph. Set up the formatting as shown in Figure 2.48.

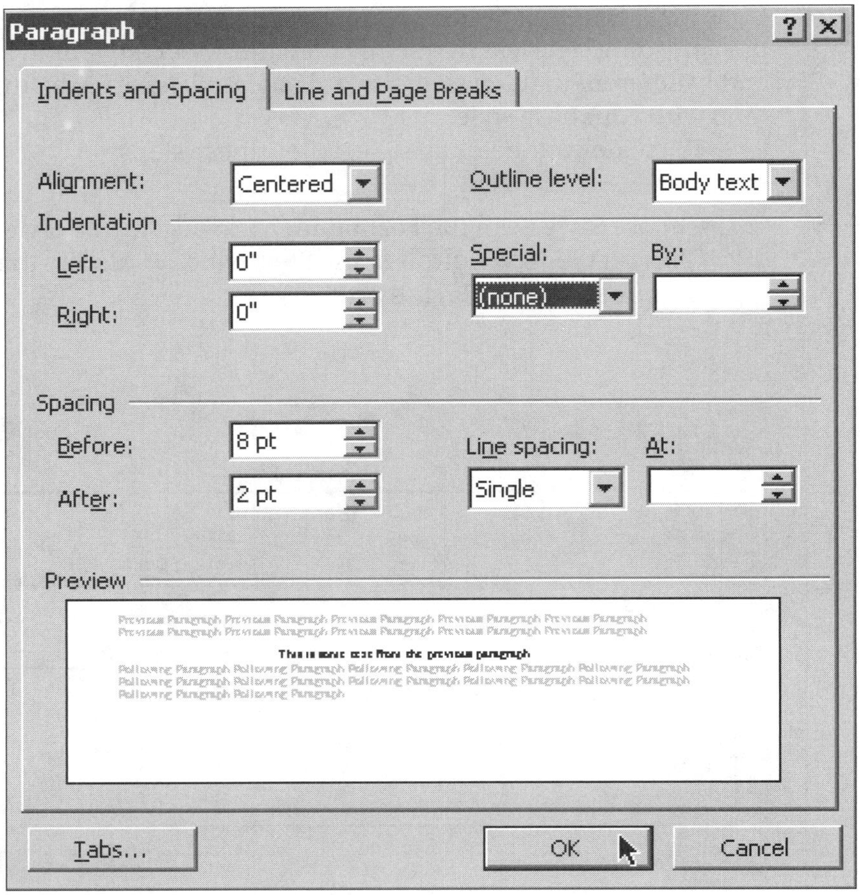

FIGURE 2.48

Be sure that there is no first-line indent set under Special, and click OK to close the Paragraph dialog box.

5. Click on **OK** in the New Style window.

The diagram in Figure 2.49 shows the relationship among the styles designed so far.

FIGURE 2.49

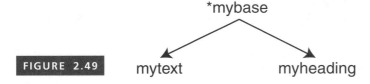

This diagram tells you that the attributes of *mybase* are passed on to both *mytext* and *myheading*. The attributes added to the styles *mytext* and *myheading* then override the attributes of the base style where changes were made.

Working with Styles

Once you have defined some styles, you need to work with them. Not only do you need to learn to apply them, but you will also want to learn how to use them more efficiently.

Mastering styles will make your day-to-day work much easier. As you create memos, worksheets, lesson plans, and other documents, you will be able to apply the formatting as you compose your documents. A personalized stylesheet is a powerful tool.

Applying Your Styles.   Once your styles are defined, applying them to text is easy.

1. In your blank document, enter at least two paragraphs. Remember, a paragraph is defined as a block of text ending with a return symbol.
2. Next, place the insertion point in a paragraph to which you want to apply the style. (When you are first using styles, you may want to highlight the text so you can clearly see which part of the text you are working with.)
3. Click the Styles box on the Formatting toolbar. If this toolbar is not visible, go to the **View** menu and select it from the list that appears in **Toolbars.**
4. Choose the style name from the drop-down menu. [Figure 2.50]

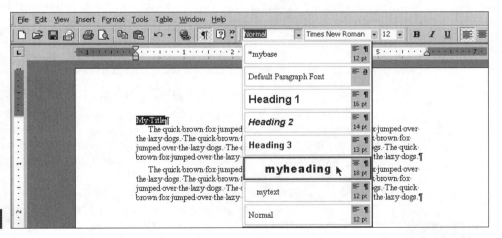

FIGURE 2.50

Repeat steps 2 through 4 for your other styles. Remember—you do not want to actually apply the base style. In fact, you never apply your base style; it is only used to connect the actual styles in your document.

If you are using a Macintosh, you are able to choose the style name from the Formatting palette. If your palette opens with the grey menu headings showing, use the disclosure triangle beside Font to open the list of options. [Figure 2.51]

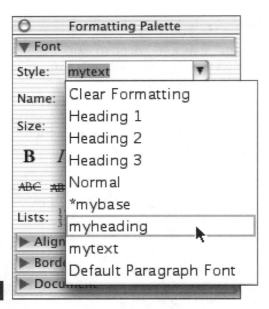

FIGURE 2.51

Why Is Based On Used?   You may be wondering why the style *mybase* was not applied to any of the text. This is because the base style serves as an anchor for other styles in your stylesheet. Because a base style is never applied to text, naming such styles in a special way—in this case, with an asterisk (*)—makes sense. The special naming makes it easy to avoid the accidental application of the base style in your stylesheet.

In Figure 2.52, each paragraph has a style applied that is connected to the base style.

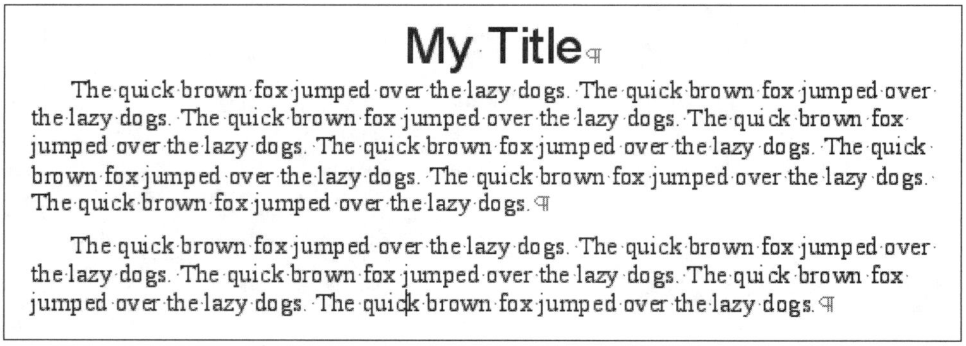

My Title ¶

The quick brown fox jumped over the lazy dogs. The quick brown fox jumped over the lazy dogs. The quick brown fox jumped over the lazy dogs. The quick brown fox jumped over the lazy dogs. The quick brown fox jumped over the lazy dogs. The quick brown fox jumped over the lazy dogs. The quick brown fox jumped over the lazy dogs. The quick brown fox jumped over the lazy dogs. ¶

The quick brown fox jumped over the lazy dogs. The quick brown fox jumped over the lazy dogs. The quick brown fox jumped over the lazy dogs. The quick brown fox jumped over the lazy dogs. The quick brown fox jumped over the lazy dogs. ¶

FIGURE 2.52

What happens if you change the attributes of *mybase*? For example, suppose you increase the type size and add italics to your base style definition. [Figure 2.53]

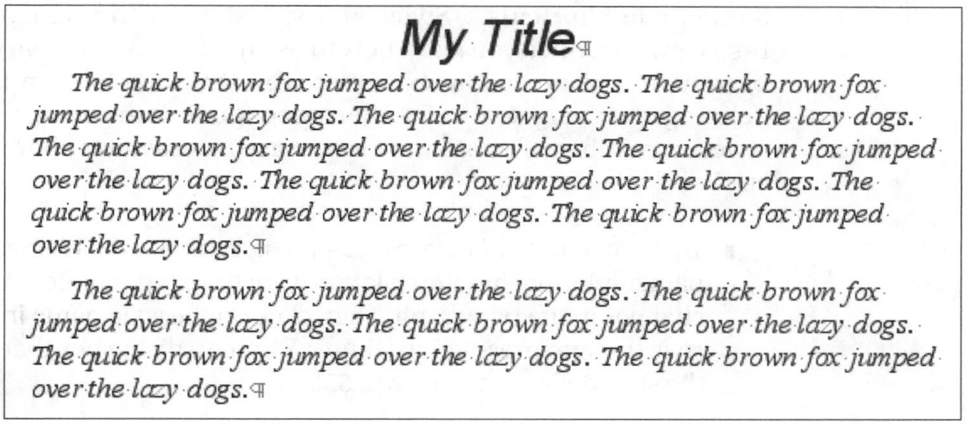

My Title¶

The quick brown fox jumped over the lazy dogs. The quick brown fox jumped over the lazy dogs. The quick brown fox jumped over the lazy dogs. The quick brown fox jumped over the lazy dogs. The quick brown fox jumped over the lazy dogs. The quick brown fox jumped over the lazy dogs. The quick brown fox jumped over the lazy dogs. The quick brown fox jumped over the lazy dogs.¶

The quick brown fox jumped over the lazy dogs. The quick brown fox jumped over the lazy dogs. The quick brown fox jumped over the lazy dogs. The quick brown fox jumped over the lazy dogs. The quick brown fox jumped over the lazy dogs.¶

FIGURE 2.53

Without making any change directly to the text, the redefined style immediately affects the document in several ways. The heading now shows italic text. It does not show a size change. The body text shows both the increased size and the italic text style.

Now, move to the **Style** window under **Format** and examine the definitions of the styles *myheading* and *mytext*. [Figure 2.54]

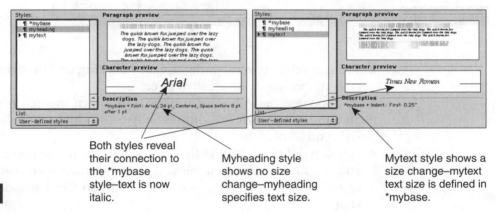

FIGURE 2.54

Both styles reveal their connection to the *mybase style—text is now italic.

Myheading style shows no size change—myheading specifies text size.

Mytext style shows a size change—mytext text size is defined in *mybase.

Note that attributes added—or removed—override the *same* attributes defined in the base style. By changing the attribute held in the base style definition, you can change every style that makes use of that particular attribute in one step.

Even if the document is 300 pages long, a change made to the base style will be applied to every paragraph making use of the attribute. For example, to change the type size of *all* of the non-heading text in this book, we would only need to change the size in the base style and the *entire* book would change.

Some Style Shortcuts.   Styles and stylesheets can seem very complex at first. However, once you learn how to use them, they can save you a great deal of time. In the preceding examples, you saw step-by-step instructions for defining and using styles. However, once you become more comfortable with styles, a number of shortcuts can be used to save you both time and key-strokes.

- To change the characteristics of a style, make the changes in one of the paragraphs that has the style you want to change applied. Make the desired changes in the paragraph. Then click on the style name in the drop-down style box and press Return/Enter. You see a dialog box that lets you change the style definition. [Figure 2.55]

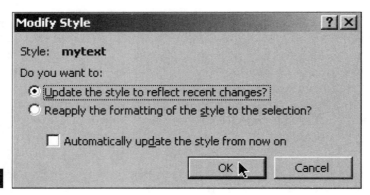

FIGURE 2.55

- You can select several paragraphs by clicking and dragging and apply a style to the entire selection at once.
- To apply a style without using the drop-down menu, press Command+Shift+S (Macintosh) or Control+Shift+S (PC) and enter the name of the style you want to use.
- You can define shortcuts to styles when you name them. For example, you might define "my small text" as "my small text, mst." Then when using the previous step, entering "mst" on the keyboard applies the style.

Technical Note: This special shortcut is only available to you if you have the For-matting toolbar visible. Also, as you use special names for the style, develop a system that allows you to easily remember what the style attributes are for each of your styles.

Another Way to Define Styles.   Some people prefer to format text the way they want it to look and *then* define a style. Even if you want to define styles this way, be sure you have created a base style as described earlier in this chapter. With your base style prepared, you can easily create new styles directly from your formatted text.

1. Begin by formatting some text in the document. [Figure 2.56]

FIGURE 2.56

In the example, the text is now in italic style and indented on the left and right margins. These attributes make it look quite different from the first paragraph.

2. With the newly formatted text still highlighted, click in the style box on the Formatting toolbar and enter a name and an abbreviation, for example: block indent,bi. You do not have to have the entire paragraph highlighted; simply be sure the pointer is somewhere in the paragraph.

3. Press the Return/Enter key, and your new style is defined.

4. Finally, you need to connect your new style to your base style. Open the Modify Style dialog box in the Style window, and choose your base style from the drop-down menu. Click OK and then Close to exit the Style window.

SUCCESS WITH STYLES

It takes time and effort to master using styles. Here are some guidelines to avoiding problems with styles.

- **Styles on all text.** Apply a style to all text in your document. Even if you only use a style once, it is worth your time to define a style. (Later you will learn how to move styles from one document to another.)

- **Based on.** Always use a base style, and as you define new styles, be sure you have used Based on correctly. (Note that you can have several base styles—perhaps one for headings, one for body text, and one for lists—but all styles should still be based on a single style.) [Figure 2.57]

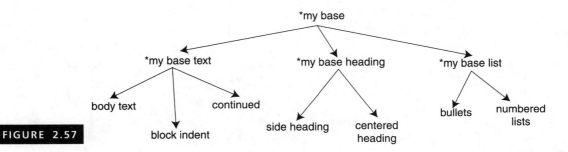

FIGURE 2.57

The book you are reading was constructed using a large stylesheet. Every paragraph of text and every graphic in the entire book has a style applied to it. Making a formatting change effective through the entire book with only one step is a matter of simply modifying the base styles used when defining the other styles. There is no question that creating documents without stylesheets is definitely the hard way to do the job. Not only can you make formatting changes quickly and easily with stylesheets, but if you create a set of documents that need the same appearance, you simply use the same stylesheet for all.

Digging Deeper

When you choose **Style** from the **Format** menu, you have access to a number of powerful tools. In this section you will learn important concepts for using styles effectively.

Keeping Those Styles Clean.   It is *extremely* important to read this next section carefully. Styles work *for* you only when they are applied consistently and correctly. If you have been using a word processor for a while, you are familiar with making formatting changes in the body of your document. If you continue to operate in this manner you will find it very difficult to become an effective user of styles. Defining or modifying a style to accommodate any formatting change is much more efficient.

So, the rule is to *always* define styles when you make any paragraph-wide changes. Do *not* change the formatting in the body of any paragraphs to which you have already applied a style unless you plan to use the revised text to define a new style.

To better understand how to solve style problems, make a change in your document *without* defining a new style. In the following example the typeface in the second paragraph was changed from 12-point Times New Roman to 14-point Zapf Chancery using the Font menu. [Figure 2.58]

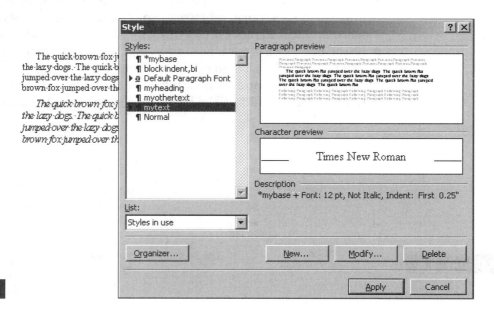

FIGURE 2.58

Now, choose **Style** from the **Format** menu. Compare the *definition* of the style (below Description in the dialog box) and the actual text you are working with (to the left of the dialog box). Because you changed the appearance of your text and did not adjust your style definition, you will find they no longer match. If this modification is something you intend to use with your paragraphs rather than your previously established definition, you need to modify the style to include this new attribute.

To modify the style definition, be sure your text insertion pointer is in the paragraph and open the Style window, then click on Modify. This opens a new window, giving you access to the drop-down list under the Format button. By selecting Font you can choose 14-point Zapf Chancery and *Word* will update the definition. Now when you use the style on new paragraphs, the text will match the formatting you have chosen.

The style correctly displays in the Current Selection part of the Style window, and any paragraph having the *mytext* style name will immediately appear with the 14-point Zapf Chancery typeface rather than the previous choice. You can make similar adjustments to any style by following these same steps. If you want to change the text appearance, be sure to adjust the style definition rather than simply changing the attributes within the paragraph.

Renaming Styles. Sometimes you want to retain the style definition, but change the name of the style. Click on the style name in the list of available styles in the Style window. Click on the Options button to open the Modify Style dialog box and enter the new name. [Figure 2.59]

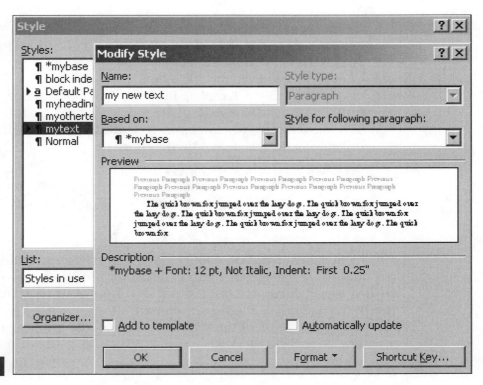

FIGURE 2.59

When you click OK, the style name will be changed in the list of styles. In addition, each paragraph that used the original name has now been changed to show the application of the new style name.

Make It Go Away.   If you want to remove a style from your stylesheet, open the Style dialog box. Click on the name of the style you wish to remove, then click on the Delete button. Note that if the style is applied to any of your text, *Word* will select a different style, usually Normal, to apply. In addition, you will be asked if you are sure this is what you want to do.

Using Styles in Other Documents

Once you have mastered the skill of creating styles, you need to establish techniques for using them in your day-to-day work. There are two different techniques for working with styles. One technique is not necessarily better than the other; choose the one that works best for you in a particular setting.

Using a Template.   Earlier, you learned how to save a template document. Recall that when you save a document as a template, all elements in the document appear whenever you open the document. In the example, there was a small graphic and the needed lines to begin a worksheet, as well as section and column breaks. The new document created from a template is named Untitled so that you cannot accidentally modify your template.

If you have a set of styles that you want to use on a regular basis, they can be saved in a template so that when you open a new document using the template, the styles are ready to use. To create such a document:

1. Define the set of styles you want in a new document.
2. Remove any text or other elements from your document that should *not* be part of your template document.
3. Choose **Save As** from the **File** menu.
4. Choose Document Template from the Format drop-down list (Macintosh) or from the Save As Type drop-down list (*Windows*).
5. Save the template with an easily recognizable name. Remember that it will automatically be saved in the *Office* Templates folder.

Your template will appear in the list of choices of new documents. If you are using a Macintosh, the template document will appear in the Project Gallery under My Templates.

Moving Styles Among Documents.   You may have created documents that you now realize would benefit from the use of your styles, or perhaps you just created a new document but did not start from your template. You do not need to recreate all your styles. If you have already created a set of styles, you can move some or all of these styles to any document using the Organizer available in the Style window.

1. Begin with a document containing styles.
2. Choose **Style** from the **Format** menu.
3. Click on the Organizer button found in the bottom left corner. A dialog box appears that lets you close and open different documents. The current or active document window is represented on the left. Generally, the "Normal" document will appear on the right.

   Close the document represented on the right by clicking the Close File button directly below the window. The button changes to Open File. After you click on the Open File button, you can browse the files on your computer to locate and open the document into which you want to put your styles.
4. The Organizer displays the list of styles in your current document on the left. Click on the name of a style you want to move to the new document, then click on Copy. The style name will appear in the window on the right, indicating it has been copied into the new document. [Figure 2.60]

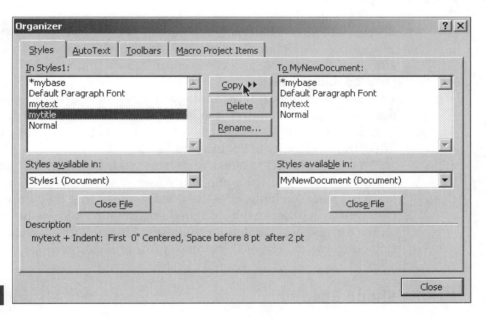

FIGURE 2.60

5. When you have copied all of the styles you want into your new document, close the dialog box. Make sure you move your base styles as well as the styles you apply.

The Organizer allows this copying of styles in either direction. Had you been working with the new blank document as the current file, the left window would appear without your styles list. This time you would use the right window to Close File—the default template—and follow the steps to locate the document you have created that contains all your styles. The copy step would move the selected styles from the right to the left window, placing the desired styles into your open, blank document.

Styles in Day-to-Day Work.   Styles only work for you if you have the stylesheets handy whenever you are ready to work. Thus it is important to place your stylesheets in an easily accessible place, such as the desktop of your computer. If you work on more than one computer, be sure that the styles you want to use are on every portable disk you use on different machines.

Different people use different approaches when working with styles. Some prefer to have one large stylesheet that includes all the styles they use in their work. Others prefer to have separate stylesheets for separate tasks. For example, you might have a set of Lesson Plan styles, a set of Worksheet styles, a set of Letters Home styles, and so forth.

When you first start using styles, getting a set of styles that works comfortably can take some time. Remember that tasks will take a bit longer as you first begin using styles. However, you will soon find that styles are a tremendous time-saver and wonder how anyone can get along without them.

INCREASING READABILITY

Several factors to increase readability of your documents have already been introduced—for example, that serif type is easier to read than sans serif type. However, the reading process is complex and many other factors influence the readability of text.

Because computer technology makes it easy to create your own teaching materials, it is important to keep factors that affect the readability of text in mind. Throughout this book, you will learn about a variety of factors that affect the readability of documents.

Learning to create effective documents is important for teachers so that students learn easily and efficiently from their materials. Students need to learn to create readable, effective documents so that they learn to communicate well with others. Well-designed documents make evaluation much easier for the teacher. Remember that these ideas fall into the category of NETS that concerns the use of Technology Communication tools.

Shape Reading

You already understand the difficulty caused by underlining your text. This effort to indicate emphasis on a word makes things more difficult to read because underlining interferes with the character set. Perhaps you feel that using all capital letters will solve this problem. Wrong. Using all capital letters causes an even worse problem.

Words are read partly by their shape. Consider the word *design*. Written with all capital letters, it has a rectangular shape. [Figure 2.61]

FIGURE 2.61   DESIGN⟶

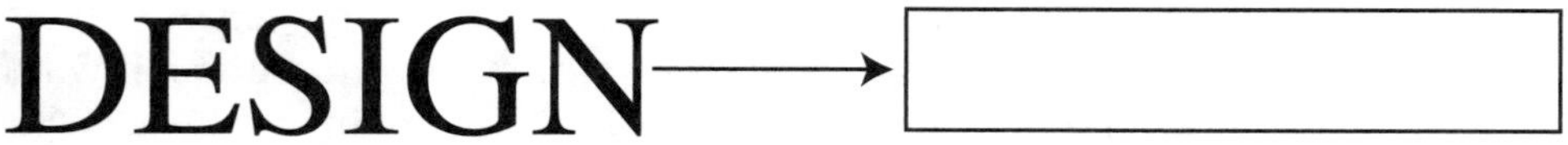

If you put several words side by side in all capital letters, they all have this same rectangular shape.

Using mixed or lowercase letters provides some variation. Look at the same word in lowercase. [Figure 2.62]

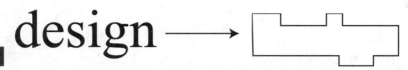

FIGURE 2.62

There is an obvious shape to the word even though you seldom stop to think about this. However, as you are reading, you make use of the shapes of letters and words to help recognize the words.

This same issue of giving shape to words is found in giving shape to paragraphs. Left-aligned text is more comfortable to read than centered or full-justified text. The straight edge on the left attracts the eye because it produces a distinctive edge, making it easy to move the eye back to the left edge of the page. The ragged right edge gives some shape to the paragraph, helping the eye to be consistent in moving down only one line as it moves to the left. As a result, the reading task is completed quickly and with little effort.

Notice how the paragraphs on the left have different shapes, whereas the ones on the right are not particularly distinctive as you move from one paragraph to the next. [Figure 2.63]

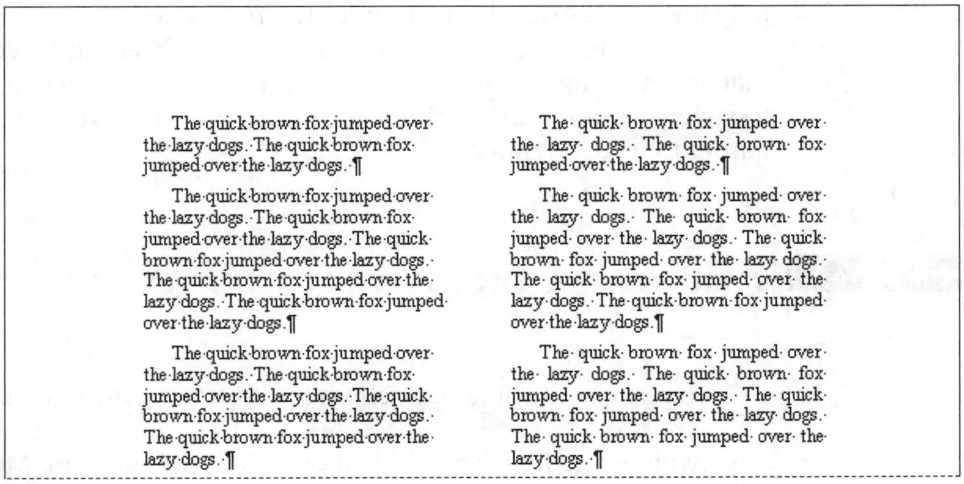

FIGURE 2.63

The·quick·brown·fox·jumped·over· the·lazy·dogs.·The·quick·brown·fox· jumped·over·the·lazy·dogs.·¶

The·quick·brown·fox·jumped·over· the·lazy·dogs.·The·quick·brown·fox· jumped·over·the·lazy·dogs.·The·quick· brown·fox·jumped·over·the·lazy·dogs.· The·quick·brown·fox·jumped·over·the· lazy·dogs.·The·quick·brown·fox·jumped· over·the·lazy·dogs.·¶

The·quick·brown·fox·jumped·over· the·lazy·dogs.·The·quick·brown·fox· jumped·over·the·lazy·dogs.·The·quick· brown·fox·jumped·over·the·lazy·dogs.· The·quick·brown·fox·jumped·over·the· lazy·dogs.·¶

The·quick·brown·fox·jumped·over· the·lazy·dogs.·The·quick·brown·fox· jumped·over·the·lazy·dogs.·¶

The·quick·brown·fox·jumped·over· the·lazy·dogs.·The·quick·brown·fox· jumped·over·the·lazy·dogs.·The·quick· brown·fox·jumped·over·the·lazy·dogs.· The·quick·brown·fox·jumped·over·the· lazy·dogs.·The·quick·brown·fox·jumped· over·the·lazy·dogs.·¶

The·quick·brown·fox·jumped·over· the·lazy·dogs.·The·quick·brown·fox· jumped·over·the·lazy·dogs.·The·quick· brown·fox·jumped·over·the·lazy·dogs.· The·quick·brown·fox·jumped·over·the· lazy·dogs.·¶

There are times when it is appropriate to use alignments other than left alignment, but for most documents stick to the basic left alignment.

The shape of several words side by side also plays a role in how easily you can read text. Look at the sentence in Figure 2.64. Can you read what it says?

FIGURE 2.64 our eyes follow the tops of letters.

If you were able to read it, did you find it difficult to read?
Now look at the sentence in Figure 2.65.

FIGURE 2.65 Your eyes follow the tops of letters

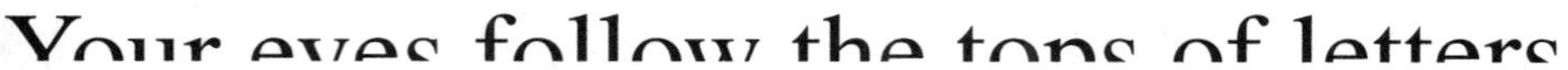

Could you read it? Researchers have concluded that reading is done in part by considering the shape of letters, words, and paragraphs. Having only the tops of the letters is easier to read than having only the bottom portion. The tops of letters provide more cues for reading. Did you experience this?

Because most people have been reading for a considerable length of time, they seldom stop to think about the role of word and paragraph shape in the reading process. Of course, ignoring these guidelines does not mean your words cannot be read, but the chance of it being read decreases rapidly. In most cases, people will stop reading or will be constantly distracted from reading without being aware of the cause.

Creating readable documents is even more important when working with children who are just learning to read. Well-designed documents will help them understand what is written *much* better.

There are other important challenges in reading to consider as you make formatting decisions. Because words written in all capital letters have less shape than words written in mixed case or lowercase, they are even harder to read. [Figure 2.66]

FIGURE 2.66 CAPITALS GIVE FEWER CUES

Here are some other guidelines for improving the readability of text.

- Avoid using light-colored text on a dark background. Many people like the appearance of light text on a black or other dark background. However, research indicates that comprehension of text drops tremendously when a dark background with light text is used.
- Keep your lines relatively short—lines longer than eight to ten words become quite hard to read. (Remember, this is line length rather than sentence length.)

- Lines that are too short cut your text into so many tiny pieces that it becomes difficult to find any meaning in the words.
- *Always* use a serif type—such as the one you are reading—for large blocks of text.

SUMMARY AND TIPS

This chapter has taken you many steps beyond beginning word processing. You will do well to stop and create your own checklist of special features to practice until they become an automatic part of your work style.

Computers put you in charge of both the content and the publishing of the document. Thus, you need to be concerned not only about the words that make up your document, but also about the appearance of your document.

Many of the options you encountered in this chapter will be helpful regardless of the type of document you are creating. Becoming skilled at letting the software do the menial tasks takes practice. Be patient with yourself.

The stylesheet is the most powerful feature of all—and undoubtedly the most underused by computer users. Do not expect to have all the steps in hand without considerable effort. Once you have the skill level that makes the use of styles comfortable, you will have moved a long way toward making the computer a powerful helper.

Because personal computers are a relatively new tool in people's day-to-day lives, most have not made enough of a transition from paper and pencil or typewriter to computer. Many still do tasks with the same mindset that they would have in using an older method. This often results in missing the real power of using a computer.

An important example is the creation of template documents, which can save you a great deal of time. By creating a new template document each time you encounter a new category of tasks, you are well on your way to using the power of *Word.* You should have template documents for letters, for memos, for different kinds of reports or papers, for lesson plans, for worksheets, for quizzes or tests—the list could be long. These documents will be automatically saved in the *Office* templates folder.

If you work on several computers, you will want to have a set of files that can be used as templates on a portable storage device, such as a floppy or Zip disk. A word of caution is in order here. If you move or save a template document created by *Word* outside of the correct *Office* folder, when you open the document to use it, your new file can only be saved as an official *Office* template document. To solve this problem, save each of your personalized templates—the files you want to use for producing customized documents—as a regular *Word* document on your removable media. Then, when you open your personal template document, immediately save it with a different name so you do not overwrite the template-like document you created for a specific task.

You should have stylesheets in each of your personal *Word* template documents. You may create new styles as you work to meet the special needs of a particular task. On a regular basis, update your personal templates by taking a few moments to incorporate your most used and new styles. Delete the styles that you seem to not need. Remember to save styles selectively and import them into any document you wish.

Another time- and frustration-saver is the spell checker. When you are creating a document, do not spend time correcting keyboarding errors. Instead, focus on getting your ideas into the document. Once you are finished with the document—or a section of the document—stop to spell check. You will be surprised at how many of your keystroke errors will be automatically located and corrected with the *Word* spell checker.

Finally, avoid re-entering the content of documents. Often beginners who have problems with a document simply throw up their hands and start over. This is a result of feeling helpless because in the past their skills were insufficient to overcome the problem. However, it is very seldom necessary to completely re-enter a document.

Documents can be translated from one word processor to another and from one platform to another. Printed documents can be scanned. Damaged disks can often be repaired. Lost documents can often be found. Keep an organized and up-to-date backup system in place. Ask for help. Keep trying new steps to problem solve rather than giving up easily, especially if you have put a long time into working on the document. Again, learn to let the computer do the work of finding, translating, and formatting the document or fixing the disk.

The power of word processing is incredible. Yet, as with many other skills, you need to practice before using the tools becomes automatic. Resist the temptation to ignore the new ideas you have encountered. You already know that you can make your document *look* acceptable when you print it by using your more comfortable bad-habits approach. Give yourself time to gain the skill level that makes using these new tools equally comfortable. Your work will soon be accomplished with less time and effort. Your work will gain the flexibility of letting you modify it quickly and easily and move it from one computer to another without fearing the results. Indeed, your publishing skills will result in much more effective communication.

The new skills and ideas that you learned in this chapter are incorporated in the ISTE Technology Standards categories of Productivity and Professional Practice and Basic Operations and Concepts. Both you and your students need to develop computer skills to function well in a world that is becoming increasingly dependent on computer technology.

Beyond the Typewriter— Word Processing Rules

This chapter introduced several new rules you should use when entering text.

1. Headers and footers should be used to organize your document.
2. Using section breaks lets you easily vary text layout choices.
3. Use automatic page numbers by inserting rather than trying to hand enter page numbers.
4. Use a stylesheet for your work and keep the stylesheet current.

5. Left-aligned text is the most readable.

6. Avoid the use of all capital letters.

7. Do not use a light color for text on a dark background.

8. Adjust the length of the line to the size of the font being used. The length of line most appropriate will hold about 8 to 10 words in the typeface you have chosen.

9. Do not use two hyphens to format text. Instead, use an *em dash* or an *en dash*. An en dash replaces the word *to* in an interval statement, for example, in "the meeting will be from 4–6 P.M. on Wednesday." An em dash provides a sentence break stronger than a comma but less important than a period. For example, in "She entered the classroom—despite the fact she was not a student—and took a seat near the door."

Mark this page in your book and review these guidelines from time to time. They will help you produce documents that communicate effectively with your colleagues and students.

Graphics Tools

The first two chapters of this book focused on learning to use the word processor in *Microsoft Office* as an aid in working with words. You learned that word processing is different from typing. You learned that *Word* contains many features that can make your work easier.

In addition to tools for working with words, *Word* has tools for working with graphics. Other *Office* components also have graphics features, which will be explored later in this book. Being comfortable with integrating and using images increases your options for producing attractive documents.

We live in a world filled with images. From television to store advertisements to electronic games to movies to magazines, we are constantly barraged by both static and moving images. To communicate effectively in today's world, you need to learn to create documents that use images as well as words. Learning to use images effectively is part of effective communication using technology, one of the categories of NETS, the ISTE-developed Technology Standards for students and teachers.

In this chapter, you will learn about three different graphics features available in *Word:* the Drawing toolbar, WordArt, and the Clip Art collection that comes with *Office.*

INTRODUCTION TO PAINT AND DRAW

Before learning what you can accomplish using the graphics tools in *Word,* you need to learn about the different types of graphics you encounter in working with digital documents. There are two general types of images, Paint and Draw. Paint images are also called bitmapped or raster images. Draw images are also called Vector images.

Most of the images you will use in *Word* will be Draw images. However, there are many Paint or bitmapped images that you may want to add to your *Word* documents. For example, photos from a digital camera are bitmapped, as are images you download from the Internet. Some applications, such as *Adobe PhotoShop,* produce bitmapped images. Images produced using a scanner are also bitmapped.

A bitmapped document is made up of many, many dots, called *pixels*—for **pi**cture **el**ement—the smallest available area on a computer screen. A Paint document stores each individual pixel that you see on the screen. If you magnify a line drawn in a Paint environment, you can actually see the individual pixels that make up the line. Often such a line is jaggy and uneven in appearance since the individual pixels are visible. [Figure 3.1]

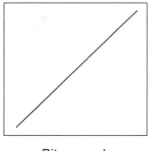 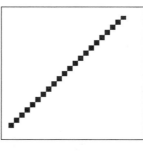 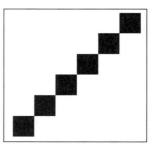

Bitmapped Straight Line	Same Bitmapped line viewed at 400%	Same Bitmapped line viewed at 1600%

FIGURE 3.1

Because the images created consist of many pixels, a Paint document requires considerable working memory and storage space.

Draw documents, on the other hand, are stored as mathematical descriptions of the lines and shapes used to create the image. As a result, Draw documents require less memory and storage space than a Paint document.

Paint and Draw images also vary in the way they print. For images intended for use in print documents, Draw images produce better results. However, many of the graphics included in this book are bitmapped graphics—Paint images. This is because actual screenshots were used in the manuscript—and any image you see on a computer screen is made up of pixels. Occasionally you may notice the jagged look common to all bit-mapped images.

You have now seen some of the differences between Paint and Draw.

- Paint images are made up of dots called pixels.
- Draw images are stored as mathematical formulas.
- Paint images have the "jaggies"—especially if they are enlarged.
- Text in Paint looks jaggy when printed.
- Draw objects can be sized without distortion or the jaggies.

An example illustrating some of the differences between Paint and Draw images follows. The image and label combination on the left were done in a Paint program; the same image was produced in a Draw program, shown on the right. In each environment, the combination of circle and text label was selected for resizing to produce the images below. We then took a screenshot to illustrate the result of these steps. What you see on the page is, of course, a bitmapped image. [Figure 3.2]

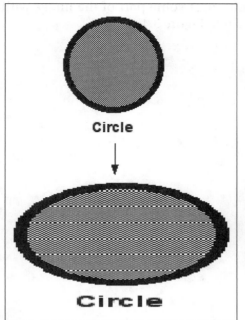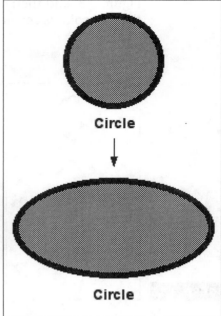

FIGURE 3.2

On the left, both circle and text change size and become distorted. On the right, the circle changes size, but the text remains the same. However, in the actual Draw document neither the text nor image shows any distortion after it was resized.

The distortion of images in the Paint environment occurs because the document contains only the specific characteristics of each dot in the original image. When you enlarge a Paint image, the computer must estimate which areas of the screen should be filled with dots to reproduce what was originally seen. If you decrease the size of a Paint image, the computer must estimate which pixels need to be thrown away. The computer can come close, but seldom can it be exact. Slight changes in size are not problematic, but changing more than 15 percent either way generally produces distortion. Keep this in mind if you add digital photos or scanned images to your document.

A Draw object is stored as a collection of attributes—think of numerical codes—and mathematical equations. When you change the object, the equation for the shape of the object is altered. However, the "codes" for color, line width, pattern, and the like remain the same. The computer can then draw the new object without guesswork or distortion.

Here is another analogy illustrating the difference between Draw and Paint images. Think of a Paint image as a piece of paper on which you want to create images with crayons. If you create something on the paper, as in

Figure 3.3, and then color over some part of the image with another color, the first color is covered up. [Figure 3.4]

FIGURE 3.3

FIGURE 3.4

The way a Paint program works is similar to this. Placing a new image or color over the first replaces the original pixels.

Next think about a Draw program. Did you ever make a collage? You collect some "stuff" and arrange it on a page to produce a work of art. [Figure 3.5]

FIGURE 3.5

You can rearrange the pieces again and again until you decide to finish the task and glue them together. [Figure 3.6]

FIGURE 3.6

Draw documents work like a collage. The pieces rearrange and resize quickly and easily—again and again. In electronic form, you can do this at any time you choose. It is not until you print the document that the elements are "glued" in place.

Think of a Paint program as a place where you work at a dot-by-dot level, changing even the smallest details if you wish. Think of the Draw program as the place you work at the object level, arranging and rearranging the objects until you have the final product. The tools that you use in *Word* are Draw tools. *Word* does not have the ability to *create* Paint documents.

THE DRAWING TOOLBAR

To begin your work with Draw objects in *Word,* go to the **View** menu, and from **Toolbars** choose **Drawing.** The Drawing toolbar appears. [Figure 3.7]

The Drawing toolbar is slightly different on the Macintosh. Your version of *Office* may display this toolbar vertically or horizontally. [Figure 3.8]

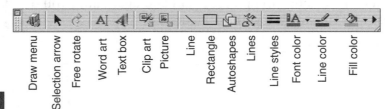

Look closely at the toolbar in your version of *Word*. Some of the icons have a small triangle next to them. Each icon with a disclosure triangle has a drop-down menu under it. You will learn about these submenus as you move through this chapter.

Technical Note: To customize your workspace to meet your unique work style, remember that these toolbars can be placed and sized in a variety of ways. If your screen has extra space to the side, placing them vertically is perhaps an advantage because it leaves more vertical screen space to display your document.

GETTING STARTED WITH DRAW TOOLS

Open a new *Word* document and be sure the Drawing toolbar is visible. To begin, we will explore simple graphics objects. Click on the Line icon, then click and drag on your page. When you release the mouse button, you see a line with a small square at each end. [Figure 3.9]

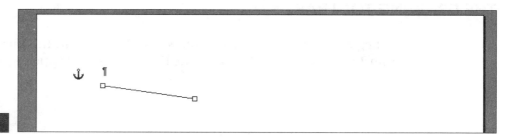

The squares are called *handles*. Handles are used to modify a Draw object. You also see an anchor symbol. This symbol is used to position a graphic on your page. There will be more about anchors later.

Next, make sure your line is selected—that is, you can see the handles. If the handles are not visible, start by clicking on the Selection Tool—the small arrow on the toolbar. Remember, the handles appear when you click on the line to select it. The handles disappear any time you click elsewhere on the page. Next, click on the Line Style or Dash Style buttons. Choose a line style that is different from the current one. When you release your mouse button, the appearance of your line changes. [Figure 3.10]

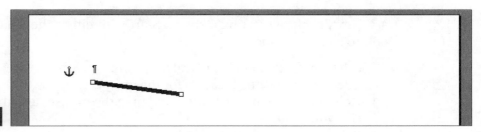

FIGURE 3.10

You can also adjust the color and pattern of the line. If you click on the small disclosure triangle next to the Line Color icon, you see a menu that lets you choose colors and more. [Figure 3.11]

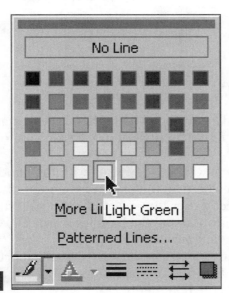

FIGURE 3.11

Explore this menu a bit and see the ways you can modify your line.

You can also turn your lines into arrows. Click on the triangle next to the Arrow Style icon. With your line selected—with the handles showing—choose an arrow style. When you release the mouse button, your choice is applied to the line. If you click elsewhere on the page, the handles and anchor disappear. [Figure 3.12]

FIGURE 3.12

Next, explore creating a shape. Start with either the Rectangle or Oval tool. To create a shape:

1. Click on the Rectangle or Oval tool icon.
2. Click at the starting location for the object.
3. Hold down the mouse button and drag the mouse until the shape is the size you want.
4. Release the mouse button. [Figure 3.13]

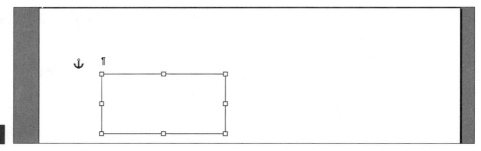

FIGURE 3.13

Again, you see white handles on the object. These handles are used when editing. You may have a different number of handles on your object than are shown in this image.

When you first create an object, it appears with the handles visible. As before, when you click elsewhere on the page, the handles disappear. When you move the pointer directly over the object, the pointer icon will change and clicking the mouse button makes the handles reappear. When the handles are showing, the object is *selected*.

To make changes to an object, you must have it selected. Once the handles are visible, press the Delete/Backspace key. You could also select the object and choose **Cut** from the **Edit** menu.

Other changes are possible. Make sure you have an object selected on your screen, and explore changing the line style and color. Use the same tools you used to modify the line earlier. [Figure 3.14]

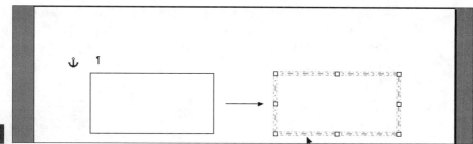

FIGURE 3.14

You can also change the fill color of the object. Make sure your object is selected, then click on the triangle next to the Fill color icon and choose a fill color. [Figure 3.15]

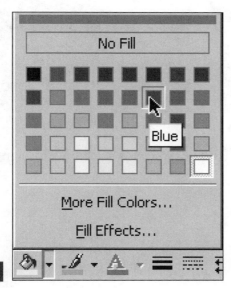

FIGURE 3.15

The More Fill colors option provides access to many more shades than those displayed. When you select a color and release the mouse button, the object you selected is filled with color. [Figure 3.16]

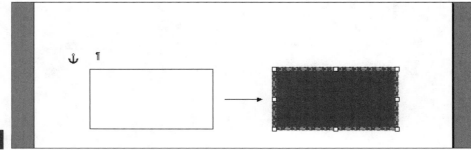

FIGURE 3.16

Other features available on the Drawing toolbar are also easy to apply. Put a shape of your choice on your page, and click on the shape to be sure it is selected. Then try clicking on the Shadow icon and select a shadow style. [Figure 3.17]

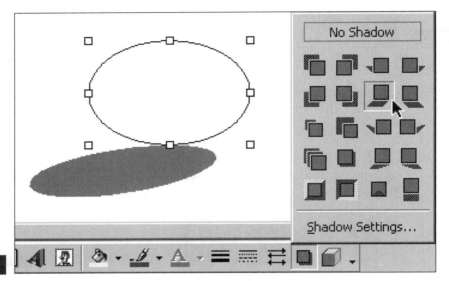

FIGURE 3.17

Next, try the 3D icon. Be sure your object is selected and then choose a 3-D style. [Figure 3.18]

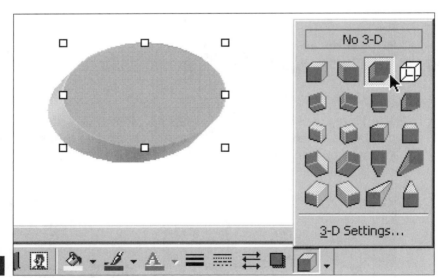

FIGURE 3.18

These two options create many interesting combinations of shapes and text.

WORKING WITH DRAW OBJECTS

Word includes many shapes that you can use much as you would clip art. Click on the AutoShapes button to see your choices. The drop-down menu provides several categories of ready-made shapes. If you are using a Macintosh, the same options are accessed using one of two buttons—the icon with three shapes on it or the icon with lines and arrows. [Figure 3.19]

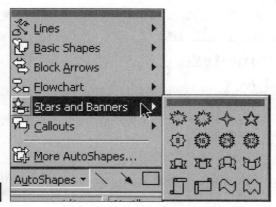

Choose a shape from the submenu from one of the categories that you would like to explore. Then click on the page. Notice that you do not need to click and drag for the object to appear. The shape can be resized by clicking and dragging a handle.

To create the shapes below, we selected the second shape on the top row of the Stars and Banners submenu. Then we clicked on a corner handle and dragged to enlarge the shape. To get the second image, we selected a 3 point line, set the color of the line to blue and selected a dashed line pattern. To get the third image, we clicked on the Fill icon and chose Fill Effects. From the next window that appeared, we clicked on the Texture tab and selected a texture we liked. [Figure 3.20]

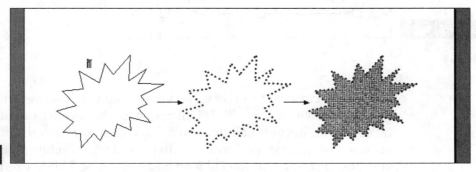

Spend some time exploring the different kinds of shapes and the many choices of colors, patterns, textures, and styles that are available. Your skills will quickly improve by exploring and experimenting with the combination of tools and options *Word* provides.

You can also add text to the graphics objects that you create. The text boxes you create using the Graphics toolbar can easily be moved on the page to combine with other Draw objects. From the Drawing toolbar, click on the Text box icon, then click on the page. You can enter text in the box that appears. [Figure 3.21]

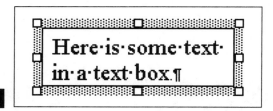

FIGURE 3.21

You can then combine your text box with the shape of your choice. [Figure 3.22]

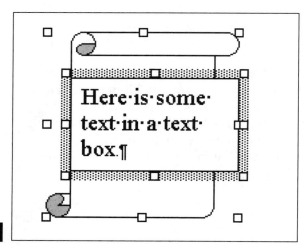

FIGURE 3.22

If you look closely at the previous image, you will discover that the text box was created with a white fill. When you place the text in front of the scroll, the fill covers whatever is behind it. In many cases, you want the object to simply appear as if the text was written onto the object. To achieve this effect, select your text box, click on the Fill icon and choose No Fill. At this point, you still have the line that defines the text box but the inside is transparent, allowing you to see the edge of the scroll behind the text box.

You can, of course, remove the box around the text. Click on the Line icon and choose No Line. [Figure 3.23]

FIGURE 3.23

Remember that the small "dots" and the ¶ mark will disappear once you print the document or click on the Show/Hide ¶ button on the Formatting toolbar.

Perhaps your shape and text box had a different problem. Maybe your shape covers the text. [Figure 3.24]

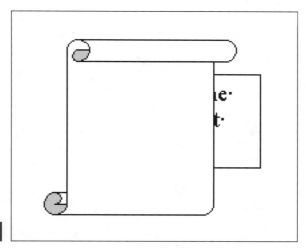

FIGURE 3.24

Items you create with the Drawing toolbar are Draw objects. Think back to the collage analogy at the beginning of this chapter. Each Draw object can be manipulated independently. When you get several Draw objects that overlap on a page, you may need to move them from one layer to another.

If you click on the Draw menu on the Drawing toolbar, you see a list of choices for working with Draw objects. If you choose Order, you see a list of choices for moving Draw objects from one layer to another. [Figure 3.25]

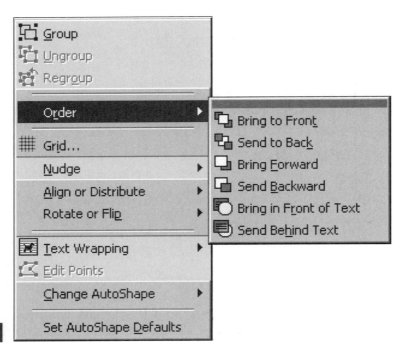

FIGURE 3.25

To explore moving objects from one layer to another, create an image that has two or three layered objects. Then select one of the objects. [Figure 3.26]

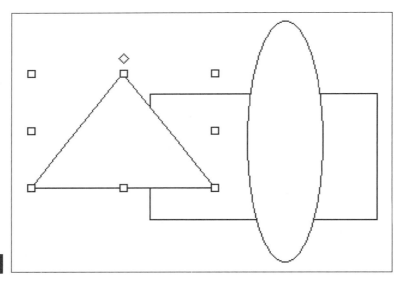

FIGURE 3.26

Open the Order submenu on the Draw menu. Change the layer in which the selected object is currently placed. For example, by choosing Move to Back with the triangle selected, the triangle moves, changing the layering of the objects. [Figure 3.27]

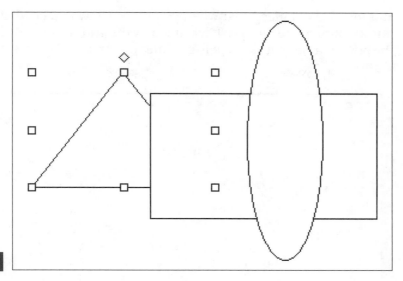

FIGURE 3.27

Take some time to explore moving objects from one layer to another so you are comfortable with the way Draw objects can be moved.

There are many other tools available for working with objects on the Draw menu. For example, you can adjust grid settings. If you choose Grid, you see a menu that allows you to change a number of settings. [Figure 3.28]

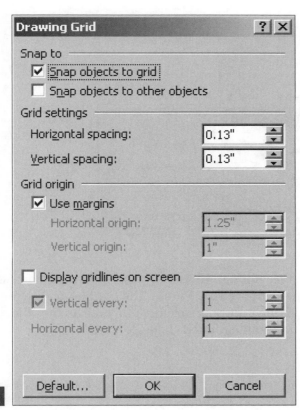

FIGURE 3.28

You may have noticed that when you move Draw objects that they "jump." The amount of the jump is determined by the grid settings. If you want to see the grid, you can check Display gridlines on screen. [Figure 3.29]

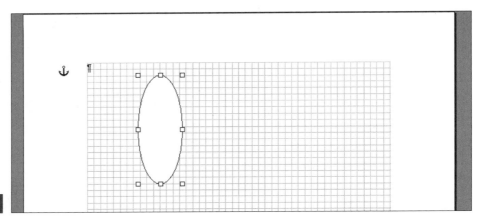

FIGURE 3.29

Changing the grid settings causes the size of the squares in the grid to change. The grid setting also affects the Nudge menu choice. If you choose Up from the Nudge menu, the selected object will move toward the top of the page the distance set for the vertical grid setting.

Next, explore the Rotate or Flip menu on the Draw menu. [Figure 3.30]

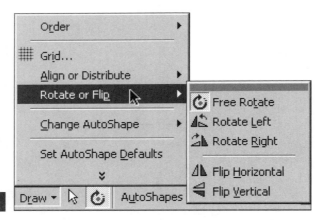

FIGURE 3.30

The first choice, Free Rotate, is also found on the Draw menu. Select an object on your page, then choose Free Rotate. The handles on the object change to green circles. With the rotate cursor, click and drag on the object. You see both the original shape and the rotated shape. [Figure 3.31]

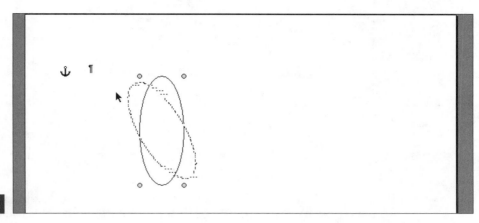

When you release the mouse button, only the rotated shape remains. The green handles disappear when you click on the shape with a different tool.

There are other choices on the Rotate or Flip menu. The Rotate Left and Rotate Right choices rotate the shape 90°. Flip Horizontal and Flip Vertical create a mirror image of the shape across a horizontal or vertical line. For example, if we flip our rotated oval horizontally, we see the shape in its new position. [Figure 3.32]

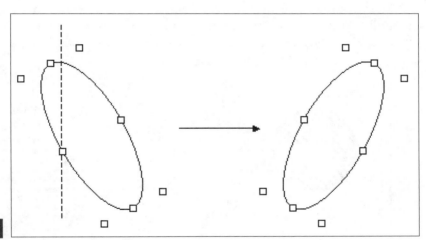

Take a few moments to experiment sizing, flipping, and rotating Draw objects.

There are three options on the Drawing toolbar that can be very useful: Group, Ungroup, and Regroup. Put a couple of objects on your page. Click on one of the objects, then hold down the Shift key and click on the second object. You see all of the handles of both objects. Then choose Group from the Drawing toolbar. You then see one set of handles for both objects. [Figure 3.33]

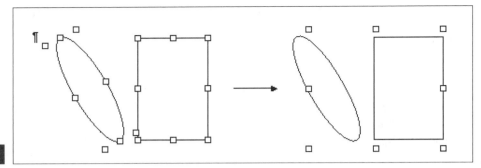

FIGURE 3.33

You can now move or modify both shapes at once because the Group option "connects" them, letting the computer treat them as a single object. Ungroup separates the object shapes back into independent shapes.

When you are working with several objects, getting them into the correct position can be challenging. On the Draw menu, the options for Align or Distribute provide convenient tools for creating graphics documents. In many cases, your final image consists of several smaller objects and positioning them quickly and easily takes practice.

Make sure you have three or four objects in your document. To select several of your objects, click on the first object, hold down the Shift key, click on the next object, and so forth. As long as the Shift key is held down, you can keep adding to the number of selected objects. Another method to select several objects is to use the Selection tool (the arrow) from the Drawing toolbar to click and drag around the objects you want to select. [Figure 3.34]

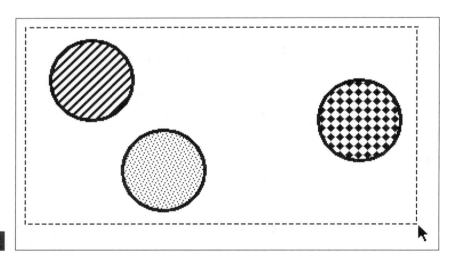

FIGURE 3.34

Once you have several objects selected, choose **Align or Distribute** from the Draw menu located on the Drawing toolbar. The menu provides a large number of choices for organizing the objects. Do not be afraid to experiment with these settings so that you can understand how they can best speed up your work. [Figure 3.35]

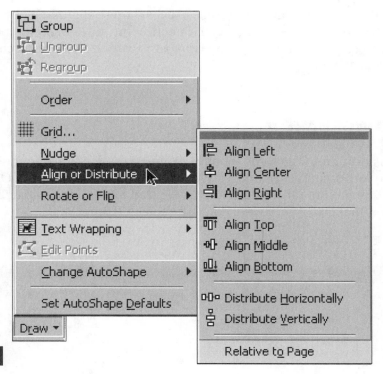

FIGURE 3.35

Suppose you have three objects similar to those shown in our example. Select them and choose Align Middle. Immediately, the organization of the objects changes. [Figure 3.36]

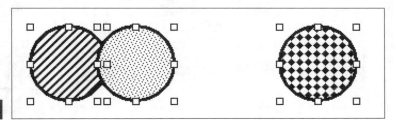

FIGURE 3.36

Again, make sure your three objects are selected. This time, click on Align center and then on Distribute horizontally. You see the spacing change. [Figure 3.37]

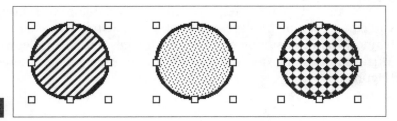

FIGURE 3.37

Did you notice that before you can access these alignment options, you must select more than one object? Spend some time experimenting with the choices on this menu. Letting *Word* assist you in placing objects can save you a lot of time.

CLIP ART AND WORDART

In addition to the tools we have explored on the Drawing toolbar, there are two other sources of images available as part of your copy of *Office*. Begin by clicking on the Insert Clip Art button in the Drawing toolbar. You see a window that gives you a wide range of choices. [Figure 3.38]

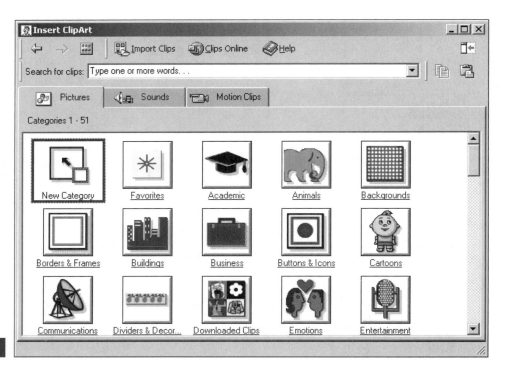

FIGURE 3.38

It is easy to add images to the Clip Art set, so the images you see may be different. The appearance of the Clip Art window also differs among versions of *Office*.

Next, click on the category of your choice. Before you choose, notice that you can scroll down to see more categories. Once you select a category, the window displays a choice of specific images. For example, we selected the Music category. Next we clicked on the image we were interested in using. [Figure 3.39]

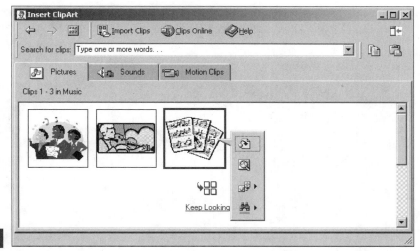

FIGURE 3.39

When you click on a specific item, you see a short menu. The top icon inserts the image at the location of the cursor on the page. The second icon allows you to preview the image. The third icon allows you to add images to this collection or bookmark those you intend to use often. Finally, the last icon lets you look for similar images.

The other kind of image you can insert into your documents is called WordArt. Click on the WordArt icon on the Drawing toolbar. You see a screen that shows the WordArt Gallery. Click on a preview to select your preference. [Figure 3.40]

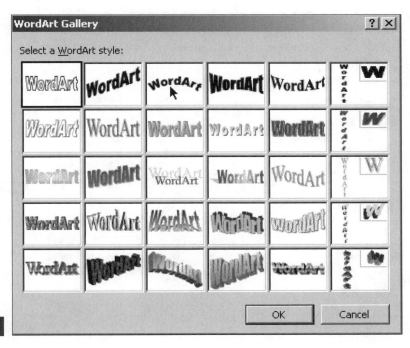

FIGURE 3.40

You then see a window in which you can enter text of your choice, and select typeface, type size, and bold or italic text style. [Figure 3.41]

FIGURE 3.41

When all of your choices have been made, click on OK.

The words you entered appear at the location of the cursor on your page, and the choices you made are automatically applied to the text. If you then click on the WordArt image, the handles appear. You also see a toolbar that allows you to make further changes in your WordArt item. [Figure 3.42]

FIGURE 3.42

Spend some time experimenting with WordArt. This powerful feature allows you to create a variety of interesting text objects for your page.

INTEGRATING TEXT AND IMAGES IN *WORD*

Once you master fundamental skills such as using styles in a word processing document and learning to use the Drawing toolbar, you are ready to combine your skills to produce more complex documents. Often, you want to create a document that includes both graphics and text. A newsletter, for example, might have a banner across the top, include several different articles with headings and subheadings, and have pictures scattered throughout the text. Newsletters are a great way to communicate with parents. They are also a good way for students to share the results of research or study in almost any discipline.

Suppose you want to design the title for a newsletter or a flyer. This part of a newsletter is often called the banner. First, locate a piece of clip art you would like to use. When you click on the clip art, you see the Picture toolbar. Take some time to explore the icons on this toolbar. [Figure 3.43]

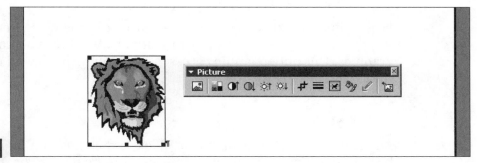

FIGURE 3.43

Next, click on the WordArt icon and create a title for the newsletter. [Figure 3.44]

FIGURE 3.44

You might choose to add other elements to make your banner more interesting.

When you are satisfied with your banner, use the Shift-click technique to select all of the elements of your banner. Then group them all into one object. [Figure 3.45]

FIGURE 3.45

If you were unable to select the clip art image you added to your page, it may be on the text layer of your page. In the next section, you will learn how to solve that problem.

INLINE AND FLOATING GRAPHICS

When you begin using graphics in your word processing documents, it is important to understand the two distinct ways that you can place your graphics. This understanding is essential if you wish to avoid needless frustration and problems.

Inline Graphics

An *inline* graphic is one that "acts" like a text character; that is, the graphic becomes part of a line of text. It moves with the text as you add or remove text characters. It "sticks" to the paragraph where it appears. The image stays between the preceding and following paragraphs if it is the only character in the paragraph.

In Figure 3.46, the graphic is inserted into the middle of a line of text, forcing the spacing to widen. Notice that when you click on the graphic, you see the handles, but the image is tightly held between the two parts of the sentence on either side of it.

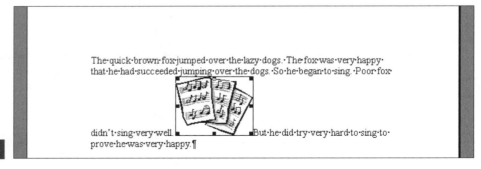

FIGURE 3.46

In Figure 3.47, the image is inserted as a separate paragraph. The image can be formatted like any other text—in this case, centered.

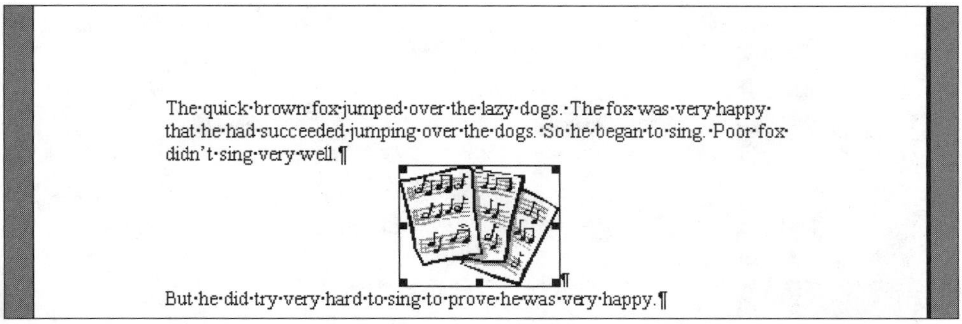

The·quick·brown·fox·jumped·over·the·lazy·dogs.·The·fox·was·very·happy·
that·he·had·succeeded·jumping·over·the·dogs.·So·he·began·to·sing.·Poor·fox·
didn't·sing·very·well.¶

But·he·did·try·very·hard·to·sing·to·prove·he·was·very·happy.¶

FIGURE 3.47

Notice that the handles are black. When you see black handles, the image will act as a single text character.

To create an inline graphic:

1. Place the text pointer in the document where you want to place the image.
2. Go to the **Insert** menu and select **Picture.**
3. Select Clip Art. In the Insert ClipArt window use the Picture tab and locate the appropriate category of images. (If you are on a Macintosh, the Clip Art Gallery appears with the available categories displayed on the left and the included images on the right).
4. Click on the image of your choice and open a menu of four buttons. Click the top button to insert the image and then close the window. (On a Macintosh, click on the selected image and use the Insert button to both place the image and close the window).
5. The selected image is visible in your document where the text pointer was positioned. Click and drag on the black handles to resize if needed.

Floating Graphics

Graphics can be put into text as *floating graphics* so that they are not affected by the text. A floating graphic is carried in its own layer and is always distinct from the text layer. When selected, a floating graphic can be placed anywhere in the document by clicking and dragging. In addition, the image may be left in a layer above the text or moved behind the text.

To create a floating graphic:

1. Select the graphic you inserted earlier. You should see the *black* handles.
2. In the Drawing toolbar, click on the Draw menu and choose Text Wrapping (on a Macintosh, from the Draw menu select Format Picture and select the Layout tab).
3. Select Square. You see the handles change to open squares. You can now click on the image and drag it anywhere on the page. The text moves out of the way of the image. When text flows around an image, text wrap is turned on. [Figure 3.48]

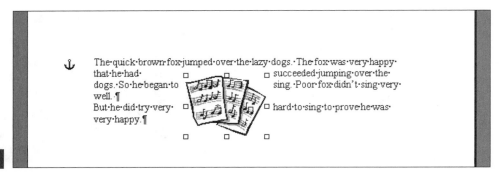

FIGURE 3.48

You can move an image from floating to inline by selecting the image and using the Drawing or Picture toolbar to access the text wrapping options. Or, if you double-click on the image, the Format Picture window opens with the needed settings available on the Layout tab.

Just as you can have an image with text wrapped around it, you can also put an image behind the text. An image behind text is often referred to as a *watermark* image. In this situation, the image needs to be made extremely light so that it does not interfere with the reading of the text.

To create a watermark, locate a very light image or use a program with paint capabilities to lighten the image.

1. Insert the image into your document.
2. Double-click on the image to open the Format Picture window.
3. Select Behind text. [Figure 3.49]

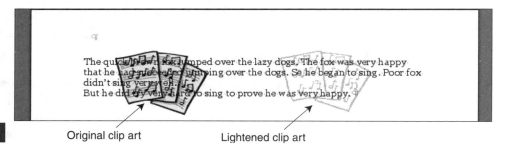

FIGURE 3.49

Original clip art   Lightened clip art

Notice that even with the lightened version of the image, the watermark does increase the effort required to read the text. To ensure that adding a watermark does not detract from your message, use them sparingly and with great care. Often, such an element merely distracts the reader rather than enhancing the communication you intend.

GRAPHICS? WHERE?

Graphics are an increasingly important part of the documents we create. There are many sources of graphics, but you must keep in mind that there are copyright issues surrounding the use of them. Check the sources of any image you use for copyright information.

So, where can you get graphics?

- As you have seen, the clip art available in *Office* has an extensive variety of categories.
- As a registered owner of *Office,* you have access to a large collection of Clip Art online. If you are connected to the Internet, you should be able to access this collection from the Clip Art dialog box.
- Digital cameras are becoming increasingly common and economical. You can take your own pictures to illustrate a document or add interest to a flyer.
- Scanners allow you to digitize almost any image. You can scan household objects, leaves, and fabric, in addition to photos.
- The Web has many sources of clip art. Images that you see on the Web belong to the Web site owner. If you use an image from the Web, be sure that you have permission to do so.
- Clip Art collections are probably the fastest and easiest source to use for graphics. A mid-range Clip-Art collection should cost less than $100, provide many thousands of images on CD or DVD, and should provide a printed set of thumbnails—tiny pictures—for you to use in selecting your image.

Graphics add a great deal to your documents' effective communication. Take the time to learn to use images appropriately in *Word.*

SUMMARY AND TIPS

The combination of Drawing tools, Clip Art, and WordArt provides a variety of options for producing attractive and useful images. You should enjoy using these tools even if you feel you are not particularly artistic. Letting the computer do the difficult work will soon have you feeling confident enough to try producing your own unique images to include in your documents.

The relationship between the text and images in a document is important. There are instances when inline graphics are best. If text gets added or deleted, the relationship of any image to the text is maintained. If you are to produce a newsletter and want to place an image and text together in a banner, it is best to create the banner using the tools accessed via the Drawing toolbar, group all the elements, and place the completed object as a floating image into your word processing document. With practice, you will soon be making these kinds of decisions with little effort.

As soon as you begin to combine word processing and images in complex ways, it's time for the tears to begin. Most likely part of your previous experience with computers was doing word processing. Perhaps you occasionally added a graphic to your document, but your primary experience is probably with entering and formatting text.

When you begin to have difficulty with a document that has both text and graphics in it, first stop and take a deep breath. Begin clicking on various parts of the document. Pay attention to the handles on images. Are they black? Are they white? Are several images grouped?

A common problem for beginners occurs when they first add graphics to a word processing document. Perhaps you have had your graphic "stuck" so that you could not move it where you wanted. Most likely, you inserted the graphic as an inline character instead of as a free-floating graphic object. If so, reread the section "Using the Drawing toolbar in *Word*" and follow the steps there carefully.

To create an inline graphic:

- Click in your text to place the insertion point where the image is to be placed.
- Insert the image.
- If you want the image in its own paragraph, use the Enter or Return key as needed.

To create a floating graphic:

- Double-click on the image.
- In the Format Picture window, click on Layout.
- Choose any of the choices *except* In line with text.
- Position the image in the text by clicking and dragging.

Meeting the Standards

Your work in this book has taken you through many steps in learning the features of *Office.* You may have found yourself becoming more comfortable and efficient in handling your computer at the same time. You might find this a good time to return to the Preface and reread the NETS technology standards presentation, or consult www.iste.org.

As a teacher or a student, it is important to consider the sequence needed to effectively master and apply the NETS guidelines. For example, it is important that you have enough practice on basic skills before you attempt to complete a complex task such as a book report or science project. If you are a teacher, plan carefully how you will sequence the activities planned for your students. If you are a student, remember to be patient with yourself and master several small steps before attempting a huge project that will leave you overwhelmed and frustrated.

Take some time to reflect on how much progress you have made toward improving your own level of mastery. Certainly, you have had many opportunities to increase your basic understanding of technology and the work you have done with graphics has increased your ability to communicate effectively. Regardless of the skill level you brought to the original tasks, you are probably progressing toward becoming a more skilled and efficient user of technology.

CHAPTER FOUR

Tables, Outlines, and Presentations

This chapter explores further features of word processing environment and introduces you to the Presentations environment. First, you will learn about tables, a powerful feature of *Word*. You will find many situations in which tables provide exactly the element you need to present information. Next, you will explore the basics of the Outline tools also found in the word processing environment.

Then you will learn about the Presentations environment in *Office*. *PowerPoint* is designed for creating presentations using the computer and a data projection device. PowerPoint can also be used to create handouts to go with a presentation or to print transparencies that you can use on an overhead projector.

These topics increase the ability of *Office* to meet your work needs. However, each is easy enough to learn that you do not need an entire chapter to be ready to make use of them.

USING TABLES

Tables are rows and columns of space in which data can be organized. A simple, empty table of four columns and two rows looks like Figure 4.1.

FIGURE 4.1

You can enter information into your table and format that information exactly as you want. There are many situations in which placing data in a table communicates your message more easily than the usual paragraph format used with most of your text. For example, if you look back at the end of Chapter 1, you will see we used a table to present the key to recognizing the buttons from the button bar. Our table contains both text and images.

Creating Tables

To begin learning about tables, open a new word processing document. There are several ways to create tables.

1. Click on the **Table** menu, select **Insert,** then choose **Table.**
2. A dialog box appears. Enter the number of rows and columns. [Figure 4.2]

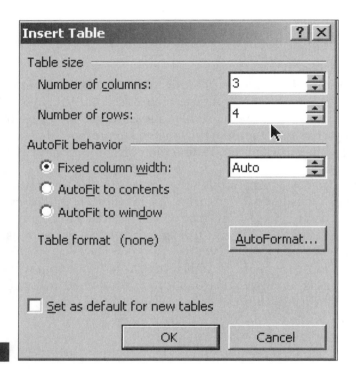

FIGURE 4.2

3. A table appears on your page with the indicated number of rows and columns. [Figure 4.3]

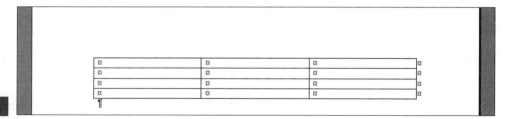

FIGURE 4.3

4. You can modify the size and shape of a table by choosing **Table Properties** from the **Table** menu. You can then click on the Row or Column tabs to change the size of the table. [Figure 4.4]

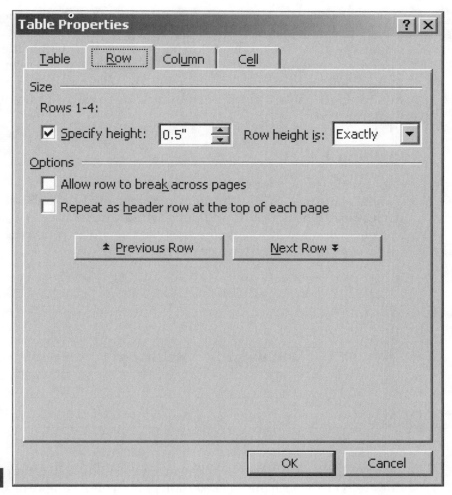

FIGURE 4.4

When you click on OK, the changes you have indicated appear in the table. [Figure 4.5]

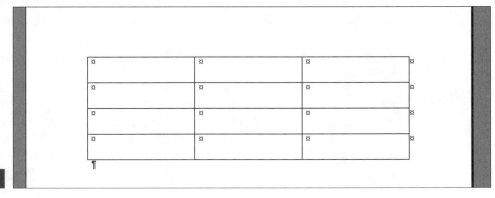

FIGURE 4.5

These steps give you the basic table size and shape, but there is still more that you can do with a table. Notice that if you did not change the shape or size of the table, the text insertion point still appears within the *first cell*—the intersection of Row 1 and Column 1—of the table. If, however, you used the arrow pointer to manipulate the table, the text insertion point is no longer visible in the table. You will need to click in the cell you want to use to begin entering text.

Editing Tables

Your table is ready for text to be entered. Click in the first cell in which you want to enter text. Within the table, you can move from one cell to an adjacent cell by using the tab key. In addition, if you are in the last cell, using the tab key creates a new row. If you use the arrow keys to move around the table, you can move left, right, up, or down cell by cell. [Figure 4.6]

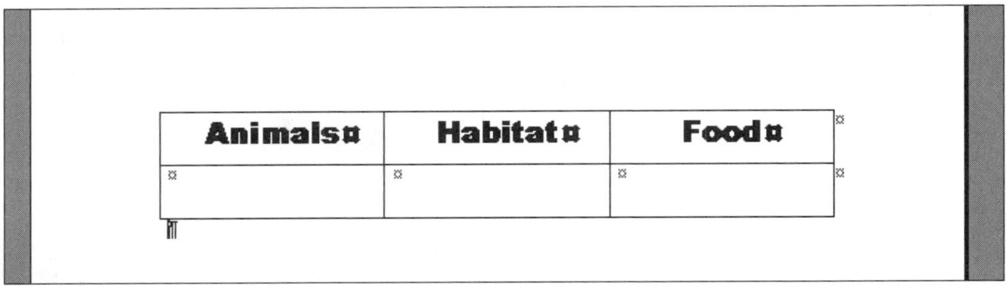

FIGURE 4.6

Finally, if you want to use a nonadjacent cell in the table, click directly in the desired cell to place the text insertion point. This flexibility provides you with the ability to build tables easily and gives you a convenient way to organize and present data. Note that the same paragraph styles created for use in a word processing document can be applied to the text in table cells.

As a teacher, creating tables for students to use in classification activities is fast and easy. You can set up tables to help your students organize material. Even setting up different tables for different groups is not complicated. If you need to present information in columns or organize matching questions, tables can help you create the material quickly and easily. It is not necessary to make the grid lines visible, so tables are extremely versatile. In addition, students will find that by creating tables many of their own tasks are made easier. Like anything else, it is simply a question of practicing until the skills have been mastered.

If you work with tables a great deal, you may want to develop a series of paragraph styles specifically for use with tables. Text in tables looks attractive and is comfortable to read if you make sure there is some space between the lines of the table and the text. You might consider putting a small extra left margin in a table with text that is left justified and perhaps a few points above the paragraph. [Figure 4.7]

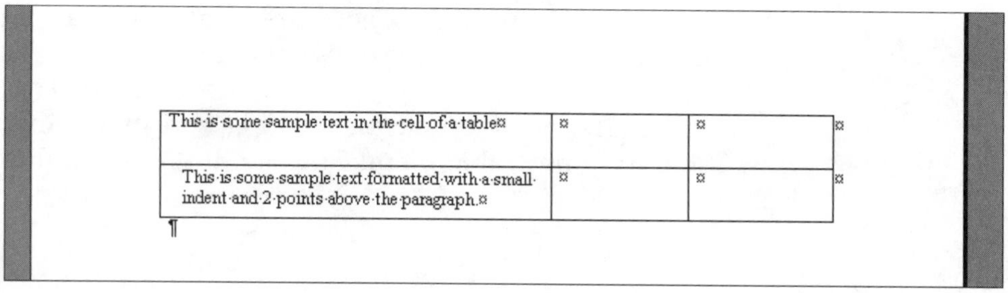

This·is·some·sample·text·in·the·cell·of·a·table☒

This·is·some·sample·text·formatted·with·a·small· indent·and·2·points·above·the·paragraph.☒

FIGURE 4.7

At any time after your table is created, you are able to change the size of the cells that make up the table. Click on a line that makes up the table. The cursor changes to an icon with two lines and two arrows. When you click and drag on a line, a dotted line appears as you move the mouse. When you release the mouse button, the line appears in its new location. [Figure 4.8]

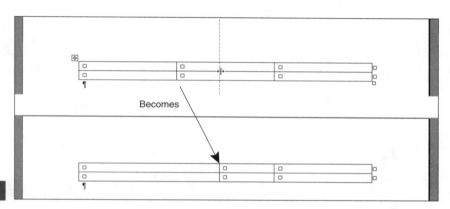

Becomes

FIGURE 4.8

Another way to change the way your table is presented is to use the options that appear in the **Table** menu in the menu bar. The following steps let you remove entire rows or columns.

1. Click and drag across the rows or columns to highlight the cells you want to delete. [Figure 4.9]

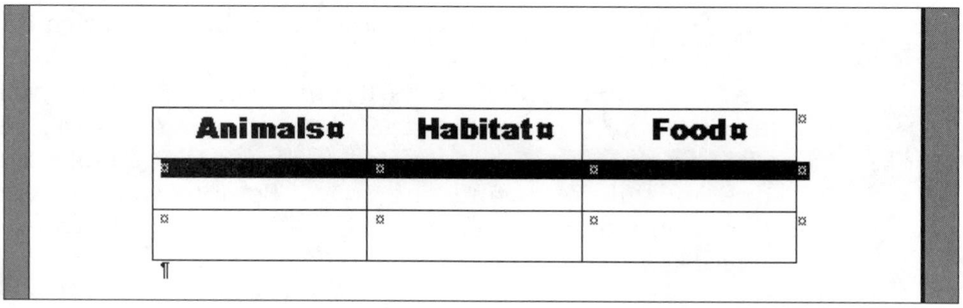

Animals¤ **Habitat¤** **Food¤**

FIGURE 4.9

2. Choose **Delete** from the **Table** menu and indicate in the submenu whether you want to delete rows or columns.

There is another method for creating and modifying tables. Choose **Draw Table** from the **Table** menu. You see the Tables and Borders window. [Figure 4.10]

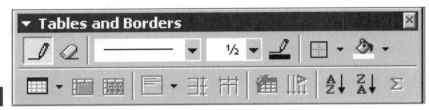

FIGURE 4.10

The Pencil tool can be used to draw an initial rectangle for your table. With the table selected, you can choose line styles, line widths, line color, and even fill color. You can use the Pencil tool to add cells to your table. [Figure 4.11]

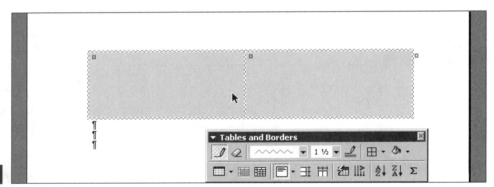

FIGURE 4.11

The tools for creating line and fill styles can be used to create a border around text or other images.

The Tables and Borders options can be used to modify any table, regardless of how you create it. Note that to select the entire table, you click on the icon at the upper left corner of the table. You can then set line and fill colors and line styles. Be sure you use the Borders submenu options to indicate which cells of the table you want to modify. [Figure 4.12]

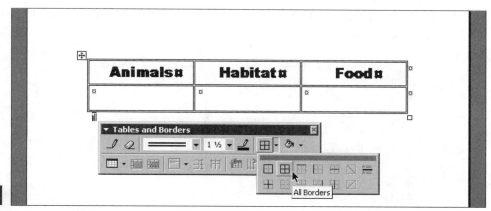

FIGURE 4.12

The Pencil tool allows you to subdivide cells and add lines to any table. Simply click and drag where you want new lines. [Figure 4.13]

FIGURE 4.13

The original cell is split into two smaller-sized cells. To create a vertical division, click and drag the Pencil tool up or down. To remove a line from your table, use the Eraser tool from the Tables and Borders window.

Take some time to experiment with these new techniques to create and modify tables. Some of these tools take practice, so take your time and be patient with yourself. Once you have the skills, you will use them a great deal.

You have already learned that you can add new text to your table by placing the text insertion pointer in the desired cell. However, you may already have text in your word document and then decide that it would be more appropriate to present the text in table format. You do not need to re-enter your text. Instead, *Word* can convert the text into a table layout for you.

1. Select the text you want to convert to a table. [Figure 4.14]

FIGURE 4.14

2. Choose **Convert** on the **Table** menu and then select Text to Table. [Figure 4.15]

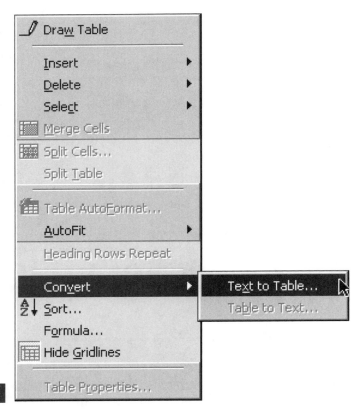

3. A table containing your text appears. [Figure 4.16]

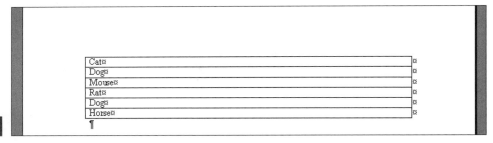

If you now select your table, you can use the Table to Text submenu from **Convert** on the **Table** menu to convert the table back to text.

When you finish formatting and sizing a table, you can use **Table Properties** from the **Table** menu to place your table relative to the text in your document. You can even wrap text around a table so that the table behaves like a floating object. Remember our discussion about floating and inline images? Tables can be treated in this same fashion. [Figure 4.17]

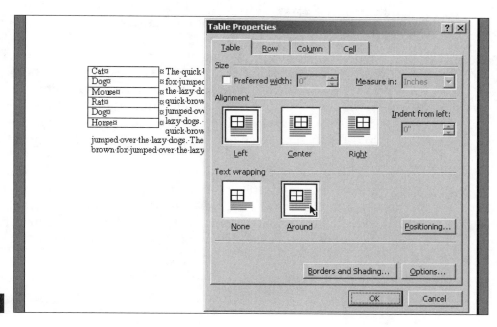

FIGURE 4.17

Notice that you choose None to place a table inline. And, although the diagram would indicate the table is left aligned, remember that you can apply any alignment you wish. Often, you will want to center align the table. Simply format the inline table object with the same tools you use for other text elements.

Take some time to look closely at all of the powerful features contained on the **Table** menu. Spend some time experimenting with the various options and note those you feel you would make the most use of in your work. Try to master some of the less obvious options to allow you to create tables that exactly meet the needs of your documents.

Think especially of what you gain by being able to insert cells in addition to deleting them. You will want to learn to merge selected cells to make fewer but larger cells in your table. For example, you might merge all the cells in the first row to contain a title across the top of your table. *Word* can also space the rows or columns in your table evenly. Create a table and take time to explore these capabilities. Only with practice will you develop the skills to quickly and easily make tables part of your day-to-day documents. Tables add power and flexibility to your documents, especially in the word processing environment. Take the time to learn to use them effectively.

CREATING OUTLINES

Outlines allow you to organize information in both a sequential and a hierarchical order. However, many people view the task of making an outline as difficult, frustrating, and not particularly useful. This is often true in a pencil-and-paper environment in which modifying the entries in an outline and changing their organization is not easily accomplished. However, creating an electronic outline is a different process. Entries in an *Office* outline can be quickly rewritten and reorganized, resulting in a smooth integration of the writing and outlining tasks.

Before you begin to consider how outlines are created, it is helpful to think about the type of text that *Word* uses to create the outline. You are already comfortable seeing text that includes a numbered or bulleted list. In fact, you have encountered several examples of such formatting as you have read this book. However, it is possible that you may not have encountered formatting that uses a character other than the standard bullet or numbering system.

The character that starts a bulleted or number list adds emphasis to your message and attracts the reader's attention. Often such characters are referred to as *symbols* or *dingbats.* In fact, you will find entire typefaces that are devoted to special characters of this kind. Stop and check the list of fonts in your **Font** menu to see if you have:

φ Symbol,
↗ Wingding, or
❈ Zapf Dingbats.

Each of the characters you see is produced using the "f" key in the appropriate typeface and each might be appropriate for a particular purpose in a document. With the built-in formatting the *Word* outliner provides, you will encounter special symbols. More importantly, since you want to modify your outlines to use word processing rules, you may want to make use of symbols of this kind.

To begin exploring the *Word* outliner, create a new word processing document and select **Outline** from the **View** menu. Enter your first topic. [Figure 4.18]

FIGURE 4.18

As you can see, the toolbars at the top of the document change.

Technical Note: Macintosh users, your toolbar may look quite different. Rather than a simple left or right pointing arrow to promote or demote entries, you may find the arrows show on a small page icon. The small double arrow will turn any indicated text into your standard body text format apart from the outline formatting.

You are ready to place the next entry into your outline. If the next entry is to be of the same level, press Return or Enter. An end-of-paragraph marker will appear and the text insertion pointer is in position to enter text directly below the first entry. However, if the next entry is to be of a different level—a subheading below the first topic—click on the right arrow on the Outline toolbar to move the entry to the right (*indent*). The right arrow *demotes* the entry to a subtopic level. [Figure 4.19]

The indent shows that the second item is a subheading related to the preceding entry but of a different level of importance. Each indent of text to the right is considered a lower level in the organization of the outline. If you move text to the left (*outdent*), the entry is *promoted* to a higher level in the organizational scheme.

Continue entering items into your outline.

- Use the right arrow if you want to make a lower-level entry—a subheading or subtopic.
- Use the Return or Enter key to continue making entries at the same level.
- Use the left arrow on the Outline toolbar to create a higher-level entry.

Note that you can move several levels at one time by clicking the arrow several times. Entries beginning in the same position are considered to be equal in importance and to be at the same level in the hierarchy of the outline. [Figure 4.20]

Our example shows a three-level outline containing two major topics. Continue to add entries to your own outline until you produce a similar example. You will become more efficient in adding entries to your outline with practice. Once you begin planning the next entry before completing the current one, your speed will increase. You will know if you need to use the

Outline toolbar choices or simply the Return or Enter key. However, unlike paper and pencil outlines, an electronic outline allows you to modifying the entries with ease.

The Outline toolbar makes it easy to move entries up or down in the hierarchy or to move entries left or right in the levels of the outline. Since outlines are generally created as you think about the topic or brainstorm ideas, you seldom get the entries in the final order on the first try. If you decide that the importance of one item relative to another is incorrect, select the item and use the left, right, up, or down arrows to change the position of one or more items.

In our example, one of our level-two entries contains two subheadings indicating that they are related but are subcategories of the higher-level entry. Let's explore the options using this particular entry. [Figure 4.21]

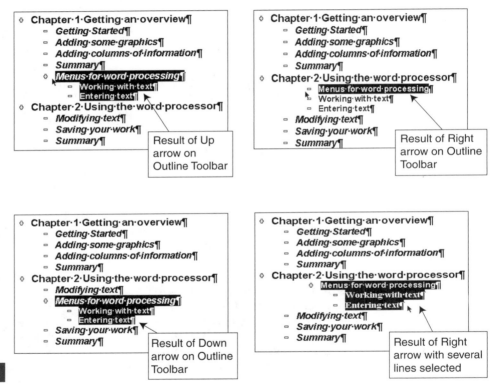

FIGURE 4.21

Take the time to explore your own outline and practice using these features of the *Word* outliner.

There is another method for moving entries in the outline. Click on a topic to move it to a new position vertically. Working in the left side of the document, click on the icon next to the line you want to move. The cursor changes to a four-way arrow. Drag the mouse up or down for a vertical move; drag the mouse left or right for a horizontal move. The cursor changes again and a line appears across the page, indicating the new location for the high-lighted entry. [Figure 4.22]

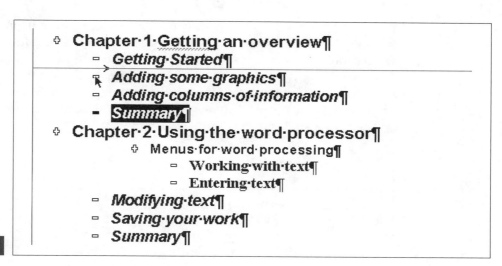

FIGURE 4.22

Release the mouse button when the bar is at the location you want. If you need both a vertical and horizontal change, complete the first move, release the mouse button, and then complete the second move.

When your outline is complete, you can manipulate it in various ways. For example, you can collapse the outline. Since your outline contains several levels of entries, the collapse feature is useful. If you click on the 1 on the Outline toolbar, the outline collapses so that you see only the first-level entries. If there are sublevels in the outline, a light underline becomes visible. [Figure 4.23]

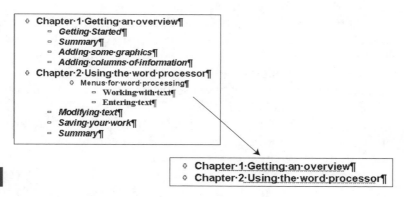

FIGURE 4.23

Collapsing the outline in this manner lets you examine the main topics and reconsider the structure of your outline.

There are still other ways to collapse the outline. If you click on the plus sign in front of an entry, it will collapse that particular entry. This allows you to close just a part of the outline. You probably made note of the plus and minus sign buttons on the toolbar. The minus sign allows you to collapse one level at a time on any particular entry you have selected. So, to collapse the entire outline, use the Number buttons. Otherwise, work with the minus sign or click directly on the icon preceding an entry.

As you would expect, you can expand the outline in much the same manner. Use the Number buttons to expand the entire outline to the level of your choice. Otherwise, select the part of the outline you want to expand. Click on the plus sign on the Outline toolbar or click on the icon preceding the entry. The highlighted section of the outline expands. If you use the Number buttons, you see only the levels you asked to see. If you use the 2 button you see Figure 4.24.

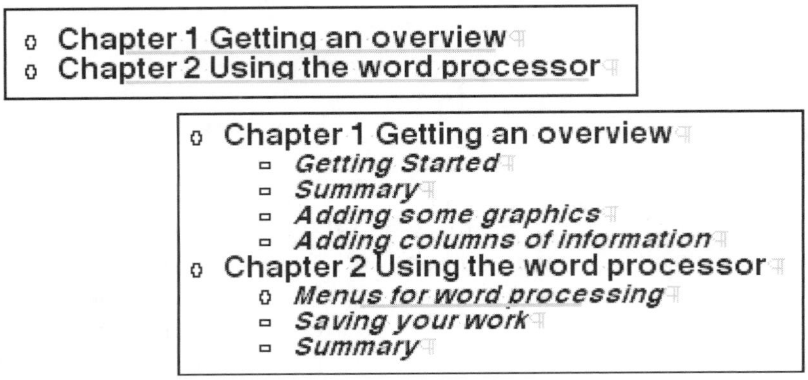

FIGURE 4.24

Did you notice in the expanded version there is a light line under the Chapter 2 entry? This indicates that in this portion of the outline there are entries at levels deeper than level two.

As a student, you probably already use outlines as you prepare material to include in a paper or project you need to complete. However, you might also find an outline provides a powerful study tool. Creating an outline for any topic you are studying helps you to remember the content more easily because you must organize it as you work. In addition, you are forced to reflect on the associations in the information you include. The outline also serves as an aid in checking your recall of the information. If you collapse the outline to show the first-level entries, you can test yourself by seeing how many items in the next levels you can recall. To monitor your progress, you can expand the outline to check that you have the items correct.

In Chapter 2 you learned that you could define styles to help control your text formatting. When you switch to Outline view, *Word* uses built-in styles to construct your outline. Click on a line in your outline. Look at the style name on the Formatting toolbar. If you are using a Macintosh, the style names are found on the Formatting palette.

You see style names such as Header1, Header2, Header3, and so forth. Because these produce text that applies typing rules and you are now using word processing rules, you probably find the large type annoying or distracting. Click on the Show formatting button; each time you click the button, *Word* switches between applying the Header styles and removing the Header styles. [Figure 4.25]

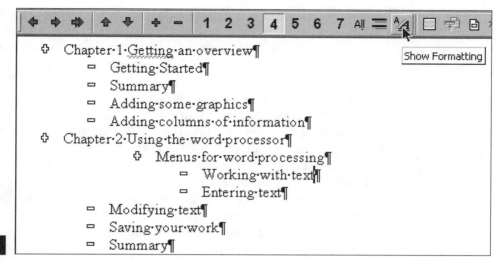

FIGURE 4.25

The long-term solution consists of using your newly acquired style building skills. You will undoubtedly want to modify the built-in Header styles using word processing rules to produce text that is comfortable and easy to read. And, of course, you only need to do the process once because you can move your styles into any document that requires their use.

USING *POWERPOINT*

The Presentation environment of *Office* is called *PowerPoint*. It is designed to make the process of creating a linear electronic presentation easy. *PowerPoint* provides the tools needed to create a set of customized slides that help you to communicate your message. Adding visual aids to the verbal component of a presentation increases the impact of your message and allows you to reach your audience in a more flexible manner.

Presenting information electronically is valuable for both teachers and students. As a teacher, you can better address the needs of visual learners and enhance ideas with images. Students can develop presentations as part of projects in almost any discipline. Further, creating presentations can be an excellent collaborative activity for students, in which they can practice communication skills, planning skills, organization of information, and much more. Students also generally enjoy creating presentations. Of course, each of these steps will move you toward mastery of the NETS for Teachers and Students developed by ISTE.

Starting a Presentation

Before you open a new presentation document, plan the design and content of your presentation. Even though that design may evolve as you develop your document, good planning on paper always results in a better final product. Although a complete discussion on design is beyond the scope of this book, there are some basic ideas to keep in mind as you explore your options in *PowerPoint*. Be aware that simply because *PowerPoint* has the ability to let you add a particular feature, doing so does not automatically increase the impact of your presentation. Recognize that you are still in charge and making the decisions relating to design rules.

Generally, your viewer interacts with your document when it is projected from your computer to a large screen. Errors become much more obvious when enlarged, so plan carefully. In addition, you need to have a constant layout for all slides so the viewer feels each slide is part of the same document. Once you decide on your grid layout, stick to it. In addition, find other elements, such as an icon or a graphic rule, that will appear in the same place on each slide. This repetition enhances communication.

Keep the text large enough to be read from a distance and avoid using large blocks of text on a slide. Again, the research clearly indicates that keeping your text dark on a light background is more effective than the reverse. Select elements because they enhance communication and avoid anything that distracts the viewer. Remember that your goal is to have your electronic document help the reader maintain their attention on your presentation and to focus on the message you are sharing. As you explore, think about this concept.

Open *PowerPoint,* select a **New** document using the **File** menu, and select Blank Presentation from the dialog box that appears. *PowerPoint* immediately asks you to create a new slide by selecting a layout from the AutoLayout options. [Figure 4.26]

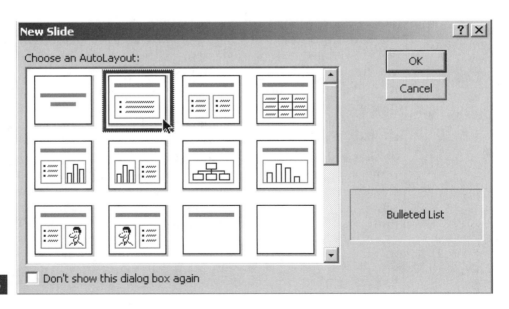

FIGURE 4.26

The layout that you choose appears on the screen. In Normal view, the screen display is divided into three parts. On the right you see the slide layout you chose. On the left you see a window containing a small icon that represents the slide you have just created. At the bottom of this area are several buttons that give you access to other views of the document—Outline, Slide, Slide Sorter, and Slide Show views. Below the slide is an area in which you can put notes to yourself—notes that do not appear on your slide. [Figure 4.27]

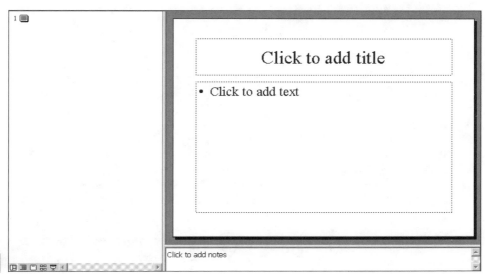

FIGURE 4.27

To begin creating a presentation, click in the area in which you wish to enter text, and enter the text of your choice. [Figure 4.28]

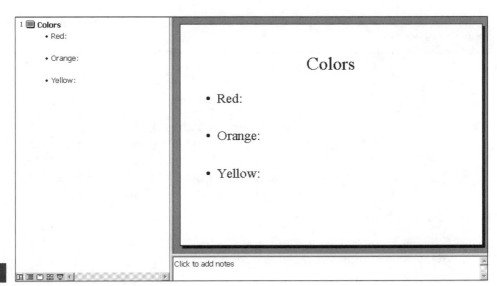

FIGURE 4.28

Notice that the text you enter on the slide appears on the left. The left side of the screen is an outline of your presentation. You can double-click on the slide icon to make the text from the slide appear or disappear. More about using this outline feature later.

In the previous chapter you learned to use the Drawing toolbar to create Draw objects. You can use all of these same tools in *PowerPoint.* If the Drawing toolbar is not visible, choose **Toolbar** from the **View** menu and select the Drawing toolbar. It immediately becomes available for use. [Figure 4.29]

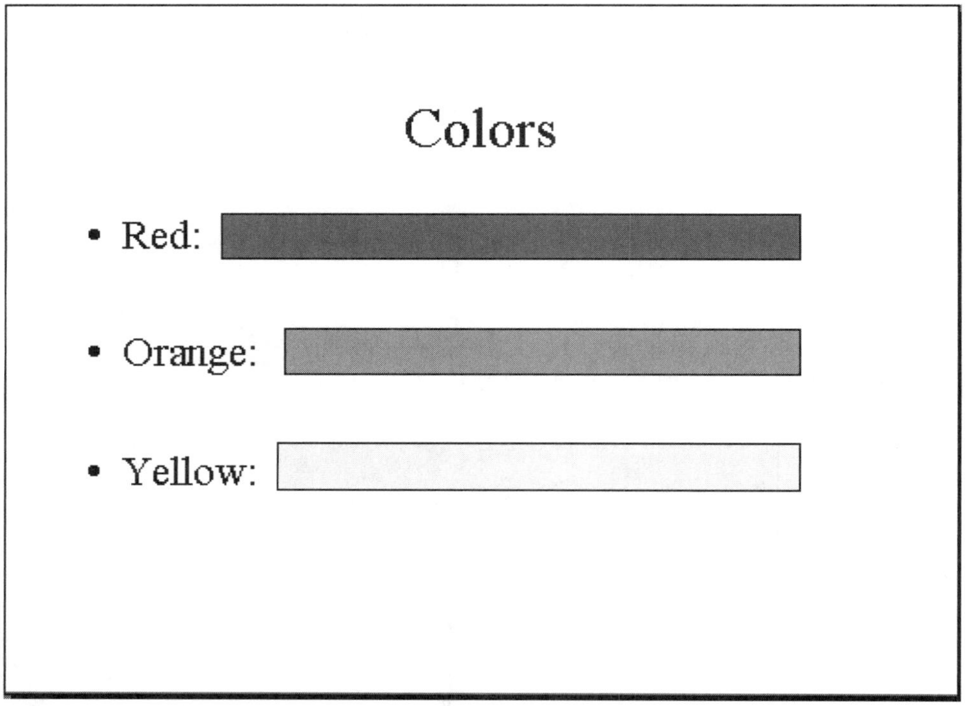

Colors

- Red:
- Orange:
- Yellow:

FIGURE 4.29

For this slide, we used the rectangle, fill, and align tools.

Did you notice that when you open up a slide layout or template, the text is already formatted? You may want to make changes in the formatting. From the **View** menu, choose **Master** and select Slide Master. You see a generic page on which you can change the formatting in this layout. [Figure 4.30]

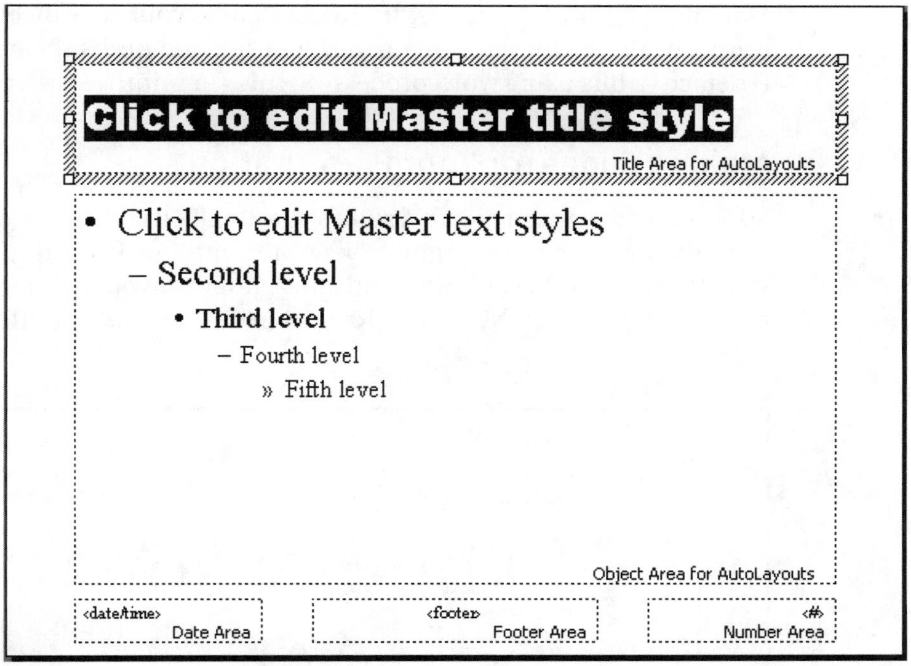

Once you are done with your modifications, use the small Close button that is visible or go back to the **View** menu and deselect the **Master Slide** option to move from the master slide back to the slides you are creating.

In the sample, we changed the title typeface from a serif typeface to a sans serif typeface. We left-aligned the title and changed the size of the text. Each time we create a new slide from this layout, the formatting we modified appears. [Figure 4.31]

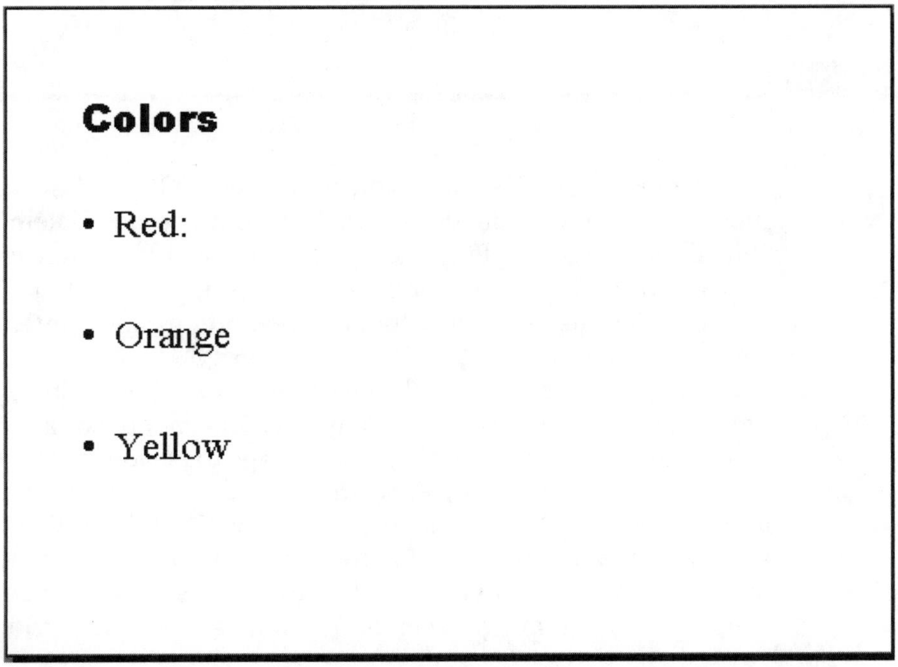

You might think of this as creating a shortcut to your stylesheet for this special purpose. Notice that our title is now left-aligned and appears in a sans serif typeface—thus using word processing rules to improve the communication.

Making Slides for Your Presentation

Suppose you want to create a slide show to illustrate a topic such as the seasons of the year. Let's begin a **New** presentation from the **File** menu. We selected a Blank Presentation and chose a slide layout from the dialog box to create the title page. Next, we added some text and clip art. [Figure 4.32]

FIGURE 4.32

As you create your first slide, you could use the Draw tools to add other elements. Try to give your slide a unified, complete look. Remember, the first slide is like the cover of a book. You want to catch the interest of your viewers by giving them some idea of the topic of your presentation. In addition, the elements on this first slide establish the margins and content area for every slide in the presentation.

Note that you used the dialog box to select a particular layout as you created your first slide. This layout may not meet your needs after you have done some work with your slide. You can change the layout at any time by accessing the dialog box from the **Format** menu by selecting **Slide Layout.** Plan ahead so you can avoid the extra work involved when you have to change your layout, but remember that the option is available.

Suppose you want each of the other slides in your presentation to have some text and an image. Keep in mind the extent of the grid, the amount of space on your slide, and the way you wish to divide that space need to be used consistently from slide to slide. The built-in layouts maintain a preset margin and content area. If you are working with a blank layout, you will need to establish your own grid.

When you are ready for your next slide, select **New Slide** from the **Insert** menu. You can select a different slide layout than your first slide if you use the grid in a consistent fashion. [Figure 4.33]

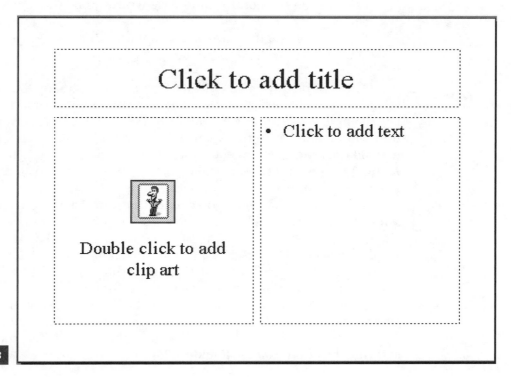

FIGURE 4.33

Now add some text and clip art—and perhaps some Draw objects. [Figure 4.34]

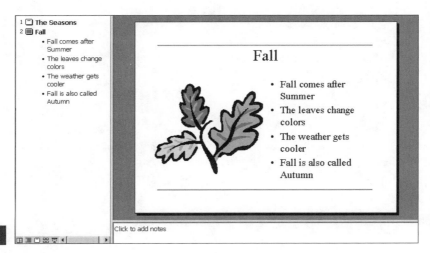

FIGURE 4.34

Notice that you can see the text on your new slide as well as a representation of your title slide in the Normal view shown here.

You can now continue to add slides to your presentation.

1. Choose **New Slide** from the **Insert** menu.
2. Choose a Slide Layout from the dialog box when it appears.
   Do not try to use a new layout for each slide. Keeping the look and feel of the slides consistent increases the impact of your presentation by maximizing the comfort and ease with which your viewers read your slides.
3. Enter the elements—text and graphics—that you want to appear on your slides.

These same three steps will allow you to add as many slides to your presentation as you wish. If you change your mind and would like a different layout applied, use the **Format** menu and select **Slide Layout.** Your new selection will be applied to the open slide. If you added elements to your slide beyond the layout, you may want to choose **Duplicate Slide** from the **Insert** menu. This is a time-saver because you only need to modify the elements that need to change.

It is possible that when you first look at your **Insert** menu, the **Duplicate Slide** item is not available. On a *Windows* computer, you may select a slide or slides in the list showing in Normal view. Once selected, you will find you can Duplicate Slides. There is also a simple keyboard shortcut. The combination of Control + Shift + D will let you duplicate a slide. These actions will place the **Duplicate Slide** option into the **Insert** menu for later use.

As you add slides, you may find it helpful to look at your presentations in several views. The icons at the lower left corner of the page allow you to switch among several views. For example, the Outline view makes the area showing the outline larger. [Figure 4.35]

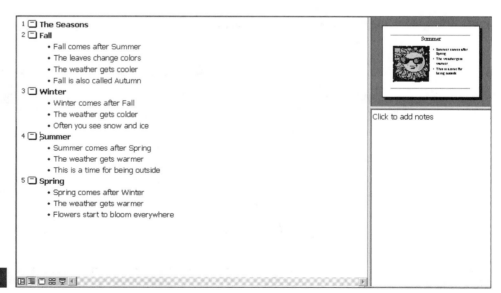

FIGURE 4.35

Reading the outline may help you identify needed changes. Any change you make in the outline version is actually changed on the corresponding slide. Each view has a particular emphasis and you will learn to use each to best advantage.

Other Presentation Features

When you are ready to preview a slide show, click on the first slide you wish to view and then click on the Slide Show view icon in the lower left corner of the screen. When you arrive at the Slide Show view and the entire screen is occupied by your slide, stay calm. Just click the mouse button to toggle through the slides. When the last one is seen, the view drops back to Normal view. Or, if you prefer, in the lower left of the slide in Slide Show view, a small menu appears. You can move directly out of the Slide Show by selecting End Show.

Sometimes you discover that the slides are not in the order you want them to be for your presentation. In our sample presentation, Spring should come before Summer. Click on the Slide Sorter view icon. Click and drag the slide you want to move to a new location. You will see a line appear at the new location. When you release the mouse button, the slide will be moved to the new location. [Figure 4.36]

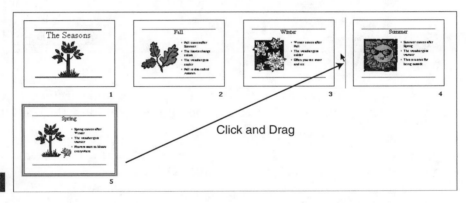

FIGURE 4.36

As you organize your final presentation, you may want to print some part of your presentation. *PowerPoint* provides many options for printing. Choose **Print** from the **File** menu. Examine the dialog box you see. Your dialog box may look different from the one below, which is from a *Windows 98* version of *Office 2000*. [Figure 4.37]

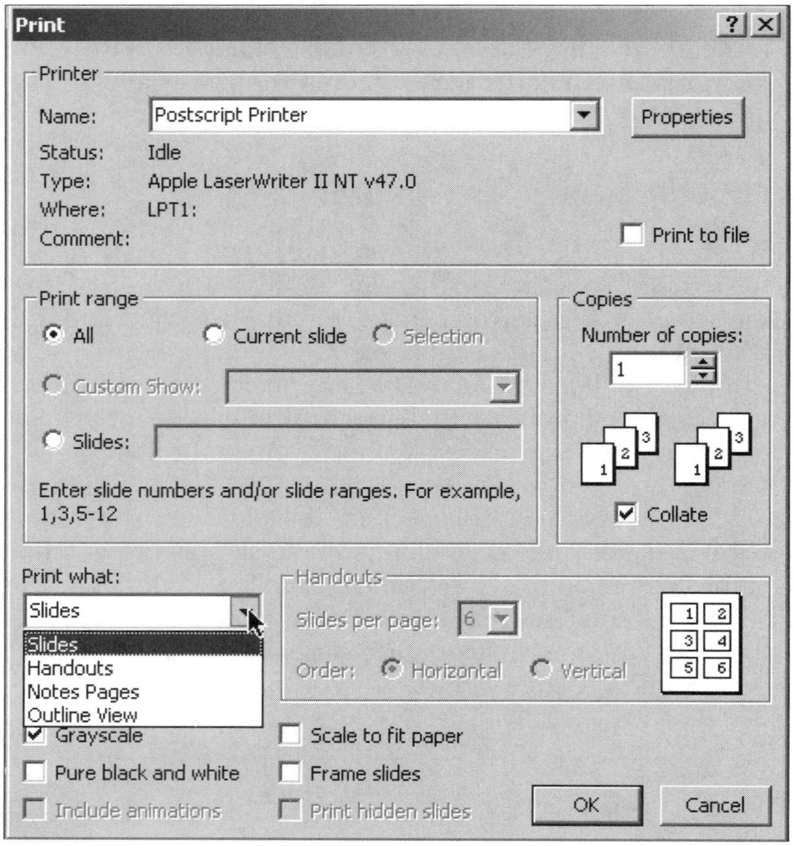

FIGURE 4.37

Notice that you can print your Slides, Notes, and Outlines. If you are using a Macintosh, these choices may be a bit more hidden. [Figure 4.38]

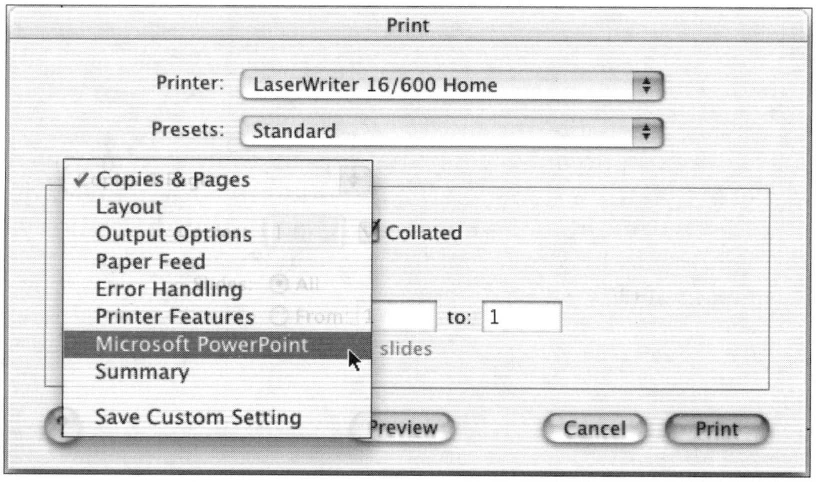

FIGURE 4.38

When you select the *PowerPoint* option, you see menus to print the Slides, Notes, and more.

Did you notice the Handouts choice in your Print dialog box? This feature lets you print small copies of your slides to use as handouts. [Figure 4.39]

Notice that you can specify the layout for your handout before printing. [Figure 4.40]

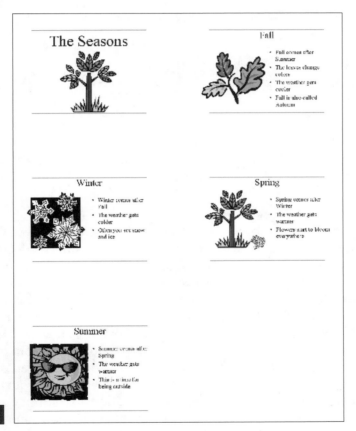

By providing handouts for your audience, they can focus on your presentation rather than taking notes. If your students make presentations, the handout format is a good way for them to share information with their classmates.

PowerPoint includes many options for how the presentation will move from one slide to another. If you choose **Slide Transition** from the **Slide Show** menu, you see the options available. [Figure 4.41]

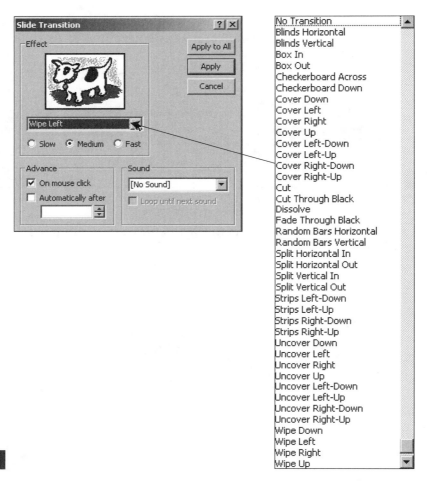

FIGURE 4.41

Transitions modify the appearance of the screen as you move from one slide to the next. Experiment with several of these transitions. Select the one you want to try and click on Apply to All. Then view your slide show by choosing **View Show** from the **Slide Show** window.

To complicate matters, transitions can be associated with individual slides rather than all the slides. Thus, you could easily have a different transition with every slide. Too many different transitions, however, are distracting to the viewer. The transition effects have been borrowed from the film industry and many of them are extremely strong—some are even distracting. Be careful that the transitions you choose in no way distract from the content of your presentation. As a guideline, if the transition is so strong that it draws the viewers' attention, it is probably too strong. Transitions should work on a subconscious level, with the viewer almost unaware of their presence. Avoid problems by planning and testing carefully. It is better to avoid transitions completely than to overuse them.

You have already explored options with text and images in your presentations. And, of course, you can move beyond the collection of images that you find installed with your version of *Office*. But there is much more that can be done to enhance your work. You can also include sounds and movies. You need to have the proper equipment to utilize these additions. If you are just beginning, you might want to leave these items until later.

Perhaps you noticed that the Clip Art collection has a tab for Sounds and a tab for Motion Clips. Click on the Sounds tab. At the top of the Insert Clip Art window there are buttons to import sounds or to get sounds online. There are only a few sounds included in your Clip Art collection, so you may want to explore the online sounds available on the Microsoft Web site.

If you click on the Clips Online button and you have an Internet connection, your computer should connect you to the Microsoft Design Gallery Live. [Figure 4.42]

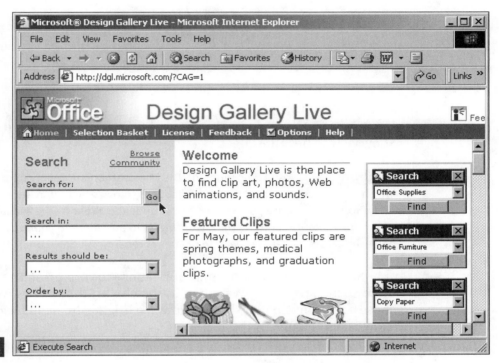

FIGURE 4.42

You can then search for the kinds of sounds you might want to use. We selected a birdsong, which we downloaded and added to the Clip Art collection. You can then insert the sound in the same manner as you insert clip art. You see a small speaker icon which you can place anywhere on the page. You can set this sound to play automatically when the slide is opened, or you can set the sound to play when you click on the speaker icon. [Figure 4.43]

If you set your sound to play automatically, you will need to use the Slide Show view to hear the effect.

Technical Note: At the moment, the Microsoft online gallery does not allow Macintosh users access to the collection of sounds, movies, and animation available to PC users. You can, of course, use movies and sounds you already have available. Place them onto your computer and use the **Insert** *menu to add them to your document. You can, however, access the large collection of images regardless of the computer you are using.*

Similarly, you can add small animations to your presentation. There are more such clips on the Web than in the clip art that comes with *Office*. We chose a motion clip that shows a flower, a bright sun, falling leaves, and then snowflakes. [Figure 4.44]

This animation involves only the images and does not affect the text.

There are also animations that you can apply to slides. Again, it is important not to overdo such features. Choose **Preset Animation** from the **Slide Show** menu to see a list of choices. [Figure 4.45]

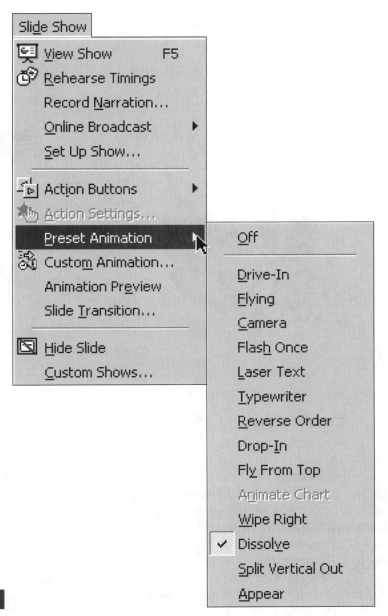

FIGURE 4.45

You can then choose the animation you would like to try. Note that we checked Dissolve.

PowerPoint lets you animate almost any element that you might include on your slide—text boxes, images, and so on. The preset animations can be applied to one or to several elements. As a result, you need to take care that you do not overuse this strong visual element. Having elements flying on and off the screen is often more distracting than helpful in sharing your message.

The animation effect applies to the selected elements on the slide that is displayed when you choose the animation. After applying the animation, you can choose Animation Preview. You see a miniature of the slide. If you have a transition applied, you first see the transition and then the animation. [Figure 4.46]

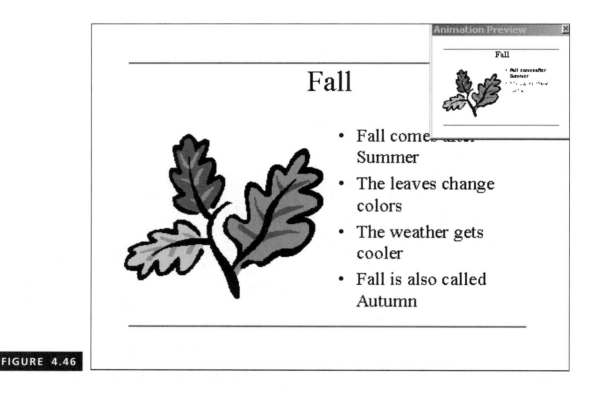

FIGURE 4.46

Once you have explored the preset animation, you may want to look at the options provided in the Custom Animation dialog box. However, again make note that having the power to add these settings does not guarantee their use adds anything positive to your communication. Having the self-discipline to avoid or limit their use is a good step forward in designing effective documents.

One other feature that can be very helpful is the ability to hide some of your slides. You can create a large Slide Show. If your presentation time is shorter than is needed to make use of the entire set of slides, you can hide some of them. Because the document still contains all the slides, you can adjust your choices for different audiences or purposes without having to redo any slides.

With the slide you want to hide displayed, choose **Hide Slide** from the **Slide Show** menu. Perhaps the easiest way to see which slides are hidden is to go to the Slide Sorter view by clicking on the icon in the lower left corner of the screen. [Figure 4.47]

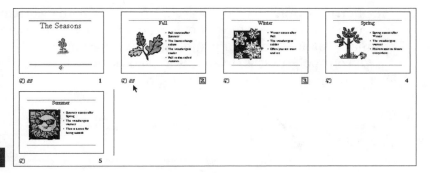

FIGURE 4.47

The icons below the slides represent such things as whether or not there is a transition with the slide. The small icon next to the arrow pointer indicates that the second slide is hidden. Can you find another slide that is hidden in the sample set shown above?

You have seen that you can choose from a set of slide layouts to make the construction of your presentation quick and simple. You can also select **Apply Design Templates,** available on the **Format** menu, to locate a collection of built-in background designs. This list depends on your version of *Office* and will look different in the Macintosh version of *Office.* These templates offer both simple and complex designs that include background colors, colored text, and other elements. These elements are placed behind those you added to your slides. [Figure 4.48]

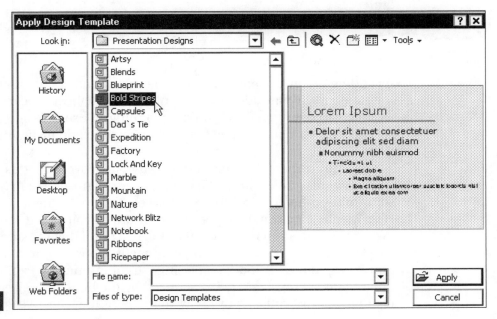

FIGURE 4.48

Just remember that having them included does not mean they have been optimized to communicate. Presentations that are too busy or flashy can easily distract your audience from the content. However, the designs do offer a starting place and provide ideas you could incorporate into your own work.

You often have much more knowledge about design that you can articulate to someone else. Be aware of your own reaction and common sense. You might be amazed at how well your instinct guides you if you let it.

If you apply a design to an existing slide show, you can easily create problems. [Figure 4.49]

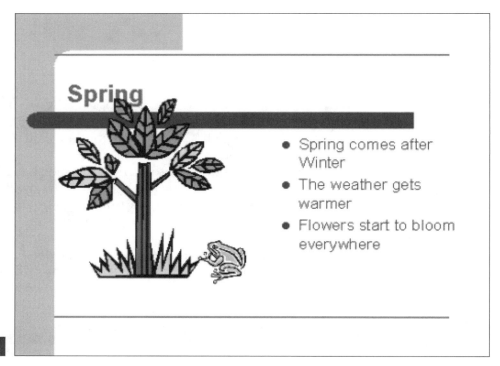

FIGURE 4.49

By adding to our current example slides, the result is not exactly helpful. All the elements that are added simply interfere with those we carefully included as we created our slides. If you are planning to use a design template, you should choose that template before you begin to add elements to your slide show.

There are many features of *PowerPoint* not covered in this chapter. Once you are comfortable with the features covered here, you may wish to explore some of the other features. Try options you find on the menu. Make use of the **Help** menu. Focus on the types of presentations you would use to make your own communication more effective. Keep in mind that the software has been created to anticipate a wide range of needs. Above all, remember that you now know quite a bit about increasing the communication ability of any document you create. Avoid being seduced by the built-in suggestions. Rely on the many things you already know about designing effective documents.

SUMMARY AND TIPS

This chapter has given you many new things to think about and perhaps access to features you have never before used. This may be an instance requiring you to return to these pages when you encounter a situation that calls for one of the features just introduced. When your skill level is high enough to make use of these special features quickly and automatically, you have made great progress in achieving some of the more advanced technology standards set by ISTE. Anything that increases your efficiency with computer basics, with making good decisions about when to apply each feature, and with maximizing your communication is a positive step toward being a power computer user.

Developing the skills to create an effective table is useful. Until you understand when a table is the best way to present information, it maybe difficult to focus at the level needed to learn and remember the steps. Tables provide greater flexibility in text organization than using tabs the way most people do. Think in terms of large blocks of data that need to be shared easily. Control of the final format is easier in a table than in the more basic tab setting approach. Note the extensive discussion on tables and return to it when you have the need.

Outlines are valuable and helpful in many situations. Their value is seldom evident until you explore the ease of reorganization and the viewing options *Office* provides. Again, when you recognize their application to some task you are trying to complete, you may need to return to the appropriate section and review the steps.

If you are responsible for sharing information with others, particularly in a formal presentation, you are well advised to master the *PowerPoint* presentation tools. The addition of an attractive and colorful slide to accompany your oral communication enhances your effectiveness as a speaker. Notice the emphasis on *enhance* and work to increase your understanding of document design, use of color, typeface choices, and layout options.

Do not expect to easily or quickly achieve success the first few times. Your first efforts may, in fact, not be helpful. Keep trying—you will find you quickly gain an understanding of what helps and what does not work. And yes, you would be advised to have a backup plan for the actual presentation, just in case. If your technology is functioning correctly, your audience will appreciate the extra effort you made in preparing your presentation. At the same time, creating transparencies or handouts from the same presentation document can serve as a backup in case of technology problems.

CHAPTER FIVE

Getting Started Using Spreadsheets

In this chapter you will begin learning about spreadsheets. The *Office* application for spreadsheets is called *Excel*. On the surface, spreadsheets look like elaborate tables. However, the similarity stops at the surface. A spreadsheet is primarily a *computational tool*. Although spreadsheets usually contain some text, the reason for putting information into a spreadsheet is to allow you to perform computations on numbers or make charts of the data.

One category of NETS for teachers as developed by ISTE focuses on assessment and evaluation. Although many available applications are devoted to electronic record keeping, it is useful to know that with a spreadsheet you can make simple record keeping documents. In addition, both teachers and students benefit from increasing their ability to interpret and communicate results of data gathering. Spreadsheet documents also include the use of the flexible chart making tools that allow you to share information in a visual format. Charts are introduced in the next chapter.

A spreadsheet contains many features that make it easy to automate computations on financial and other numeric data. A spreadsheet is such a powerful aid to working with numeric data that in the early 1980s many people bought their first computers just to gain access to this single tool.

Besides being used in accounting, spreadsheets are routinely used in math and science and are an excellent aid to all kinds of computations. In this chapter we include an example of data collection such as might be incorporated into a science lesson that includes an experiment. As you read through this chapter, you may want to complete each step in our example. Or, if you prefer, modify the steps to create your own spreadsheet.

GETTING STARTED WITH *EXCEL*

To begin working with spreadsheets, open *Excel* and create a new blank document. Examine the grid of rows and columns. Your screen may look slightly different, but these same elements will appear. You may also see the label Book1 displayed in the title bar of the document window. [Figure 5.1]

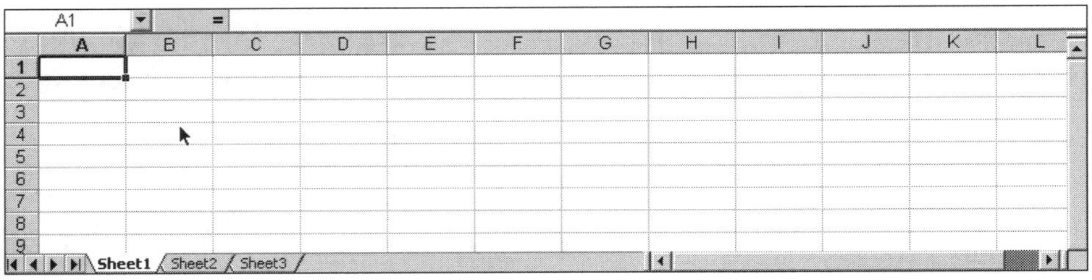

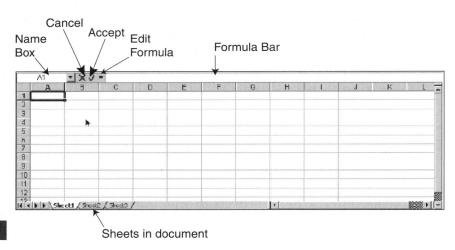

FIGURE 5.1

Your documents are spreadsheet *books* consisting of *sheets.* The default set-tings start you with three sheets, as shown.

Your work with spreadsheet documents is easier if you learn the spe-cialized vocabulary as you go. The term *cell*—the intersection of a row and column—is used to refer to a single rectangle in a table. That same term is used to refer to a single rectangle in a spreadsheet.

Notice that across the top of the grid the columns of the spreadsheet are lettered A, B, C, and so on. After the first twenty-six columns, they are lettered AA, AB, and so on. Down the left side of the grid, the rows of the spreadsheet are numbered 1, 2, 3, and so forth.

Because each row and column in a spreadsheet has a label, the labels provide a way to identify each cell. For example, cell B5 is in the second col-umn, fifth row down. This row and column designation is the *cell name* or *cell address.* [Figure 5.2]

FIGURE 5.2

Sheets in document

When you move the mouse pointer and click inside any cell on the spreadsheet, a border appears to show the cell is selected. This cell is called the *current cell* and its cell address appears in the upper left corner, in the Name box. When you open a new spreadsheet document, the current cell is the first row of the first column, as shown in our example.

Technical Note: On the Macintosh, if you have *Office 2001,* you see a small icon between the Accept and Edit Formula buttons. This button gives you direct access to an electronic calculator, which looks and operates much like a handheld version.

Creating a Spreadsheet

Spreadsheets are useful in many disciplines. This part of the chapter uses an example from a student science experiment. In this experiment, students fill an identical set of various containers with boiling water, then measure the temperature of the water at one-minute intervals. The data will allow the students to compare how fast the water in each of the different containers cools.

Once students have collected their data, they can record it in a spreadsheet. Open a new spreadsheet document. To enter data into a spreadsheet, click on the cell you want to use. As you enter data, it appears at the top of the screen in the box called the Formula bar and in the cell rectangle. Pressing Return or Enter accepts your entry by placing the data into the appropriate cell and moves the pointer down one cell in the column. If you want to move to the right, use the Tab key to both accept your entry and move to the next cell in the row.

As you begin to enter data, you see two buttons appear to the right of the Name box. Another way to accept an entry is to click on the button displaying the check mark—called the *Accept button*. This method does not move the pointer to a new cell. If you do not want to keep your entry, click on the *x* next to the Entry bar. This *x* is called the *Cancel button* and will remove your entry from the cell. Again, this action does not cause you to leave the current cell.

Begin entering data into a spreadsheet such as the one in Figure 5.3. Press Return or Enter to accept the entry and move to the next cell in a column or press the Tab key to move across a row. You can also use the arrow keys to move from cell to cell. Moving to another cell automatically accepts your most recent data entry, just as if you had clicked the Accept button.

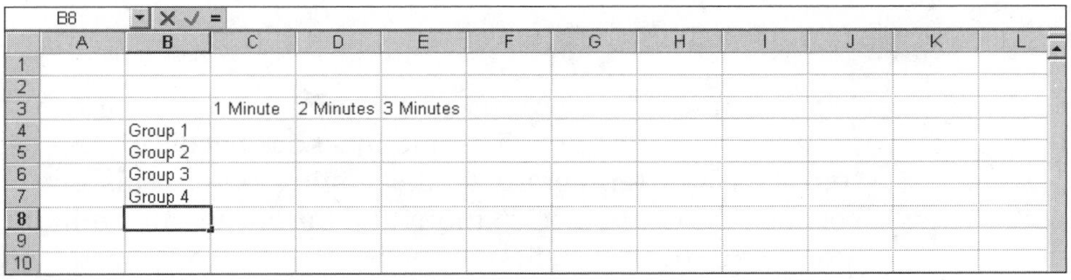

FIGURE 5.3

Notice that the entries are automatically left justified.

As you enter numbers and words into your spreadsheet, there may be an entry that has too many characters to fit into the cell. If the entry is *text,* the extra text displays in the next cell to the right, such as the entry in cell B4. If the entry is a *number,* the entire cell will be filled and then the number will either be rounded off or changed to exponential format—*scientific notation.* [Figure 5.4]

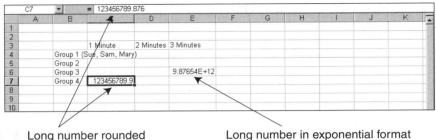

FIGURE 5.4 Long number rounded   Long number in exponential format

If you wish, *Excel* can adjust the column width to fit the data. Click on several cells in the column where the text does not fit and choose **AutoFormat** from the **Format** menu. Once the window appears, click on the Options button and deselect all options except the Width/Height choice. [Figure 5.5]

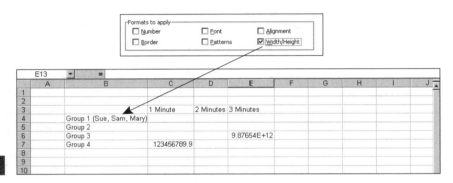

FIGURE 5.5

As you can see, the column widens to contain the entire text entry.

To set up our spreadsheet to meet our needs, we need a column for our starting water temperature—the boiling point. This entry should appear between the Group designations and the entries for 1 minute. To insert a column in this position, click on the letter at the top of your spreadsheet where the new column is needed. In our example, we need an empty Column C, so we click on the label to highlight the entire column. Next, choose **Columns** from the **Insert** menu. The data in your spreadsheet moves to the right, giving you a new column.

We want to put the boiling point of water in the now empty Column C. There is a shortcut for filling a number of cells with the same entry.

1. Enter the number in the first of the cells.
2. Click on the cell containing this number.
3. A small handle appears at the lower right corner of the current cell. This is called the Fill handle.

4. Click and drag this handle across the block of cells that you want to have the same value. (Take care, because this action can enter the data down the column and across the row at the same time.) [Figure 5.6]

C4	▼	= 212					
	A	B	C	D	E	F	G	H
1								
2								
3			Immediate	1 Minute	2 Minutes	3 Minutes		
4		Group 1	212					
5		Group 2						
6		Group 3						
7		Group 4						
8			215					
9								
10								

FIGURE 5.6

When you release the mouse button, the selected cells will all fill with the same value. In our example, the selected cells in Column C will be given this value. This same technique will work to fill rows or blocks of cells with the same value. This technique is particularly useful if you have a large number of repeated entries.

If you prefer, you can fill rows and columns by choosing **Fill** from the **Insert** menu. Using the **Fill** menu or using the Fill handle have the same result. You will soon learn which approach best suits your work style. For now, complete the task of entering the remainder of your data in the spreadsheet. [Figure 5.7]

F8	▼	=					
	A	B	C	D	E	F	G	H
1								
2								
3			Immediate	1 Minute	2 Minutes	3 Minutes		
4		Group 1	212	210	205	193		
5		Group 2	212	211	203	195		
6		Group 3	212	209	204	198		
7		Group 4	212	211	202	193		
8								
9								
10								

FIGURE 5.7

Editing the Contents of Cells

Working with the cells of a spreadsheet is similar in many ways to working with words and paragraphs in a word processor. You can use the usual techniques of **Cut, Copy,** and **Paste.**

To select a single cell, simply click on it. Other kinds of selections are also easy—just click or click and drag. [Figure 5.8]

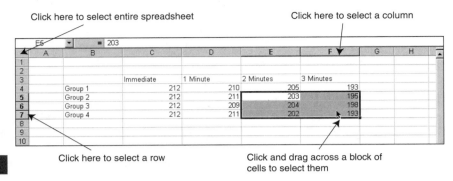

FIGURE 5.8

When you have selected a cell or group of cells, you can use **Cut, Copy,** or **Paste** just as you would with text. If you want to paste more than one cell, be sure you click in the upper left corner of the location where you want your selection to appear. [Figure 5.9]

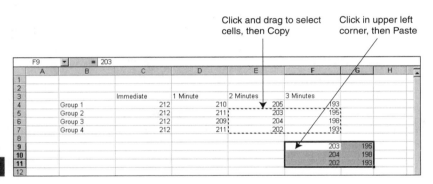

FIGURE 5.9

If you want to remove entries completely, use **Clear** from the **Edit** menu rather than **Cut.** Once you have taken this step, the data is gone unless you immediately use **Undo Clear** from the **Edit** menu.

FORMATTING IN SPREADSHEETS

As you were entering numbers into your spreadsheet, you may have tried to enter a dollar sign for monetary values. However, the dollar sign does not appear in the cell. In *Excel,* currency values are formatted for you, as are other types of numbers.

Select the spreadsheet cells in which you want a dollar sign displayed and choose **Cells** from the **Format** menu. Then click on the Number tab and choose Currency. [Figure 5.10]

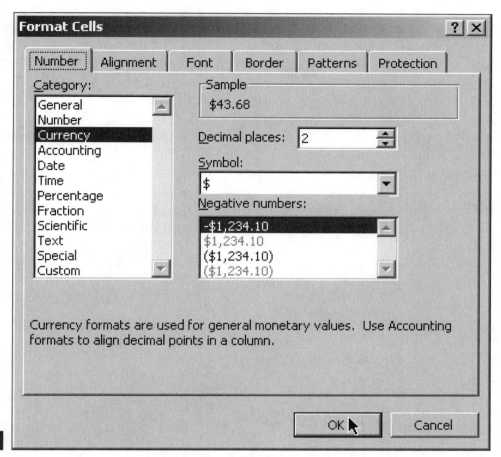

FIGURE 5.10

Dollar signs now appear in the selected cells. You can also adjust the formatting for date and time entries, for percent, for scientific notation, and for many others.

Technical Note: Be sure you select cells and not just the text in a cell when you want to apply Number formatting. If you select only the text, you may see only a Font tab.

Look carefully at the Format Cells dialog box. You can adjust the alignment, change the font, add borders, patterns, and more. Changing the text appearance from the default settings can make the spreadsheet easier to read. [Figure 5.11]

		Immediate	1 Minute	2 Minutes	3 Minutes		
Group 1		212	210	205	193		
Group 2		212	211	203	195		
Group 3		212	209	204	198		
Group 4		212	211	202	193		

FIGURE 5.11

Just remember the guidelines for producing text that is comfortable and easy to read. In this situation, making the labels distinctive from the data itself also helps the reader to easily understand your document.

Suppose you realize that the initial presentation is not particularly effective and you decide to make some changes. Highlight the entries in your spreadsheet that you want to change. There are a variety of choices on the **Format** menu. You can adjust rows or columns, as well as the entire sheet you are working with, and more. [Figure 5.12]

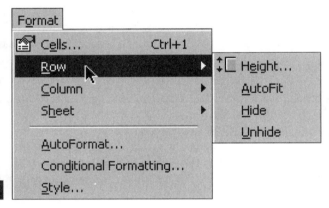

FIGURE 5.12

Experiment with some of the choices on this menu to see what options are available.

Rather than depending on the AutoFormat options, you can manually change the width of individual columns or the height of individual rows. Place the mouse pointer exactly over the line that serves as a column or row boundary where the labels appear. The pointer changes to a tool that allows you to manually resize an individual row or column. The row or column will resize as you click and drag the boundary line. [Figure 5.13]

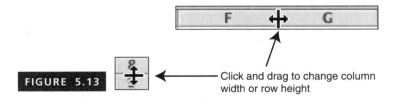

Click and drag to change column width or row height

FIGURE 5.13

Resizing in this manner allows you to customize rows and columns individually.

You can change the color of text in spreadsheets by choosing Color from the Font tab of the Format Cells dialog box. You can also use color in a cell or groups of cells. To add a border to a cell or group of cells, select them and choose the Border tab from the Format Cells dialog box. Check the settings to control the placement of borders. To add color to borders, choose the color you want from the drop-down menu. [Figure 5.14]

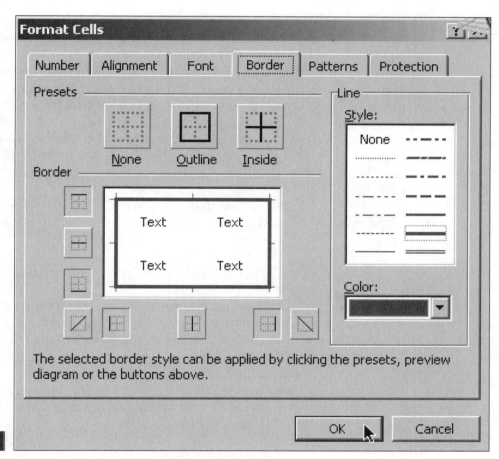

Check the layout of the lines you want in the preview and make adjustments if you need to before you leave the dialog box. Of course, you can always return to this dialog box to modify further.

You can also fill cells or blocks of cells with color and patterns.

1. Select the cells you want to fill.
2. Select **Cells** from the **Format** menu and open the Format Cells dialog box.
3. Click on the Patterns tab.
4. Choose the color you want.
5. If you wish, choose a pattern. [Figure 5.15]

		Immediate	1 Minute	2 Minutes	3 Minutes
Group 1		212	210	205	193
Group 2		212	211	203	195
Group 3		212	209	204	198
Group 4		212	211	202	193

FIGURE 5.15

Be very careful with fill colors and patterns. They can obscure your data and make your spreadsheet hard to read. Sometimes it helps to make the text bold. Keep in mind that dark text on a light background is best and if you intend to print, make the color even lighter than what works on the screen. Printing increases the intensity of the color by almost 20 percent.

Experiment with modifying the formatting in your spreadsheet to make the data it contains more attractive and readable. Using formatting options that allow the reader to easily distinguish between the column and row labels and the data you enter makes it easier to read and understand the information.

Just as you have learned that you can create and use styles to control your formatting in the word processor, you can also define special styles for spreadsheets.

1. Click on a cell in which you have added some formatting such as a border, pattern, or even typeface change.
2. From the **Format** menu, choose **Style.** You may need to use the disclosure arrow at the bottom of the list to find this option. Once the Style dialog box is open, you see some of the properties of the selected cell.
3. Modify the formatting, if you wish.
4. Give your style a name.
5. When you want other cells have this same appearance, select the cells, choose **Style** from the **Format** menu, and select the style name from the drop-down menu to apply it to the new cell.

Note that there is a Merge button in this dialog box. This button lets you bring styles from other documents into your current document.

USING FORMULAS IN SPREADSHEETS

So far all you have done with a spreadsheet is to enter information manually and format the data. The power of a spreadsheet, however, lies in its ability to do complex calculations rapidly.

Column G in the example spreadsheet could contain the difference between the first and last measurements taken in our experiment. Instead of calculating this number by hand, you can create a formula to have the calculation automatically done by the software.

Formulas are entered in much the same manner as numbers.

1. Click on the cell in which you want a formula (in the example, cell F4).
2. Enter the formula in the Formula box.
   A formula always begins with an equal sign (=). You want to find the difference between the initial boiling point of water to the final reading, so enter = C4 – F4.
   Note: Be sure you put a space on each side of the minus sign. Otherwise, *Excel* may think that you have entered a word with a hyphen.
3. Click on the Accept button.
4. The formula immediately appears in cell G4.

The next step is to use formulas to find the difference for the other entries in our spreadsheet. You can write a formula for each of the other cells in Column G, repeating the steps you just completed. However, here is a situation where the Fill handle is powerful.

1. Click on cell G4.
2. Click on the Fill handle and drag down the column.
3. The appropriate formulas and thus values are added to the spreadsheet. If you click in a computed cell, the value appears in the spreadsheet and the associated formula is shown in the Formula bar. [Figure 5.16]

G7	▼	=	=C7 - F7						
	A	B	C	D	E	F	G	H	I	J
1										
2										
3			Immediate	1 Minute	2 Minutes	3 Minutes				
4		Group 1	212	210	205	193	19			
5		Group 2	212	211	203	195	17			
6		Group 3	212	209	204	198	14			
7		Group 4	212	211	202	193	19			
8										
9										

FIGURE 5.16

Notice that the formula in each cell is adjusted automatically by *Excel* to use the correct cells for the calculation.

4. Next, enter the labels and apply the formatting that you want for the computed data. [Figure 5.17]

H3	▼	=							
	A	B	C	D	E	F	G	H	I
1									
2									
3			Immediate	1 Minute	2 Minutes	3 Minutes	Temp Change		
4		Group 1	212	210	205	193	19		
5		Group 2	212	211	203	195	17		
6		Group 3	212	209	204	198	14		
7		Group 4	212	211	202	193	19		
8									
9									

FIGURE 5.17

In the previous example, all the steps of the computation that the spreadsheet needed were manually entered in the Entry bar. However, *Excel* comes with a large number of formulas, providing a way to have you complete the task with even less time and effort.

Another step in analyzing the experimental data might be to average the readings recorded by each group. You can make use of the included average function.

1. Click in the cell in which you want the formula (in the example, cell C8).
2. Choose **Function** from the **Insert** menu. [Figure 5.18]

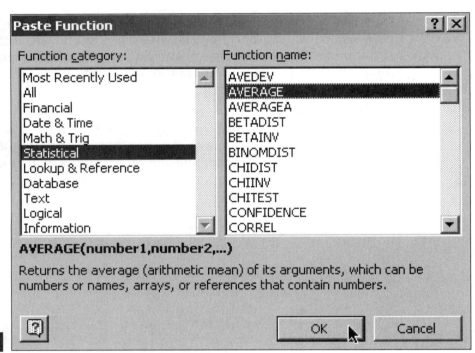

FIGURE 5.18

From the list of available options selet a Function Category and Function name.

3. A dialog box appears that lets you indicate the cells you want to use in the calculation. [Figure 5.19]

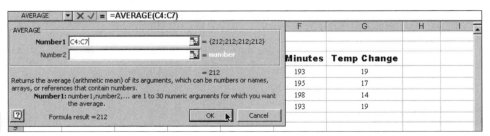

FIGURE 5.19

4. The formula appears.

In this case, *Excel* guessed what cells you wanted to average. Notice that the starting and ending cells are separated by a colon (:), and the dialog box shows what values are used to compute this average.

Now you can click in cell C8 and use the Fill handle to drag across the appropriate columns to add the Average formula to all of the columns. Finally, format the new entries in whatever way you prefer. [Figure 5.20]

		Immediate	1 Minute	2 Minutes	3 Minutes	Temp Change
Group 1		212	210	205	193	19
Group 2		212	211	203	195	17
Group 3		212	209	204	198	14
Group 4		212	211	202	193	19
Average		212	210.25	203.5	194.75	

FIGURE 5.20

You may wish to check or view the formulas you have included in your spreadsheet. *Excel* includes a keyboard shortcut that will suppress the number value and show the formula instead—Control + Tilde (~). The tilde key is usually located on the upper left corner of your keyboard. The formulas appear in the cells where they are applied. You can check them from the screen or print the sheet to check them against your calculated value.

VALUABLE SPREADSHEET FEATURES

At this point, your explorations in the *Excel* environment have given you a great start with these powerful tools. However, as you would expect, there are many other options available in *Excel*. Explore these other options; you will be able to make spreadsheets an important part of your "technology toolbox" only if you practice.

■ **Fill handle** for sequences and repeated patterns of data. This feature allows you to fill rows and columns with repeated patterns. This feature helps you enter times, dates, number patterns, and more. Enter data in one cell, then enter the next item in an adjacent cell. Use the Fill handle to fill the row or column. Note that as you drag the handle, you see the values that will be inserted. [Figure 5.21]

Dates	3/15/2003	3/22/2003	3/29/2003	4/5/2003	4/12/2003	4/19/2003
Times	11:15 AM	11:30 AM	11:45 AM	12:00 PM	12:15 PM	
Sequence	2	4	6	8		

FIGURE 5.21

Recall that you can also use **Fill** on the **Insert** menu to accomplish the same task.

■ **Absolute** and **Relative** Reference. When you use the Fill options, the spreadsheet changes the cell names appropriately. This is because all of the formulas you have entered so far are *relative* to other cells in the spreadsheet. *Excel* records the position of the cells used in a formula relative to the cell containing the formula. As you copy the formula to the new cell, this description is also carried. The new formula adjusts to use the correct cells.

Sometimes, however, you want to enter a formula that will keep the same cell value regardless of how you modify your spreadsheet or where you place the formula. In the example, this might be a row that contains the difference between the boiling point of water and the average values. [Figure 5.22]

	A	B	C	D	E	F	G	H	
				Immediate	**1 Minute**	**2 Minutes**	**3 Minutes**	**Temp Change**	
1									
2									
3			Immediate	1 Minute	2 Minutes	3 Minutes	Temp Change		
4		Group 1	212	210	205	193	19		
5		Group 2	212	211	203	195	17		
6		Group 3	212	209	204	198	14		
7		Group 4	212	211	202	193	19		
8		Average	212	210.25	203.5	194.75			
9									
10				Boiling Point of Water		212			
11									
12				Difference between Average and Boiling Point:					
13									
14									

FIGURE 5.22

The formulas for these computations are shown in Figure 5.23.

> 1 minute: F10 - C8
> 2 minutes: F10 - D8
> 3 minutes: F10 - E8

FIGURE 5.23

To calculate the difference, *every* formula has an F10 in it. The F10 is called an *absolute reference. Excel* uses a $ in the formula to indicate an absolute reference. Thus, the formula that should go in cell C13 is shown in Figure 5.24.

FIGURE 5.24 F10 - D8

The first $ indicates that the F should not be changed. The second $ indicates that the 10 should not be changed. Since there are no such characters associated with the D8, *Excel* knows to change this cell name relative to the placement of the formula.

Now you can use **Fill Across** in Row 13 with the formula containing both absolute and relative references. The formulas that will be filled in look like this as they are displayed on the Formula bar. [Figure 5.25]

FIGURE 5.25 | F10 - D8 F1- E8 F10 - F8

Recall that you can use the options for numbers in **Cells** from the **Format** menu to modify the way numbers are displayed. [Figure 5.26]

			Immediate	1 Minute	2 Minutes	3 Minutes	Temp Change	
4		Group 1	212	210	205	193	19	
5		Group 2	212	211	203	195	17	
6		Group 3	212	209	204	198	14	
7		Group 4	212	211	202	193	19	
8		Average	212	210.25	203.5	194.75		
10				Boiling Point of Water		212		
12				Difference between Average and Boiling Point:				
13				1.75	8.5	17.25		

FIGURE 5.26

For example, you could change the number of decimal places used in the numbers. For some situations, such an adjustment results in a display of entries that is much easier to read.

Note that cell F10 contains the boiling point of water in Fahrenheit. Perhaps you wonder why we did not just use the number in the formula. By entering this constant into the spreadsheet formula, we can use this same spreadsheet for readings taken in centigrade by merely changing the number in F10.

SUMMARY AND TIPS

Spreadsheets are intended for data used in computations. In the "real world," spreadsheets are usually extremely large documents involving multiple uses of the data. For your present needs, focus on extending your comfort level in *Excel* one step at a time. Just using a spreadsheet to maintain some of your own records can assist you in learning to use a spreadsheet more efficiently.

The ability to utilize formulas makes a spreadsheet work as a calculation tool. The list of included formulas is extensive. Before you start manually creating the formulas you need, think about their purpose. If you are attempting an ordinary or common calculation, chances are the necessary formula is ready and waiting for your use.

The rules for formatting text still apply if you want to create documents that communicate effectively. Taking the time to organize the data in a cohesive and structured manner is vital. Adding color and other distinctions to the entries can help you share the concepts contained in the document.

There are many shortcut tools available. Because users so often focus on the idea of getting the task done, they neglect to recognize that the time spent learning to use the available tools will eventually pay off. The power of the Fill handle is provided to speed a very repetitive but frequently encountered task.

You have been cautioned to save your work frequently in *Word,* and you have certainly realized that you must also save your spreadsheets frequently and carefully. Of course, a systematic naming scheme is essential to ensure the ease of storing, locating, and using the files you create.

Beware of believing the results of a spreadsheet just because it behaves like a large and complex calculator. It is easy to enter formulas incorrectly and thus produce incorrect results. The computer is not smart. It does not question any number that appears as a result of what you enter. Although the spreadsheet software automates many tasks for you, it does not think. Thinking is your job. For a spreadsheet to be a valuable tool, you must think carefully about the problem you are solving and at least spot-check your results. Many errors can be avoided by simply asking yourself if the entries in the spreadsheet are reasonable and make sense in the context in which they appear.

Striving to increase your skills with the computer and software is a good step toward achieving many of the milestones identified in the NETS technology standards. With each progression, you move closer to the time when you handle the technology automatically. At such a point, you can focus all your attention on the contents, details, and relationships of the material you are producing. While you are busy with the intense thinking and decision making involved in the communication, you will find yourself applying the features and design decisions allowed by the technology to maximize the benefits of your time and efforts.

CHAPTER SIX

Spreadsheet Charts and More

In Chapter 5 you learned how to enter data into a simple spreadsheet and format the spreadsheet attractively. In addition, you learned how to use formulas to automate computations in your spreadsheet. However, you often want to share the information in a spreadsheet with others. Finding meaning in a display of numbers can be difficult. Changing the information to a visual format is one way of helping others quickly understand the content. Displaying the data in a visual format is made easy in *Excel*. This chapter focuses on creating charts (graphs) from the information in your spreadsheet.

SOME TIPS AND TECHNIQUES

Before focusing on charts, this section reviews some of the options available in most *Office* applications that are particularly useful in *Excel*.

Customizing Your Screen

The spreadsheet example used in the preceding chapter easily fits on a single screen. However, spreadsheets can quickly become large enough to be difficult to view and manage on the screen. Thus, it can be helpful to learn new ways to look at your spreadsheet.

- Choosing **Zoom** from the **View** menu allows you to look at your spreadsheet in different magnifications. [Figure 6.1]

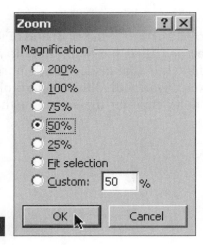

FIGURE 6.1

175

Setting the Zoom to 50 percent displays the spreadsheet at half the size you normally see it. [Figure 6.2]

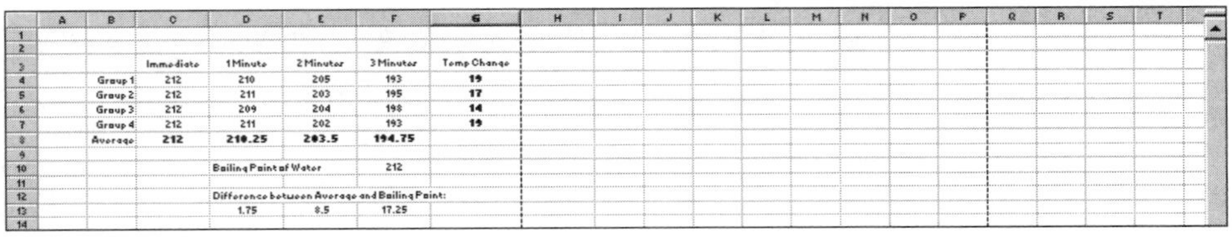

FIGURE 6.2

- Choosing **Full Screen** from the **View** menu causes your spreadsheet to use the full available space on your screen. This allows you to see as much of your spreadsheet at one time as possible.
- Choosing **Page Break Preview** from the **View** menu allows you to see where page breaks will occur when you print your spreadsheet. Depending on the layout of your spreadsheet, you may be able to click and drag on the page break lines and move the breaks to a better position before printing. [Figure 6.3]

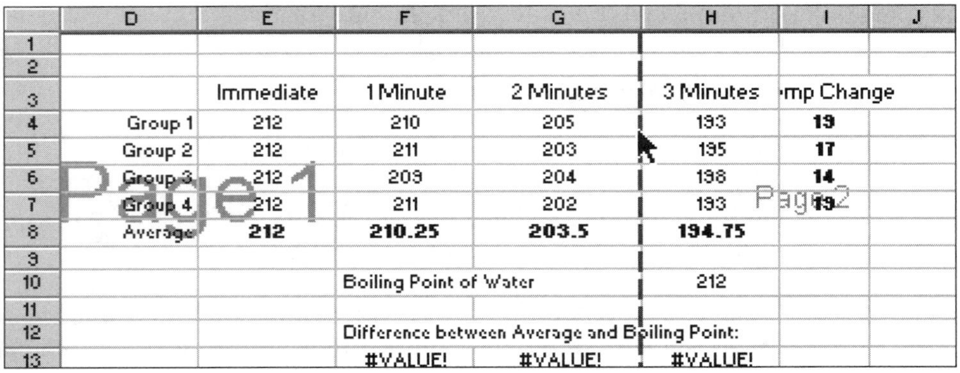

FIGURE 6.3

- At the top of the vertical scroll bar and at the right end of the horizontal scroll bar is a small rectangle called the Scroll box. If you click and drag this box, you can split the spreadsheet both horizontally and vertically. This can allow you to work with different parts of your spreadsheet that are otherwise not visible on the screen at the same time. [Figure 6.4]

	A	B	C	D	E	F	D	E	F
1									
2									
3			**Immediate**	**1 Minute**	**2 Minutes**	**3 Minutes**	**1 Minute**	**2 Minutes**	**3 Min**
4		**Group 1**	212	210	205	193	210	205	19
5		**Group 2**	212	211	203	195	211	203	19
6		**Group 3**	212	209	204	198	209	204	19
7		**Group 4**	212	211	202	193	211	202	19
8		**Average**	212	**210.25**	**203.5**	**194.75**	**210.25**	**203.5**	**194**
9									
10				**Boiling Point of Water**		212	**Boiling Point of Water**		21
11									
12				**Difference between Average and Boilin**			**Difference between Average and**		
13				1.75	-203.5	-194.75	1.75	-203.5	-194
14									
12				**Difference between Average and Boilin**			**Difference between Average and**		
13				1.75	-203.5	-194.75	1.75	-203.5	-194
14									
15									
16									
17									
18									
19									
20									

Sheet1 / Sheet2 \ Sheet3 /

FIGURE 6.4

Because the sample spreadsheet fits on one page, it is not obvious how this feature is helpful. In this example, you might choose to put the results of a second experiment on the page below the first. Of course, you might instead choose to put the results of another experiment on a separate Sheet in the Workbook document.

Searching and Sorting

Unlike the sample spreadsheet document in Chapter 5, spreadsheets normally contain a large amount of information. When you use a large spreadsheet, it becomes difficult to locate specific entries or navigate from one position to another. *Excel* helps you by providing two ways to search for information. One method is to use **Go To** from the **Edit** menu. When you enter a cell address, you are moved directly to that cell. Remember that a cell address is a column letter followed by a row number.

You can also search in a spreadsheet by using **Find** from the **Edit** menu. When you search for numbers, you need to distinguish between the numerical data and the formatting on the screen. For example, you *see* the entry $24.45 but you *search* for the entry 24.45.

In certain circumstances, you may want to reorganize the order of rows or columns. For example, you want a budget spreadsheet changed so that the expense items are organized alphabetically. To reorganize, click and drag across the columns and rows you want to rearrange. Select **Sort** from the **Data** menu. Pay close attention to the Sort dialog box. Be sure you are sorting the right items in the right direction. [Figure 6.5]

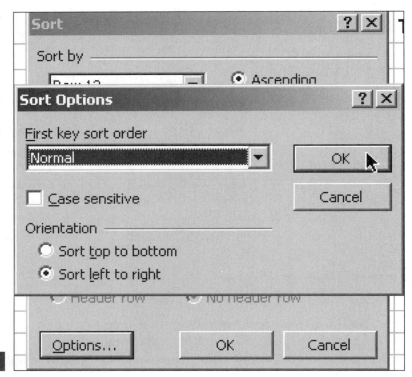

Exercise care when sorting in a spreadsheet. You can quickly lose the relationship among rows and columns with an incorrect sort, so always save your work before you sort. If the result of your sort is not what you intended, close your file without saving to move back to your earlier version.

MAKING CHARTS (GRAPHS)

Excel allows you to display information in various forms. Some people are very good at looking at a table of numbers and "seeing" various relationships in the data. However, most people are much better at understanding a graphical representation that emphasizes the patterns in the data. *Excel* makes it easy to create a variety of charts from your data.

Creating a Chart

Open your spreadsheet document. To create a chart of spreadsheet data, select the part of your spreadsheet you want to convert to a graphical format. Choose **Chart** from the **Insert** menu. A dialog box opens that lets you create a variety of chart types. As you can see from the Chart type list, *Excel* offers many choices. [Figure 6.6]

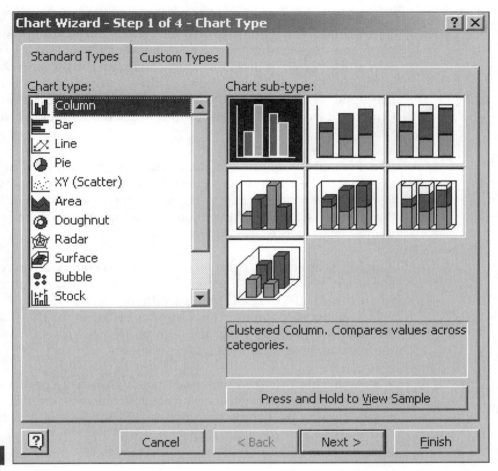

FIGURE 6.6

Selecting the Chart Type

Different kinds of charts are used to represent different kinds of information. The type of chart you select depends on two things—your data and the information you wish to share. When you actually create a chart, try several options before making your decision. Your major goal is to present the information in a way that informs or conveys the ideas and patterns the data indicate. You should have in mind the kind of chart or charts you hope to create from your spreadsheet even as you are designing it.

The following gives you some information on each type of chart available in *Excel* with some "rules of thumb" to keep in mind when choosing a chart type.

■ **Column** or **Bar.** Used to represent discrete data such as grades on tests, cost per unit, or people with different hair colors. The primary strength of such charts is their ability to show comparisons. For example, you might compare the averages for a series of tests that your class has completed.

■ **Line.** Line graphs are often used when there are a lot of data points to represent that have some functional relationship among them. For example, if your spreadsheet is statistics kept for players on a basketball team over some period of time, the chart can reveal the player who is most consistent for the time period shown. Think of this chart as a way to illustrate the trend or pattern in your data. In the spreadsheet example used in Chapter 5, you might use a line chart to see the temperature decrease over time.

■ **Pie** and **Doughnut.** Pie charts are generally used to show the percentages that make up a whole. A pie chart could be used to show what percentage of students got As, Bs, Cs, Ds, or Fs on an assignment or in the class. A doughnut chart is similar but allows more than one series to be presented in a single chart.

■ **XY (Scatter).** This chart format is used to compare two related but different sets of data to see if patterns exist. Clusters of data sometimes appear when this format is used. Using a different symbol for each category can reveal relationships among the categories of data in the chart. You most often find this chart type in statistical reports. They are a good choice for representing data points from science experiments.

■ **Area.** This format is often used to show growth in a particular category of data. For example, an area chart nicely illustrates the population change of a city or country over some time period. Fluctuations in growth rate can be easily observed.

Excel also includes a number of other less used chart types, including Radar, Surface, Bubble, Stock, Cylinder, Cone, and Pyramid. Once you are more advanced and looking for ways to extend your skills, you might enjoy exploring these different forms of representing data. However, we suggest you first work to maximize your skill level with the more common chart types.

For each of the types of charts available in *Excel,* there are numerous features that can be changed. In the beginning most of your needs can be met by using bar, line, and pie charts.

The Spreadsheet Layout

Without question, your most effective charts are created when you plan ahead. Before you add any data to the spreadsheet, try to anticipate what information you might want to chart. Plan for your chart by making appropriate choices for your data placement. In addition, include labels that give the content of your spreadsheet some meaning. Even the experiment example, despite the simple entries and overall concept, includes short concise labels that describe the data.

You should put labels on *all* of your rows and columns. It is also important that your labels are in only one row or column. You are also less likely to have problems if you keep your labels next to your data in your spreadsheet. If you want to provide a slight separation between the labels and data, make use of the options for formatting the text within the cells. Remember, you can apply Space Before and Space After to paragraphs to ensure a bit of space around the text entry.

Select the Data

Before a chart is started, decide what information you wish to communicate with the reader, and try to decide what type of chart is best suited to share this information. This example will chart the experiment data for the Group 1.

1. Click and drag across the first row of data *including the labels.* [Figure 6.7]

	A	B	C	D	E	F	G	H
1								
2								
3			Immediate	1 Minute	2 Minutes	3 Minutes	Temp Change	
4		Group 1	212	210	205	193	19	
5		Group 2	212	211	203	195	17	
6		Group 3	212	209	204	198	14	
7		Group 4	212	211	202	193	19	
8		Average	212	210.25	203.5	194.75		
9								
10				Boiling Point of Water		212		
11								
12				Difference between Average and Boiling Point:				
13				1.75	8.5	17.25		

FIGURE 6.7

Note that we have selected the data for the Group 1 and have not included the temperature change column. Including the change does not make sense. Remember that our goal is to produce a graph representing the raw data collected by Group 1.

2. Choose **Chart** from the **Insert** menu. [Figure 6.8]

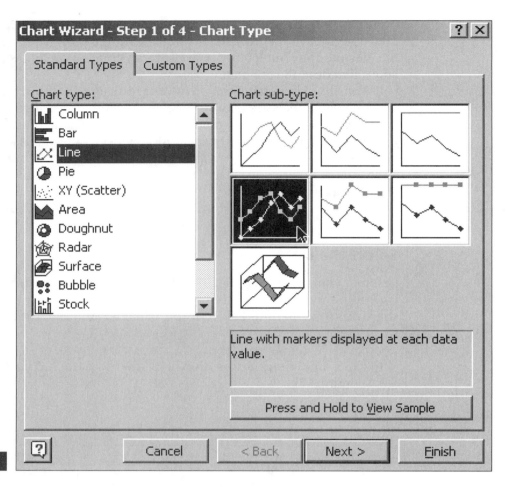

FIGURE 6.8

3. Click on Line chart in the left part of the dialog box and then select the type of line chart you want on the right. For now, click on Finish in the Chart Wizard dialog box.
4. Your chart appears on top of the spreadsheet. [Figure 6.9]

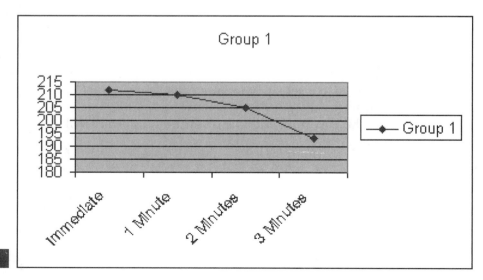

FIGURE 6.9

To create this example, we clicked Finish as soon as we picked the type of chart we wanted. If you click Next, you find other options for customizing or modifying the way the Chart Wizard completes your charts. If you wish, stop and explore these options. However, you will learn how to modify your chart outside of the Chart Wizard in the next section.

MODIFYING YOUR CHART

The chart we have created does a good job of representing our data. You can easily discern the direction of temperature change. You can also see approximately how much temperature change occurred. However, the chart can still be improved. Is it obvious the chart represents changes in the temperature of the water samples?

Modifying a Title

Adding a title helps the reader to quickly connect the data in the chart to a context. Did you notice that when your chart appeared, a Chart toolbar also appeared?

To add a title, follow these steps.

1. Click on the drop-down menu on the Chart toolbar.
2. Choose Chart Title. [Figure 6.10]

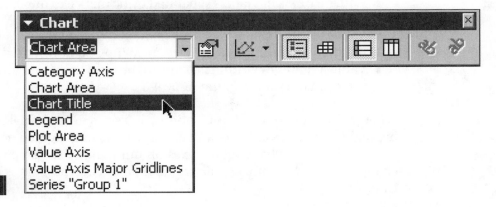

FIGURE 6.10

3. The title currently on your chart is highlighted. Enter a meaningful title. As you enter the text, notice that it appears on the Formula bar rather than in your chart. [Figure 6.11]

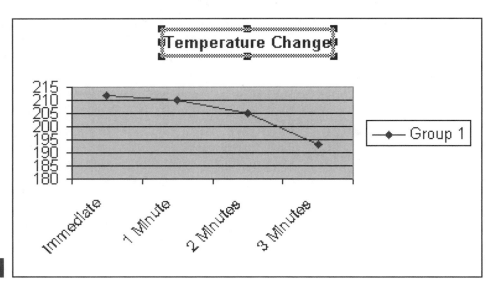

You must hit the Return or Enter key to move the text into your chart. Using a simple but meaningful title makes the chart easier to understand.

Adjusting Axes

You can adjust both the horizontal and vertical axes in your chart. If you examine the drop-down menu on the Chart toolbar, you see several choices that relate to the axes of your chart.

- **Category Axis** has labels separated by tic marks. In our example, it is the horizontal (bottom) axis.
- **Value Axis** has values on it that allow you to read the data points on the chart. In our example, it is the vertical (up and down) axis.
- **Value Axis Major Gridlines** refers to the lines that are drawn in the chart out from the values on the Value Axis.

When you choose one of these options, you see a different part of your chart highlighted, and are able to make changes to the highlighted portion.

Let's explore changing the axes on our graphs. The steps below reflect changes we made in our sample graph. Try applying these steps to your graph as you read.

1. Choose Value Axis from the drop-down menu on the Graph toolbar.
2. The vertical axis is highlighted—you can see the handles at each end of the axis line.
3. Next, display the Format Axis dialog box so you can make changes in your axis. Be sure the axis is selected. Go to the **Format** menu and choose **Selected Axis.** The Format Axis dialog box appears. [Figure 6.12]

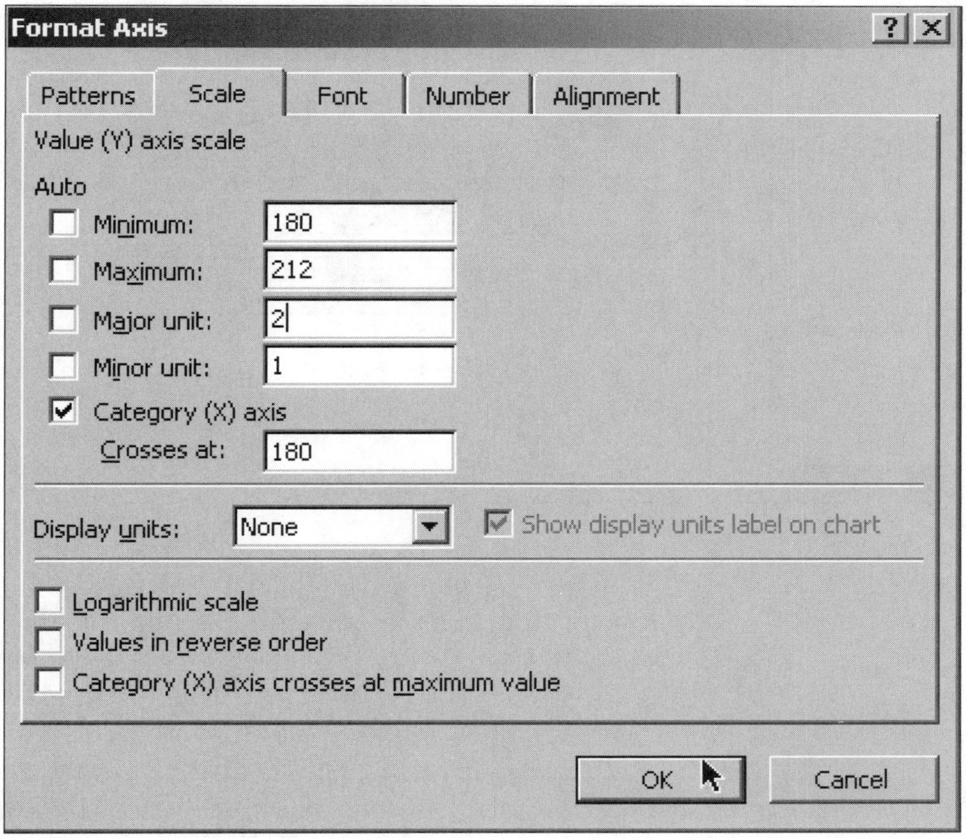

FIGURE 6.12

There is a faster way to access the Format Axis options. Move your mouse over the axis and its labels. When you see the words "Value Axis" appear, double-click to bring up the Format Axis options.

There are many adjustments that can be made to the vertical scale. While most are self-explanatory, take note that you can change the tic marks and lines from the Patterns tab.

Technical Note: The Format Axis dialog box opens to display the tab choices of whatever was being viewed when the dialog box was closed. As a result, you may see a different tab displayed on your screen.

4. To create a chart that gives a bit more accuracy, use smaller units. These settings are located on the Scale tab. *Un*check the Auto column where the changes will be made. [Figure 6.13]

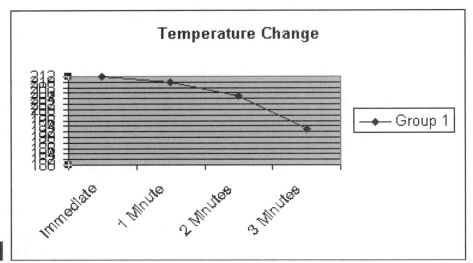

FIGURE 6.13

There are now more numbers on the vertical axis, but they are so close together that they are quite hard to read. Click near the outer edge of your chart to stretch the chart from the top or bottom. [Figure 6.14]

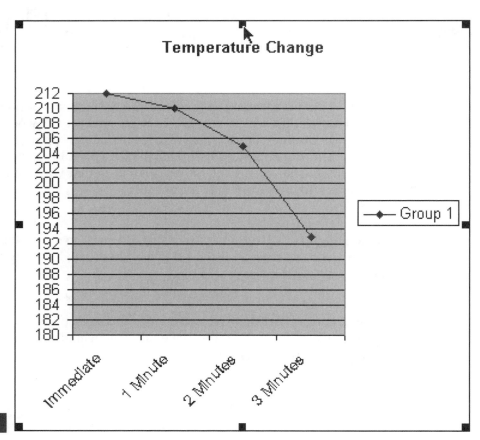

FIGURE 6.14

This simple change in step size on the y-axis helps the reader to find the value that is attached to the points in the chart. In other situations, you may need to adjust the minimum or maximum to achieve the clarity you want.

Controlling Labels

Earlier in this chapter, you learned to add a title to a chart. You can modify the title formatting by double-clicking in the title to open the Format Chart Title dialog box. Or, go to the **Format** menu and choose **Selected Chart Title.** The dialog box gives you access to options for changing your text appearance. If you click on the title so that the selection handles become visible, you can click and drag the title to a new position on the chart.

The legend included in your graph is also essential in helping your reader easily understand your chart. Move the mouse over the legend box and wait until the word *legend* appears, then double-click. When the Format Legend dialog box appears, you can choose the placement and adjust the appearance of your legend text. [Figure 6.15]

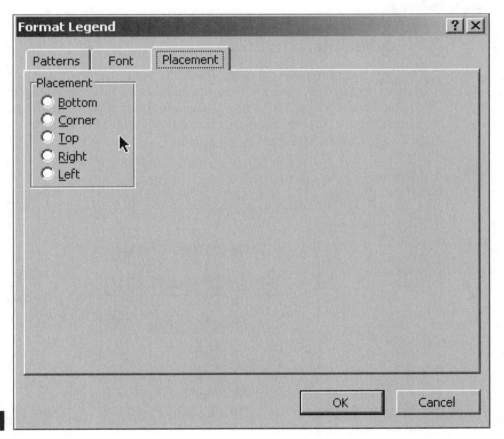

FIGURE 6.15

As you did with the title, you can click and drag the legend into place. [Figure 6.16]

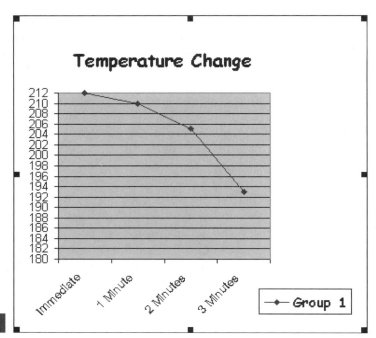

Other Characteristics

You have seen several ways to modify your chart. When you double-click on an area of the chart, the Format Chart dialog box appears for the specific area you have selected. The changes you make apply only to that particular part of the chart. Having the correct terms in your mind will enable you to keep track of your work more easily. [Figure 6.17]

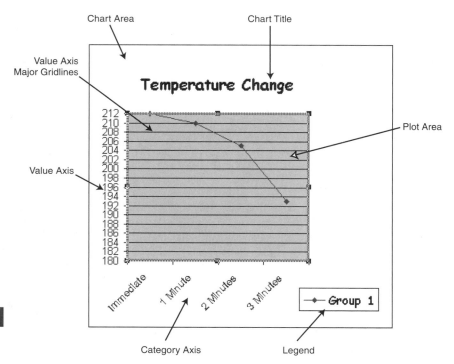

In previous sections you learned how to change the labels, legend, and title on your chart. You can also make changes in such attributes as the color of your chart. For example, if you double-click on the Plot Area, you see the Format Plot Area box as shown in Figure 6.18.

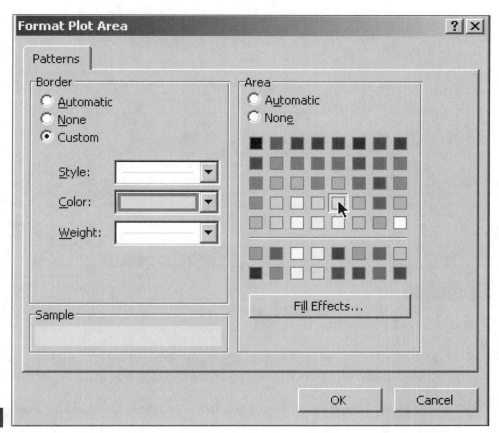

You can adjust the color and line features of the area in which your data is charted. Similarly, you can adjust the color and line characteristics of the chart area. Using color on your chart can increase how well it communicates, but too much color can distract from the data itself. [Figure 6.19]

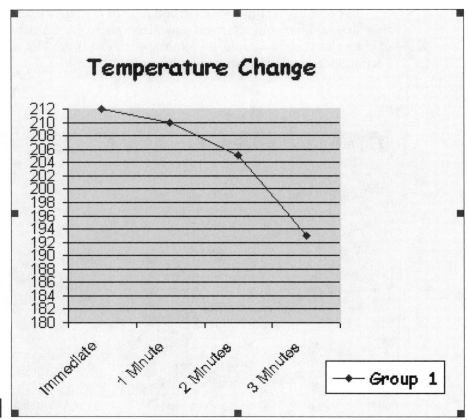

FIGURE 6.19

It will take considerable thought and practice before you can use color effectively. In addition, if you are printing grayscale rather than color, you will need to learn what combinations of color translate into contrasting grays. In the beginning, keep things simple and remember the earlier guideline of placing dark elements on a light background for easy reading. It is far too easy to make your chart more difficult to read.

A CHART PROBLEM: NONADJACENT DATA

The initial creation of a spreadsheet is complex. It is impossible to anticipate and plan for every possible application you might make of the data. From the example, suppose that you want to compare the readings that Group 1 recorded with the readings that Group 4 recorded, without including the readings from Group 2 and Group 3. Stop and look at the position of these columns. It is not obvious how to create such a chart from this spreadsheet.

If we click and drag across the Group 1 and Group 4 readings to highlight the data for charting, we also get Groups 2 and 3. How do you solve this problem?

1. Click and drag across the labels and the data associated with Group 1.
2. Hold down the Control key (Command key on the Macintosh) and click and drag across the data for Group 4.
3. Choose Insert Chart. [Figure 6.20]

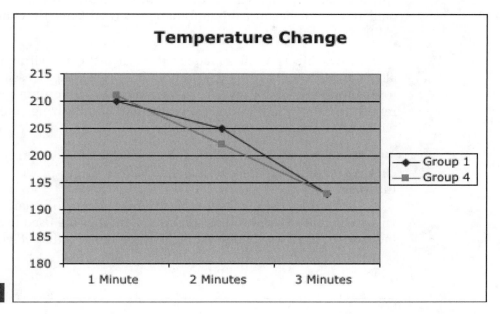

FIGURE 6.20

This technique gives you the flexibility to make a wide variety of charts from the same data.

MORE TIPS

As you can see, there is an almost limitless combination of types and settings for charts available. The more time you spend experimenting with charts, the better you will understand how to use these features. Here are a few tips and reminders that may help you work more efficiently with charts.

■ **Multiple Charts.** You can have more than one chart in your spreadsheet document. When you save the document, all of the charts will be saved with it. Zooming out and comparing two or three charts is a good way to decide which one communicates your message most effectively.

■ **Deleting Charts.** To remove a chart from a spreadsheet, simply click on it so that you see handles. Then choose **Cut** from the **Edit** menu.

On the PC, you may find the tags that appear to identify parts of the chart interfere with easily deleting the chart. Click on the chart and drag it a small distance until the four-way arrow cursor appears. Then, immediately choose **Cut** from the **Edit** menu.

- **Sizing Charts.** Charts can be sized. Click on the chart to select it, then click and drag any of the handles and resize just as you would any other graphic object.

- **Linking Charts and Spreadsheets.** When you change the data in your spreadsheet, any charts in the document automatically change to match the data. Be careful, because this automatic link is broken if the chart is moved to a different document.

- **Draw Objects.** Charts made in the spreadsheet environment are actually Draw documents. You can paste them into word processing documents to illustrate a concept you are communicating. If you are responsible for reporting data, using a *Word* document and emphasizing your information with selected charts is extremely effective.

- **Modifying a Chart.** Charts are Draw documents. You have seen that clicking on different areas of the chart allows you to provide formatting to that part.

    You can also use the Draw tools to add elements to a chart. You practiced with many of the Draw tools earlier and here they are used to add a label to indicate the units used to measure the water temperature. [Figure 6.21]

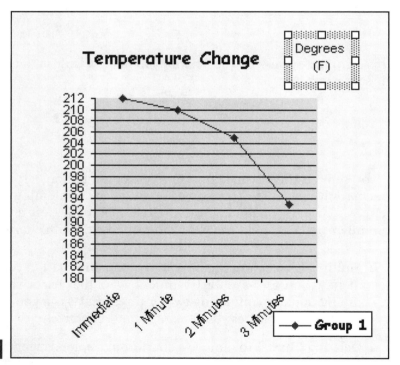

FIGURE 6.21

Move the elements of the chart to make room for the label close to the information associated with it. [Figure 6.22]

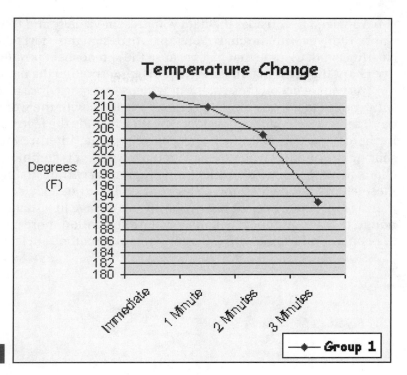

The ability to use Draw tools to modify a chart gives you even more flexibility when creating charts. As your skill in designing effective documents increases, you will more and more want to use these options to control the appearance of your charts.

SUMMARY AND TIPS

This chapter has given you tremendous help in understanding why and how to convey the message in the spreadsheet data in a visual format. There are so many simple options to enhance your charts that your problem may be deciding on the options that work most effectively. If you have never had reason to create charts before, it will take time to gain the insights you need to make the correct decision quickly. If you have struggled to create charts without the assistance of a spreadsheet, you will already be more than willing to push the provided buttons to complete the task.

While it is easy to recognize the way *Excel* makes decisions in creating the charts, you need to maintain the control of your own presentations. The automatic charts are simple to use, but even adding one or two specific steps, such as adding a title and changing the labels on the axes, increases the effectiveness of your communication. Keep trying options without worrying about making mistakes. *Excel* is quite happy to delete and build charts until you have the one you need.

One danger with spreadsheets is the ease with which you can make charts. It is much too easy to create a chart that has little or no meaning. While the spreadsheet automates the process of making charts, it does not think for you. You need to consider the data you present visually and the message you want to convey with the chart. Your job is to design the chart to communicate clearly. Do not assume that just because the spreadsheet produced an attractive chart, the resulting image is helpful in interpreting the data.

As you reflect on these many new steps for using *Office* to communicate with your readers, take time to connect the tools with the work you do each day. The NETS guidelines developed by ISTE include the features just covered in the category of collecting and analyzing data, interpreting results, and sharing the findings with others. In today's world, it is common to encounter charts in newspapers or on television programs. Learning to understand how these charts are created increases your ability to quickly comprehend the message in someone else's chart. Sharing a message in visual format in addition to text and numbers will make your information more easily accessible to people comfortable with different styles and methods of learning.

CHAPTER SEVEN

Getting Started Using *Access*

You have now seen several of the environments in *Office*. You have been practicing to master your new skills and maximize the value of owning your copy of *Office*. This chapter deals with the database application *Access*. (Note: The Macintosh version of *Office* does not include *Access*.)

So what is a database? A database is a collection of information. There are many kinds of printed databases, such as telephone books and dictionaries, that we use all the time. A card file of recipes or research notes is a database. Your personal address book, a class list, or a list of customers is a database. Obviously, databases play an important role in our day-to-day lives, although few people think about the fact that they are using databases.

As computers have become more and more a part of our lives, so have electronically stored databases. Companies purchase such databases and use them for target marketing. As a result, we all get junk mail—and junk e-mail—from each company that purchases a database containing our contact information.

In this chapter you will explore two interrelated topics: creating simple databases and searching and sorting your database to find information you need. In the next chapter, you will learn how to print reports from *Access*.

UNDERSTANDING DATABASES

There are a number of terms used with databases that have specific meanings. Before you create your first database, it is helpful to learn some general database vocabulary and some vocabulary specific to *Access*.

Let us start by looking at your telephone book. You can find a person's name, mailing address, and phone number. These three pieces of information make up a single *record*. The term *record* is used to describe a collection of information that is related in some way. The name, address, and phone number are the *categories* of information in the record.

After a careful examination of the telephone book, it is apparent that some records do not show an address entry. A telephone customer can choose to have only a name and telephone number in the publication. Even though the telephone book reserves the same categories for each person—a record—it is not necessary to put data in every category.

Think about the traditional address book that you might have for your friends and family. In this address book—database—records might contain the first name, last name, street, city, state, postal code, and phone number associated with each person. Each record could contain seven different but related pieces of information—categories.

In an electronic database you divide records into one or more categories of information called *fields*. Thus, an electronic database of your friends and family would have at least seven fields: first name, last name, street, city, state, postal code, and phone number. If you decide to have several telephone numbers in each record, then you need to add more fields.

Technical Note: Computer programs that allow manipulations of data in a database are technically called *database management systems.* However, the word *database* is now commonly used to refer both to the collection of information and to the software used to work with the collection of information.

When a database is stored electronically, it is easy to use the computer to store, access, search, and sort the information. Powerful electronic database programs are prevalent throughout our society. Governments use databases to keep tax and property records. Businesses use databases to track inventory, organize names of customers, and record sales information. Schools use databases to keep student grades, textbook inventories, and fee schedules. The success of such organizations is increasingly dependent on making effective use of their electronic databases.

Databases can be as useful to individuals as they are to organizations. You can keep address lists, holiday card lists, household inventories, or records of collections of books, CDs, or DVDs. These lists can be printed, sorted, or used with other computer applications.

CREATING A DATABASE

Access creates database files that consist of a number of different objects such as tables, reports, and so on. Regardless of how many objects you decide to include, you will still have just one file to store. Of course, you will remember to continue your practices of backing up your file and using incremental saving to safeguard your work.

To begin your exploration of *Access,* open the application from the **Start** menu. From the dialog box that appears, choose Blank Access database. [Figure 7.1]

FIGURE 7.1

If you already have the application open, choose **New** from the **File** menu to open the following window. Be sure you have clicked on the General tab, then choose the icon labeled Database. [Figure 7.2]

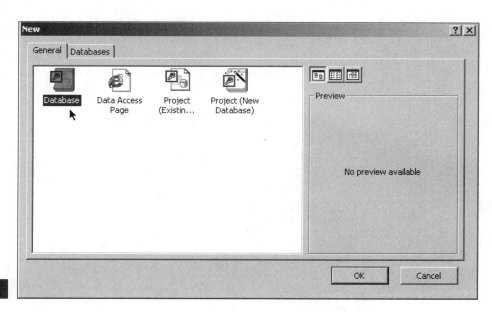

FIGURE 7.2

Once you click OK, a new dialog box opens.

Regardless of your first step, when you click OK, a new dialog box appears allowing you to specify a name and location for your database. Unlike files created in the other applications in *Office,* naming and saving the file precedes entering any information. [Figure 7.3]

FIGURE 7.3

As you complete this step in *Access,* you can accept the name that *Access* provides or you can create a name that helps you recognize the file's contents or purpose.

Once the file is saved, the database window appears. A great deal of your work will be done from this window. It organizes the many pieces that will make up your final database and displays tools for interacting with your database. [Figure 7.4]

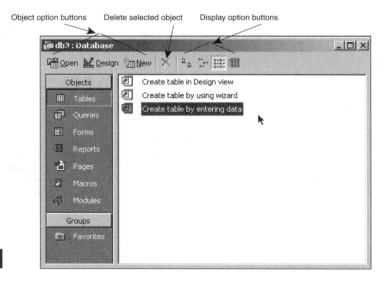

FIGURE 7.4

Before continuing, take the time to notice the items that are visible in this window. *Access* database objects are started using the buttons in the list on the left. Once you select the kind of object you want, the buttons along the top provide assistance in interacting with and creating them. The list on the right contains options for creating new ones and the name of all such objects you have added to the database. At this point, you have no objects in your first database.

Your first object will be a table. Make sure you have the Table button selected on the left. New tables can be made in several ways, but for now, double-click on Create table by entering data. You then see a new, blank table. *Access* files may consist of many such *tables*—rows and columns of data established by defining fields as containers for your data. The table as displayed is in the Datasheet view. [Figure 7.5]

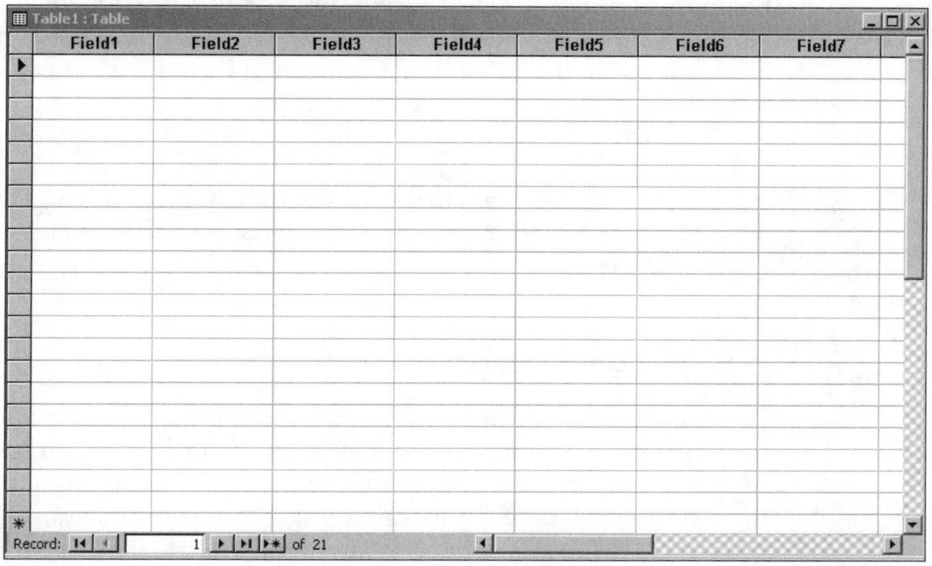

FIGURE 7.5

Keep in mind the terms introduced at the beginning of the chapter and examine this special table carefully. In this view, you can see that a table consists of several fields, the special containers for your categories of information. The names of fields appear at the top of the columns. Each row represents one record in your database. At the moment, no fields have been defined and no records have been entered.

Your next step is to save the table as part of your database. From the **File** menu, select **Save.** Enter a name for your table in the small dialog box that appears and click OK. Remember, since you may want to have more than one table in this database, using a name that conveys something about the content is helpful. After you have set the name and clicked OK, a dialog box will appear reminding you about using a *primary key* to identify the table. A primary key is a way for *Access* to be able to interact and identify entries in your table. For now, click on Yes to let *Access* supply this for you. It will be a sequential number used for each record you place in this table.

Once you let *Access* supply an identifier, the table changes in appearance. From this beginning you will be able to add the fields you intend to use. [Figure 7.6]

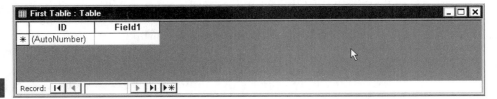

FIGURE 7.6

Obviously, your table is not yet ready for data entry, but you are now ready to begin designing the set of categories—fields—in your new database. If you stop to examine the database window, you will see that the name of your table now appears in the list of items associated with the database.

Technical Note: Once you are more familiar with *Access* and the objects in a database file, you may want to explore other methods of creating a table. This method is used because it gives you an immediate concept of how the elements that make up a table will appear.

Designing a Database

To create a successful database, you need to think carefully about why you are going to create a database and plan its contents before you spend a great deal of time entering data. The manner in which you can enter and organize the information will determine the usefulness of your final document. The database must be flexible enough to allow you multiple ways of accessing the data it contains. Designing a database is a skill that takes practice and thoughtfulness. The example, and your first database, will be quite small, but it provides practice with the same decisions you must make when you are working with large data sets.

Define your fields carefully. When you name your fields, it is best to keep the names simple, with an obvious relationship to the data you plan to put into them. As you define fields, you also need to think about the type of information to be put in each field. Will the data be numbers only? Dates? Names? Graphics? Or will your field include only a check mark?

It is time to set up the first table in our database with specific field names and field types that control the kind of data each field will hold. If you closed the first table when you saved it, go to the database window—most likely it is still open behind your table—and select the table from the list. If you cannot find the database window on your screen, go to the **Window** menu and select the database window by the name you gave to your database. Click on your table name to select it and click on the Design button. If your first table is still open, click the Design button in the database window. [Figure 7.7]

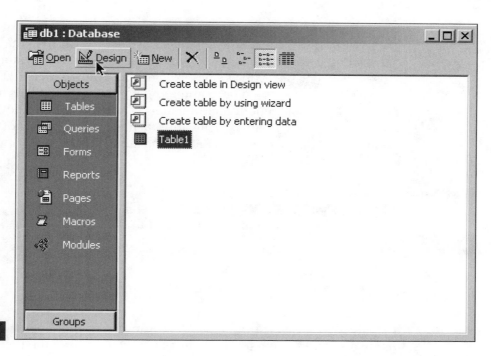

Using the Design button gives you access to a view in which you can enter names and decide on the data type for your fields. The Description entries are optional but can be used to remind you of your original intention for the entries in each field. This is helpful later if you want to modify the database in some way. Take time to decide on the topic and organization for the database you plan to create. Once you have identified the basic categories for your database, you are ready to start creating it by entering the names and types of fields. The example will be an annotated book inventory. [Figure 7.8]

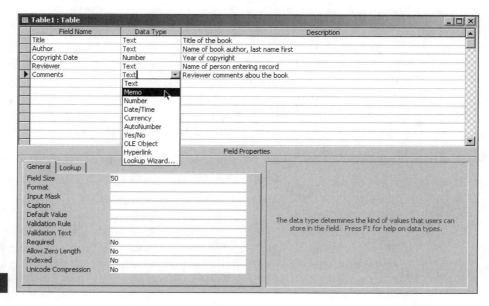

The Data Type list is accessed by the small disclosure arrow that appears in the Data Type cell. Each time you make a selection, the information shown in the lower left corner changes to provide details about the data type. As you close this dialog box, you will be asked to save your changes.

Note that you could have entered the names of the fields into the original table showing generic field headers. Double-click on the field headers and enter you own names. This approach, however, does not allow you to choose the data type for each field in the table. [Figure 7.9]

FIGURE 7.9

The decisions you make during the creation of the fields are important to the effectiveness of the database. For example, suppose you want to create a name and address database. Perhaps you plan to have the first field contain both the first name and the last name in a single field called Name. This organization lets you easily create mailing labels or merge the name into letters or documents. However, you will not be able to sort this database by last name. If you need to locate all the records that have Smith as the last name, this task will be very difficult.

A name and address database is more flexible if you use two fields to contain names. Create both a Last Name and a First Name field in your database. This provides the ability to easily sort by last name or by first name as required. In addition, there are still ways available for you to place the complete name in address labels or letters.

Adding Data

As you work through this chapter, create any kind of database that interests you. The database demonstrated in this chapter is a database of books. This is something you might try in your classroom. As students read books—perhaps for book reports—students enter information about each book they read, including some brief comments about the book. Gradually, you will accumulate a large database that your students can use to help decide what books they want to read.

To move from the Design view of the table and back to the Datasheet view, close the Design view. You will be prompted to save your changes. Double-click the table name in the database window to re-open the table in datasheet view.

The cells in the table can easily be resized. Click on the lines between field names to adjust the width of the fields. The double arrow cursor that appears allows you to drag the column border left or right. [Figure 7.10]

FIGURE 7.10

Table1 : Table					
Title	Author	Copyright Date	Reviewer	Comments	

Recall that a record is a collection of information, often of different data types. You are ready to enter data into your database. Enter some data in the first record of your database table. [Figure 7.11]

FIGURE 7.11

Table1 : Table					
Title	Author	Copyright Date	Reviewer	Comments	
While the Bear Sleeps	Matthews, Ca	1999	Susie	ies from around the world	

Notice that if the information you enter into a field is longer than the width of the field, the data scrolls off the left edge of the field. However, the data is still there.

If the records you are entering have several fields with the same or similar data, you may want to select **Copy** from the **Edit** menu. You can then paste the record one or many times. For example, if you are entering many books by the same author, you can put the author's name in place in a blank record. **Copy** and **Paste** this partially completed record several times. Go back to each record and add the information needed to complete each record.

After you have entered several records, look at the bottom left corner of the Datasheet view of your table. You see the Navigation buttons. These buttons provide information about the database and make it easier to move around within the data table. Try each of the buttons so you understand how to use them to navigate in your data table. [Figure 7.12]

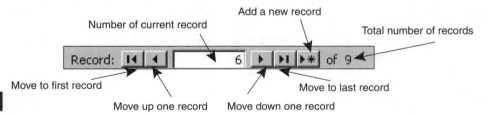

FIGURE 7.12

When you have finished entering the data into your sample database, correct or modify it if needed. It is a good idea to use **Spelling** from the **Tools** menu to check the spelling of your database entries. And of course, make sure to continue your habit of saving frequently and changing the file name in incremental saves.

EXAMINING YOUR DATABASE

Now that you have finished entering your records, take a few minutes to check your table. If necessary, you can use the scroll bars to move through your database to display the remainder of the fields and records. At this point, you may want to modify the width of the columns by clicking and dragging between the field names. [Figure 7.13]

FIGURE 7.13

Title	Author	Copyright Date	Reviewer	Comments
While the Bear Sleeps	Matthews, Cait	1999	Susie	Fun stories from around the world
Harry Potter and the Prisoner of /	Rowling, J. K.	2001	Ned	There is some scary stuff in this bool
Harry Potter and the Chamber of	Rowling, J. K.	2000	Nada	This book was really exciting. I wante
Harry Potter and the Sorcerers S	Rowling, J. K.	1999	Juan	The book has more detail than the m
Buster Bear Twins	Burgess, Thort	1921	Sam	Fun story about a bear family
Little Women	Alcott, Lousia I		Sarah	Loved this book about 4 sisters. Can1
The Secret Garden	Burnett, France		Sally	This is an old fashioned book, but I re
Black Beauty	Sewell, Anna		Hannah	Wonderful story about a horse.
Heidi	Spyri, Johanna		Marie	Story about little girl living in the mou

You may also want to change the order in which the columns appear in your database. Click on the field name and drag either left or right. The selected column moves to a new location. Note that moving a column does not change the order of the fields in the Design view. Use the **View** menu to move between **Design view** and the table—**Datasheet view.**

EDITING YOUR DATABASE

Databases tend to be documents that are constantly being modified. Regardless of careful planning, you often need to update your data or change the field structure of your document. Changing data is relatively simple. You can do so by clicking directly into the cell and editing the text as you would in a word processing document. Changing fields, however, is potentially problematic because such changes can affect the data already present.

Editing Records

You can change the text in a record by clicking on the text in any field and changing it, much as if you were working with a word processor. You can duplicate entire records so that you only have to modify part of the data in the record. The standard **Cut, Copy,** and **Paste** functions can also be used with particular information in a field.

To select a range of adjacent records, click and drag over the small boxes to the left of the records. [Figure 7.14]

Table1 : Table				
Title	**Author**	**Copyright Date**	**Reviewer**	**Comments**
While the Bear Sleeps	Matthews, Cait	1999	Susie	Fun stories from around the world
Harry Potter and the Prisoner of /	Rowling, J. K.	2001	Ned	There is some scary stuff in this bool
Harry Potter and the Chamber of	Rowling, J. K.	2000	Nada	This book was really exciting. I wante
Harry Potter and the Sorcerers S	Rowling, J. K.	1999	Juan	The book has more detail than the m
Buster Bear Twins	Burgess, Thort	1921	Sam	Fun story about a bear family
Little Women	Alcott, Lousia I		Sarah	Loved this book about 4 sisters. Cant
The Secret Garden	Burnett, France		Sally	This is an old fashioned book, but I re
Black Beauty	Sewell, Anna		Hannah	Wonderful story about a horse.
Heidi	Spyri, Johanna		Marie	Story about little girl living in the mou

FIGURE 7.14

When you have selected one or more records in a database, you can **Cut** or **Copy.** You can then paste a copy of these records at the end of your database table by choosing **Paste Append** from the **Edit** menu. The pasted records appear at the end of the database table. [Figure 7.15]

Table1 : Table				
Title	**Author**	**Copyright Date**	**Reviewer**	**Comments**
While the Bear Sleeps	Matthews, Cait	1999	Susie	Fun stories from around the world
Harry Potter and the Prisoner of /	Rowling, J. K.	2001	Ned	There is some scary stuff in this bool
Harry Potter and the Chamber of	Rowling, J. K.	2000	Nada	This book was really exciting. I wante
Harry Potter and the Sorcerers S	Rowling, J. K.	1999	Juan	The book has more detail than the m
Buster Bear Twins	Burgess, Thort	1921	Sam	Fun story about a bear family
Little Women	Alcott, Lousia I		Sarah	Loved this book about 4 sisters. Cant
The Secret Garden	Burnett, France		Sally	This is an old fashioned book, but I re
Black Beauty	Sewell, Anna		Hannah	Wonderful story about a horse.
Heidi	Spyri, Johanna		Marie	Story about little girl living in the mou
Harry Potter and the Prisoner of /	Rowling, J. K.	2001	Ned	There is some scary stuff in this bool
Harry Potter and the Chamber of	Rowling, J. K.	2000	Nada	This book was really exciting. I wante
Harry Potter and the Sorcerers S	Rowling, J. K.	1999	Juan	The book has more detail than the m

FIGURE 7.15

At each step, Access will ask you to verify the action and, of course, if you use **Cut** you are reminded this cannot be undone.

Technical Note: You cannot use **Cut** to completely remove an entire column from the database. Removing a column is equivalent to removing a field from the database.

The **Edit** menu also includes the standard **Find** and **Replace** features. These allow you to search for and replace items in your database table just as you can in *Word.* Another useful option on the **Edit** menu is the **Go To** feature, which can be used instead of the navigation bar in the datasheet view.

A powerful feature in *Access* is the ability to hide selected columns in the database table. Click on the field name or names and choose **Hide Columns** from the **Format** menu. In Figure 7.16, we hid the three center columns.

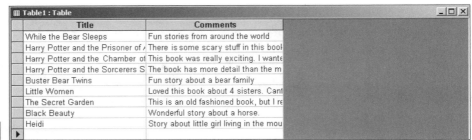

FIGURE 7.16

When the columns are hidden, the data is still there. If you select **Unhide Columns** from the **Format** menu, you see a list of all the fields. Select which fields you want to be visible by checking the box to the left of the name of the field. [Figure 7.17]

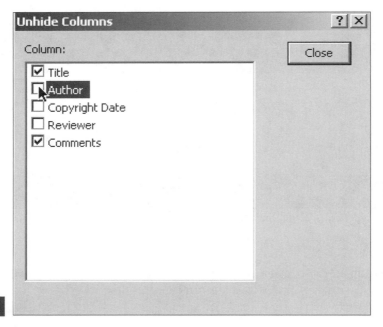

FIGURE 7.17

You have seen how to enter information into a database and how to modify that data. You have also seen that many of the tools available in other parts of *Office* are also available in *Access.* Your work with databases has progressed step-by-step, but there is much left to learn.

Editing Fields

You need to know how to modify, add, and delete fields in a database. These capabilities are particularly useful when experimenting with the initial database design. You create a database, enter data to produce several records, and then test the database to see how well it works. Can the database be used the way you planned? Should you change the organization? Even if you are satisfied at the moment, you may change your mind later.

You will probably find that the design of a new database needs to be modified a couple of times before it serves the purposes you have in mind. Perhaps some fields are not really necessary. This means that some data being gathered will not be used—a waste of data entry time and computer storage space. Perhaps additional fields are needed to solve problems you did not originally anticipate. For example, suppose you have entries such as "Sam," "Pat," and "Terry" in the Reviewer field. Later, when you decide to share your database with another teacher, you want to include the reviewers' last names. You need to be able to add a new field to the database.

To modify the field structure of your database, select **Design View** from the **View** menu. You see the list of fields instead of the data. If you want to enter a new field at the end of the current list of fields, just add it as you did when you created the database.

If you want to enter a field between two existing fields, click on the box just to the left of where you want to enter a new field. Then choose **Rows** from the **Insert** menu. Enter the field information just as you did earlier.

You may decide the name or type of field you created needs changing. To make changes in field names or descriptions, simply click in the appropriate cell and enter the correct information.

You can also remove fields in Design view. Click on the box at the left of the field name to select the field you want to remove. Choose **Cut** from the **Edit** menu. You are prompted to rethink your decision. [Figure 7.18]

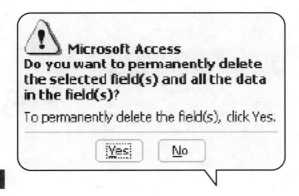

FIGURE 7.18

Be very sure you no longer want to keep the data before you click OK. Removing a field removes any data that occurs in the database in the field you are deleting. A simple mistake can be costly.

SORTING

One of the main reasons for storing data electronically in a database is that information stored in electronic form can be easily reorganized or searched for specific items. To explore sorting, click on the field name in your table that you want to sort. Then click either the Sort Ascending or the Sort Descending icon on the button bar. [Figure 7.19]

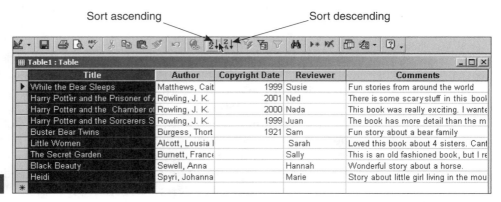

FIGURE 7.19

When you click on the button, the records in your database are in the order you selected by the field you selected. In this example, the sort occurs in ascending alphabetical order by book title. [Figure 7.20]

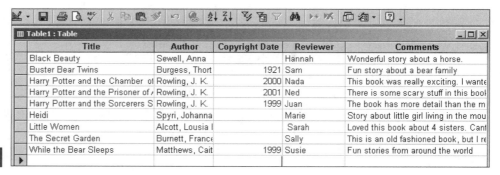

FIGURE 7.20

Examine the sorted database we have been working with. Do you see a problem? Look at the Author column. Can the database be sorted by the authors' last names? Why not? This is an example in which you might have used an Author Last Name *and* an Author First Name field.

SEARCHING

You are now familiar with the process of creating a database and entering data. Entering and editing data are not much different than using a word processor. Adjusting the fields in your database is not particularly complex once you learn which menu items and windows to use. Sorting data is a simple one- or two-step process.

The real value of a database is in being able to search the information effectively. The steps required to locate specific data require some careful thought. In this section you will begin to explore searching for information in a database. Learning to find information efficiently in a database is a complex task requiring considerable practice.

Because we can only show short examples in this book, it is easy to miss the importance of learning correct search strategies. A large database is of value *only* if you have the ability to locate the information helpful to you. If you have a small database you can—if necessary—simply look at the contents of the file to find the desired information. But real-world databases have hundreds, thousands, or even millions of entries. You certainly do not want to have to look through such a database entry by entry to find needed information.

If you have explored the World Wide Web and done a search for information, then you know that good searching techniques are necessary for finding the information you require. Think of the World Wide Web as an enormous database of Web sites. When you go to a search engine on the Web, you are searching this enormous database much as you will be searching an *Access* database.

Several different methods for searching for information in a database will be explored. The first is easier, but less flexible. The second is more complex, but gives you greater ability to refine your search.

Searching Using Find

Earlier in this chapter we mentioned that you can use **Find** and **Replace** in a database. Replace can be used to make corrections throughout a database, but Find can be used to locate particular data in the database.

Choose **Find** from the **Edit** menu. Notice that you can specify not only what to search for but where to search. You can also look for part or all of the information in a field. If you click on the More button, you can also specify whether to search Up or Down in the database. [Figure 7.21]

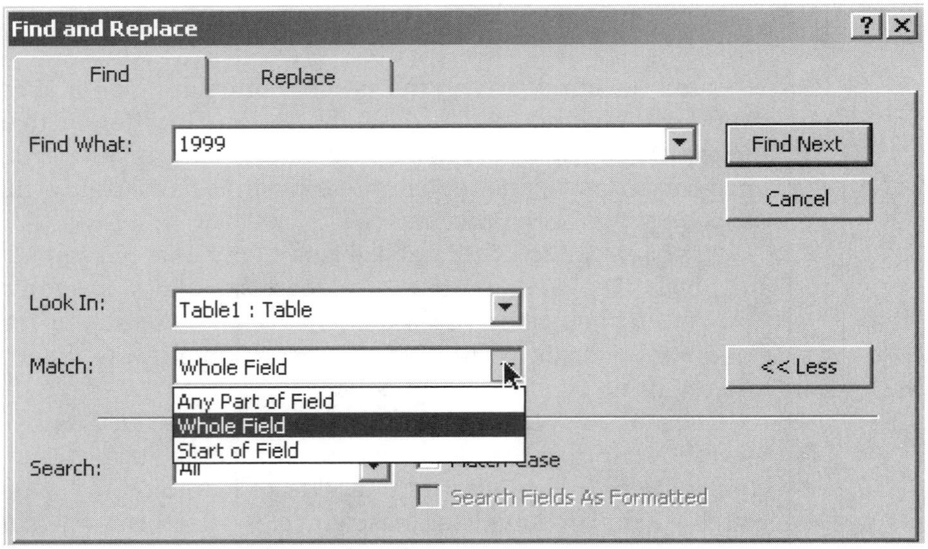

FIGURE 7.21

This kind of searching lets you quickly and easily locate a particular piece of data. The disadvantage is that it only locates one record at a time. It does not give you a way to see how many records contain the data you are searching for. In a small database it's easy to count as you search, but in a large database this is an impractical way to search for data.

Searching with a Filter

Using a filter solves the problem of keeping track of how many records match the criteria for which you are searching. A filter creates a mini table of matching records. A number of different searches are demonstrated below.

Filter by Selection.   This type of filter allows you to select a data item in your database and then apply the filter so that you see only those records containing that piece of data. [Figure 7.22]

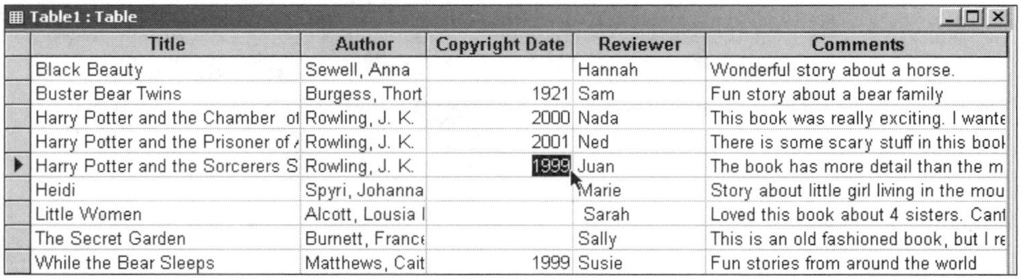

FIGURE 7.22

Title	Author	Copyright Date	Reviewer	Comments
Black Beauty	Sewell, Anna		Hannah	Wonderful story about a horse.
Buster Bear Twins	Burgess, Thor	1921	Sam	Fun story about a bear family
Harry Potter and the Chamber of	Rowling, J. K.	2000	Nada	This book was really exciting. I wante
Harry Potter and the Prisoner of /	Rowling, J. K.	2001	Ned	There is some scary stuff in this bool
Harry Potter and the Sorcerers S	Rowling, J. K.	1999	Juan	The book has more detail than the m
Heidi	Spyri, Johanna		Marie	Story about little girl living in the mou
Little Women	Alcott, Lousia		Sarah	Loved this book about 4 sisters. Cant
The Secret Garden	Burnett, France		Sally	This is an old fashioned book, but I re
While the Bear Sleeps	Matthews, Cait	1999	Susie	Fun stories from around the world

Once you have selected the data for which you want to search, choose Filters then **Filter by Selection** from the **Records** menu. Our example selects the 1999 entry in the Copyright Date field. The table changes to display only those records that contain the selected data. [Figure 7.23]

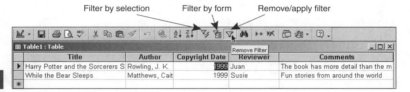

FIGURE 7.23

At the bottom left corner of the window, you see the number of records found by the filter next to the Navigation buttons.

You can easily return to the view that shows the entire database table. Select **Remove Filter/Sort from the Records** menu or click on the Remove Filter icon to display the entire database table again. [Figure 7.24]

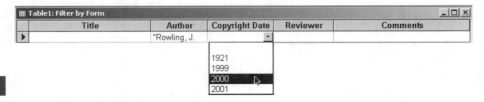

FIGURE 7.24

When you release the mouse button, the entire database table reappears.

Filter by Form.   Another way to search is to filter by form. First, be sure that the entire database is visible by removing any previous filters. If you have an extra blank record at the bottom of your database, place the cursor in one of the fields of the blank record. Filter by Form lets you choose more than one criterion. Choose **Filter by Form** from the **Record** menu.

You see a blank record with your field names at the top of the table. When you click in a blank cell, a drop-down menu shows the choices for that field. In the Author field we selected Rowling, J. Then, because you can select items from one or more fields we added the copyright date of 2000. [Figure 7.25]

Table1: Filter by Form				
Title	Author	Copyright Date	Reviewer	Comments
	"Rowling, J.			

1921
1999
2000
2001

FIGURE 7.25

With these criteria, only one record will be selected. Click on the Apply Filter icon—the same icon you use to remove a filter. [Figure 7.26]

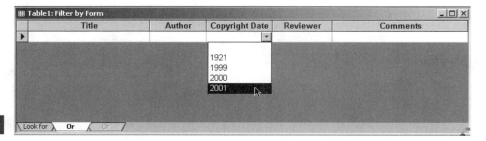

FIGURE 7.26

Another way of describing this filter is to say that it looked for all records containing "Rowling, J. K." *and* all Copyright Dates containing "2000."

There are times when you want to search for more than one entry in the same field. For example, suppose you wanted to search for a couple of copyright dates. Begin the search in the same way. After you have chosen the Author entry and the Copyright Date entry, click on Or on the tab at the bottom of the table. Then select a different year from the Copyright Date field. [Figure 7.27]

FIGURE 7.27

When you click on the Apply Filter icon, you see records that meet all of the criteria you selected. [Figure 7.28]

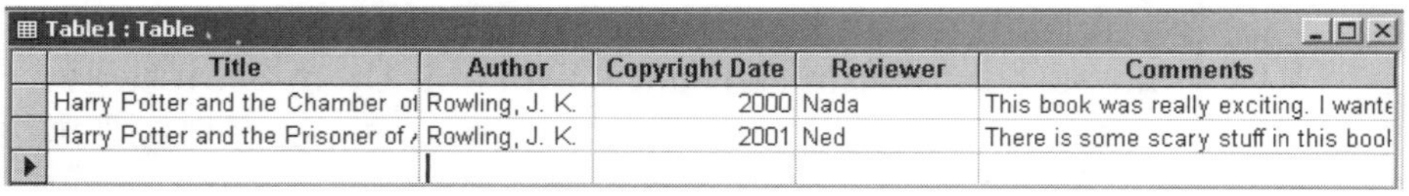

FIGURE 7.28

You can describe this filter as looking for all records that have the value of both Author as "Rowling, J. K." *and* Copyright Date as "2000" *or* both Author as "Rowling, J. K." *and* Copyright Date as "2001."

Filter Excluding Selection.   You can also filter to leave out records with specific data. Display all the data in your database table. Select the criteria that are to be used for eliminating records. Then choose **Filter Excluding Selection** from the **Records** menu. For example, suppose we filter for all records that do not contain "Rowling, J. K." When you apply the filter you see all of the records except those having Rowling as the author name. [Figure 7.29]

Title	Author	Copyright Date	Reviewer	Comments
Black Beauty	Sewell, Anna		Hannah	Wonderful story about a horse.
Buster Bear Twins	Burgess, Thort	1921	Sam	Fun story about a bear family
Heidi	Spyri, Johanna		Marie	Story about little girl living in the mou
Little Women	Alcott, Lousia l		Sarah	Loved this book about 4 sisters. Can't
The Secret Garden	Burnett, France		Sally	This is an old fashioned book, but I re
While the Bear Sleeps	Matthews, Cait	1999	Susie	Fun stories from around the world

FIGURE 7.29

Another way of describing this Filter is to say we are searching for all records *not* containing "Rowling, J. K."

Using an Advanced Filter/Sort

The searching and sorting methods you have seen so far are quite easy to use. They will work for many kinds of simple searches, but there is a more sophisticated sorting and searching choice on the **Filter** menu. When you choose **Advanced Filter/Sort** from the **Records** menu, you see a dialog box that allows you a great deal of flexibility. [Figure 7.30]

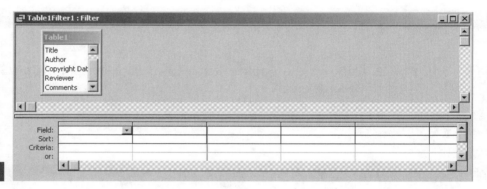

FIGURE 7.30

The dialog box you see may not be empty. It may contain choices you made when using a previous filter. You can delete those choices when you are ready to create a more advanced filter. In this section you will see a number of ways you can use this more advanced capability.

Locate the First Half of the Alphabet. Suppose you wish to locate the records for the books in your database having a title beginning with a letter preceding the letter *N* in the alphabet. Database searches can be done using numbers or characters. You just need to find a way to state the criteria in a manner *Access* can understand.

1. From the **Records** menu choose **Filter→Advanced Filter/Sort.** The dialog box lets you first choose the field that you wish to use, in this case the title.

    The first half of the alphabet is everything beginning with letters "less than N." (Letters can use "less than" in this manner: a<b<c<…) [Figure 7.31]

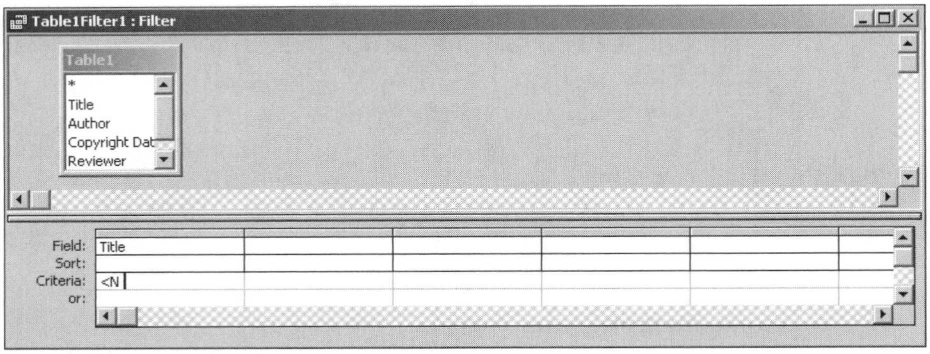

FIGURE 7.31

Note that when you enter <*N* and press Return or Enter, the software adds quotation marks on either side of the N, indicating that it is searching letters. [Figure 7.32]

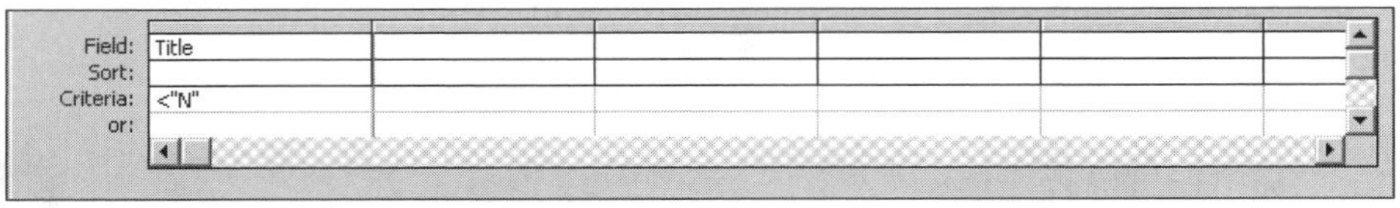

FIGURE 7.32

2. Click on the Apply Filter icon or choose **Apply Filter/Sort** from the **Records** menu.
3. You see only the database records with the titles that start with a letter in the first half of the alphabet. [Figure 7.33]

Title	Author	Copyright Date	Reviewer	Comments
Harry Potter and the Prisoner of /	Rowling, J. K.	2001	Ned	There is some scary stuff in this book
Harry Potter and the Chamber of	Rowling, J. K.	2000	Nada	This book was really exciting. I wante
Harry Potter and the Sorcerers S	Rowling, J. K.	1999	Juan	The book has more detail than the m
Buster Bear Twins	Burgess, Thort	1921	Sam	Fun story about a bear family
Little Women	Alcott, Lousia I		Sarah	Loved this book about 4 sisters. Cant
Black Beauty	Sewell, Anna		Hannah	Wonderful story about a horse.
Heidi	Spyri, Johanna		Marie	Story about little girl living in the mou

FIGURE 7.33

Remember, this is a search, *not* a sort; although the titles are all in the first half of the alphabet, they are not in alphabetical order.

Did you notice that the number of records located is visible in the navigation bar that is displayed along the bottom of the datasheet view of your table? In addition, this number is followed by the word *filtered* to remind you that you are looking at a partial set of records in the database.

Both First Half of the Alphabet and Copyright in the 21st Century. This next example examines a more complex search using the Advanced Search for two criteria.

1. From the **Records** menu, choose **Filter→Advanced Filter/Sort.**
2. Enter your search criteria in the appropriate field boxes.
   The same statement from the previous example is used as an entry with the Title field—"less than N."
   The second statement, to select a number that is 2000 or above, is entered with the Copyright Date—"greater than 1999." [Figure 7.34]

Field:	Title	Copyright Date
Sort:		
Criteria:	<"N"	>1999
or:		

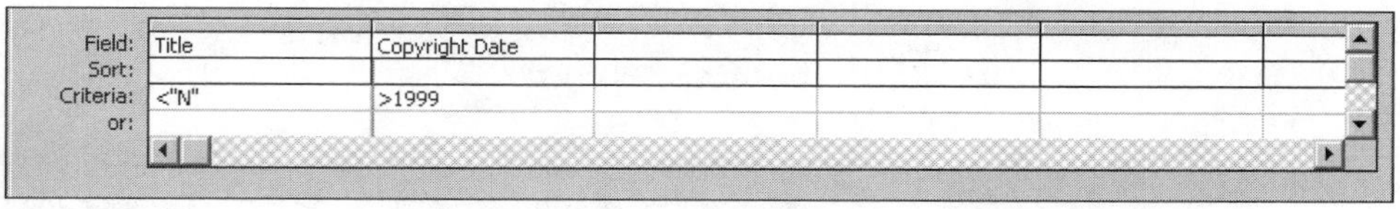

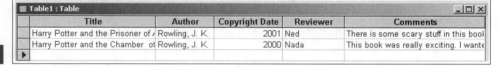

FIGURE 7.34

Note that by asking for two criteria you are using "AND" to search—both of the criteria must be met. You will learn more about the term AND later in this chapter.

3. Click on the Apply Filter icon.
4. Examine your results to be sure that your search is working correctly. Do you have only numbers greater than 1999 in the Copyright Date field? Are the book titles showing those you expected to see? [Figure 7.35]

Table1 : Table

Title	Author	Copyright Date	Reviewer	Comments
Harry Potter and the Prisoner of /	Rowling, J. K.	2001	Ned	There is some scary stuff in this bool
Harry Potter and the Chamber of	Rowling, J. K.	2000	Nada	This book was really exciting. I wante

FIGURE 7.35

Once you have completed a search and finished with the results, you may want to complete a second search on your database. Remember that you can again see the entire database table by clicking on the Remove Filter icon or **Remove Filter/Sort** on the **Records** menu.

Omitting Data. It is also possible to set up a search that works by omitting specific data.

1. Choose the Field name you wish to use and enter the search criterion.
   Let's search the database in such a way to remove any records having "Rowling, J. K." in the Author field. [Figure 7.36]

Field:	Author
Sort:	
Criteria:	Not "Rowling, J. K."
or:	

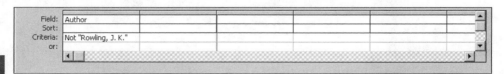

FIGURE 7.36

Notice that we used the word *not* before the data that we wish to omit. In this case we had to put quotation marks about the entire entry because there was other punctuation in the entry.

2. Click the Apply Filter icon or select **Apply Filter/Sort** from the **Records** menu.

3. Examine your results to be sure that your search is working correctly. If the name of Rowling, J. K. appears in your author list, something is wrong. Remember that your search criterion entry must be exactly like the entry in the database. This means you must be careful here with punctuation marks. [Figure 7.37]

Title	Author	Copyright Date	Reviewer	Comments
While the Bear Sleeps	Matthews, Cait	1999	Susie	Fun stories from around the world
Buster Bear Twins	Burgess, Thort	1921	Sam	Fun story about a bear family
Little Women	Alcott, Lousia		Sarah	Loved this book about 4 sisters. Can
The Secret Garden	Burnett, France		Sally	This is an old fashioned book, but I re
Black Beauty	Sewell, Anna		Hannah	Wonderful story about a horse.
Heidi	Spyri, Johanna		Marie	Story about little girl living in the mou

FIGURE 7.37

Locate Records with the Copyright Either 1999 or 2000.   You have seen a search that looked for records with two criteria: Title < "N" AND Copyright > 1999. You have also seen how to omit data using NOT. The other frequently used word in more complex database searches is OR. This allows us to look for records containing one criterion OR another criterion.

1. Choose **Advanced Search/Sort.**

2. Choose the Copyright Date field. For the criterion, put =1999.
   Click at the bottom of the window where you see "or." Add the second value of "=2000" to the search criterion. [Figure 7.38]

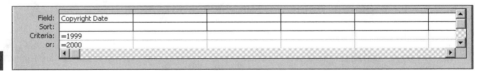

Field:	Copyright Date				
Sort:					
Criteria:	=1999				
or:	=2000				

FIGURE 7.38

3. Click on the Apply Filter icon and examine the results as shown in Figure 7.39.

Title	Author	Copyright Date	Reviewer	Comments
While the Bear Sleeps	Matthews, Cait	1999	Susie	Fun stories from around the world
Harry Potter and the Chamber of	Rowling, J. K.	2000	Nada	This book was really exciting. I w
Harry Potter and the Sorcerers S	Rowling, J. K.	1999	Juan	The book has more detail than th

FIGURE 7.39

The word OR is being used in the sense of "one or the other or both" to create the search results. Having either condition true, or having both conditions true at the same time, results in the record being highlighted.

Using Queries

Access is a relational database intended for use with huge, complex collections of data. In a relational database, there are ways that you can connect each table in the database. In our example, our booklist was intended for student use in a class. We might also add a table to our database that includes purchasing information for each of the books in question. Then, using the power of the relationship, we could locate data that will combine the two tables. However, this is far beyond the steps we need for most applications in the classroom.

So far, our examples have made use of the tools at a much simpler level that meets the needs of most users in classroom settings. The Advanced Filter feature allows you to do very complex searches. The one problem with these searches is that you cannot save them. There is a feature in *Access* that lets you create more advanced searches and to save them.

Go to the Database window and, from the list of items on the left, click on Queries. From the two options available, select Create query in Design View. You see a window that allows you to set up advanced searches and sorts. [Figure 7.40]

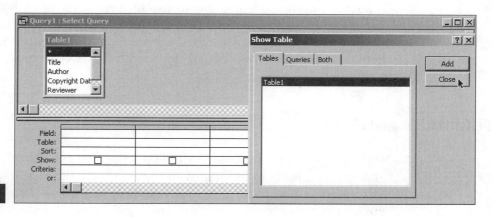

FIGURE 7.40

A query can be set up across several tables and from this window you can add the tables you wish to use. You then set up criteria for the fields in tables. You can combine queries by adding previously saved queries to the list. By now you are undoubtedly recognizing the complications implied by these options.

If you need more complex criteria, there is an Expression Builder that will allow all manner of complex expressions to be built. A Build button appears in the toolbar when you have the Query window open. When you click on the Build button, you see a long list of choices. [Figure 7.41]

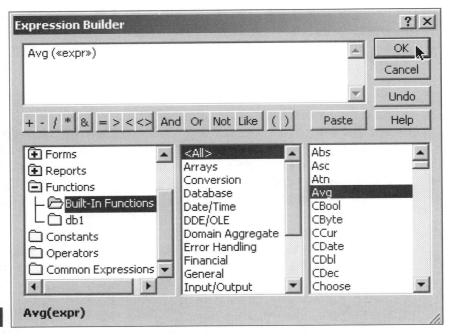

FIGURE 7.41   **Avg(expr)**

Here we have selected "Avg" for Average.

Using queries is beyond the scope of this book. If you wish to learn more about conducting more complex searches, go to the **Help** menu. Look up *Expression Builder* to learn how to use that feature. Look up *Query* to read more about using this feature. However, until you are comfortable using the tools introduced earlier and you are constantly encountering situations where you need even more control for searching, this part of *Access* can be left unexplored.

SUMMARY AND TIPS

Databases are nothing more—or less—than collections of related data. Although we use them frequently in the things we do each day, you may be quite unfamiliar with the concept of creating and using your own. With the steps you have been given, you will quickly gain the necessary skills to confidently approach the problem of using a database when necessary.

At the outset, databases seem straightforward. You enter the data. You sort the data. You search the data for what you want. Simple. However, as you begin to use the more sophisticated features of the database, problems inevitably arise.

The initial design of a database is very important. As you design a database, think about the questions you might want to answer using your database. This requires careful thought and understanding of the way databases are structured. For example, if you want to know the sum for a field in your records, you have to store that data in a format allowing you to add values. You cannot add the entries if you place them in text fields. Do not set up fields without careful thought about their content and application of their content.

Enter a few records of sample data and do some searches before committing large amounts of data to the database.

One of the most frustrating parts of *Access* is creating the criteria for searching when you are completing advanced searches. Think about the filters you want and take care that you are indicating the correct search options. It will take considerable practice until you can find exactly what you want in the database with a minimum of time and effort.

You have been introduced to many new concepts for working with collections of data stored in digital format. The NETS indicate high expectations for students to work efficiently with quantities of information. Any time a person makes use of the World Wide Web using an Internet connection, he or she is being challenged to relate to information in a database. The simple Find and Filter searches demonstrated here provide the basics of simple searches on the Web. Without getting into the complex mathematical concepts that are being applied within *Access*, you can focus on reaching new levels of competency using technology.

CHAPTER EIGHT

Using Databases to Represent Information

In Chapter 7 you learned how to create a database and enter data into it. You also learned how to sort your database and search for information. All of the tasks described in Chapter 7 are electronic onscreen tasks. Indeed the electronic form of databases is used a great deal. For example, when you use a library database to locate resources, you generally work in an electronic mode.

However, databases are also used to print information. The junk mail that fills our mailboxes is a result of the ability to enter names and addresses into a database and easily create form letters for particular groups of customers. Mailing labels on the same junk mail are printed using the same database in a different way. In education, you may need to use information from your database to send letters or reports to parents or produce reports for a class project. All of these needs can be met using the report feature in *Access*.

The fact that you can view the same database in different ways is one of the more powerful characteristics of a database. At the same time, this capability can be confusing for those using databases for the first time. When you look at a word processing or graphics document, the same window can display everything in the document. Of course you can change the formatting of the document, but part of the document does not disappear or reappear as a result of your reformatting. Databases are different. When you change the layout of a database, you are usually changing the part of the database that will be visible.

In this chapter you will learn to use your database to produce printed reports. Since your needs vary, the concept of different field data types to make the container more flexible is explored. You will also learn to use *Access* databases in combination with *Word* to create "merged" documents. However, reflect again on the need to consider these tasks before you begin to create your database so that you have the data entered in a manner that can easily allow you to use it to complete the many tasks you have in mind.

EXPLORING DIFFERENT DATA TYPES

In Chapter 7, you learned that when you create a database field you can also specify the type of data you plan to put in it. The field types in *Access* provide different ways of displaying data. In addition, the type partially determines the kind of interaction possible once the data is entered.

Open the database window and click on the Tables button in the left side of the Database window. Then choose Create Table in Design View to view the window where you can define both field names and field types. In the cell for Data Type is a drop-down menu that displays the many types of fields your database can include. [Figure 8.1]

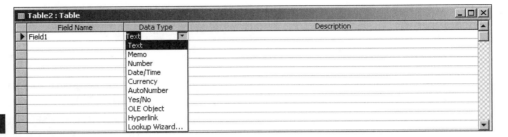

FIGURE 8.1

You have already seen that you can enter both numbers and text into a text field. However, there are times that you want to format your numbers in particular ways or create other types of fields. In this section you will learn about some of the data types that you can have in your database.

Text and Memo Data Types

You have used text fields in creating a table of data. Perhaps you noticed that the Comments field in the sample database was of data type Memo. What are the differences between these two types of data?

When you set up a text field, you can enter text characters and numbers, but the length of the field is limited. [Figure 8.2]

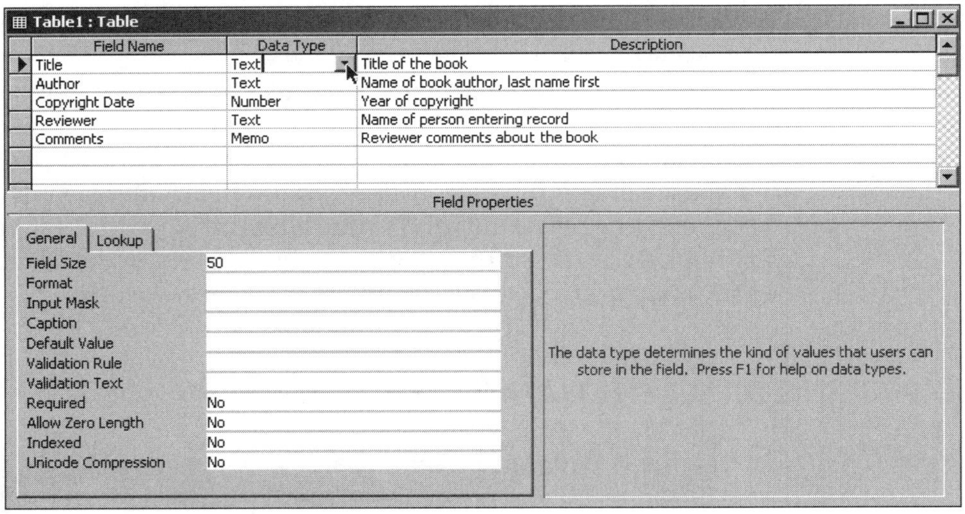

FIGURE 8.2

Note that the field size is set to 50 by default. You can change that number if you so desire. A text field can contain up to 255 characters, so you can adjust the number in the field size to be any number between 0 and 255 characters. If you try to enter more characters than the field size allows, *Access* will stop you.

If you want more text to be allowed in a field, you should use a data type called *Memo*. A memo field does not have the same size limitation as a text field. A memo field can hold up to 65,535 characters. This is the appropriate data type to use when you have fields such as the Comments field in which students may want to write more than a few words.

Date and Time Data

You have used a numeric field. There are a number of settings for the format for number data. In general, you will not want to change this setting; however, you may want to enter a default value, which will be automatically entered in the field. For example, if your students were entering only recent books, then putting a recent year in the Copyright Date field will save data entry time. It will only be necessary to change those few that do not match the year you have set into the field. [Figure 8.3]

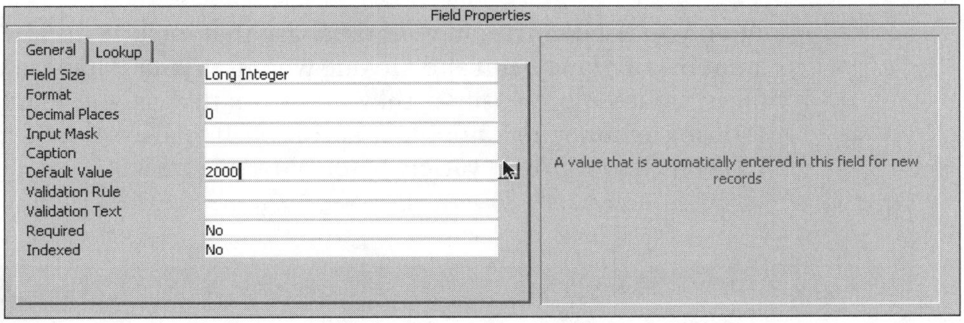

Field Properties

General	Lookup
Field Size	Long Integer
Format	
Decimal Places	0
Input Mask	
Caption	
Default Value	2000
Validation Rule	
Validation Text	
Required	No
Indexed	No

A value that is automatically entered in this field for new records

FIGURE 8.3

Some number entries have special uses such as the way you might enter the date or the time. Since this is a frequent occurrence, *Access* includes a special field type for such entries. Suppose you add a Date and Time field to your Book database. Such an entry might be useful to track student work. Once you have the field type selected, click to the right of the Format option in the General tab available below the list of created fields. There are some settings you might wish to change in this Field Properties window. [Figure 8.4]

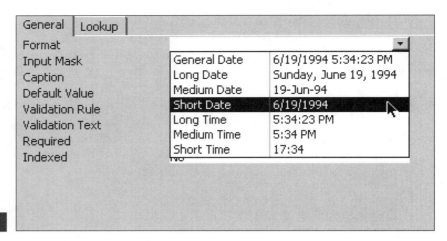

FIGURE 8.4

From the variety of date and time formats available, select the format you wish to use. *Access* will then require data in that field to be entered in a manner that matches your chosen format. You may want to use the Description option to remind yourself what option you plan to use.

Currency Data Type

Often you need entries in your database that include numbers representing amounts of money. You and anyone who uses your database will understand these values more easily if they are formatted as you would expect when showing a monetary amount. To accomplish this, use the Currency data type. You can choose from a variety of formats. [Figure 8.5]

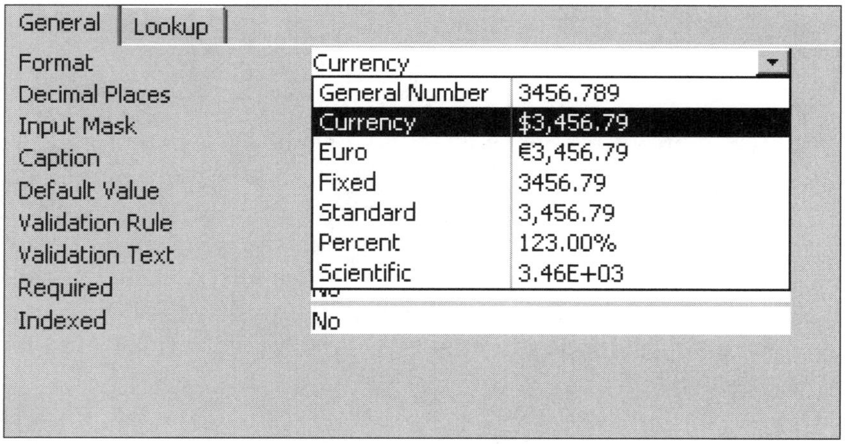

FIGURE 8.5

Note that this data type can also be used to display numbers as percents.

Even though the format you choose shows two places after the decimal, you still have to specify the number of places after the decimal. [Figure 8.6]

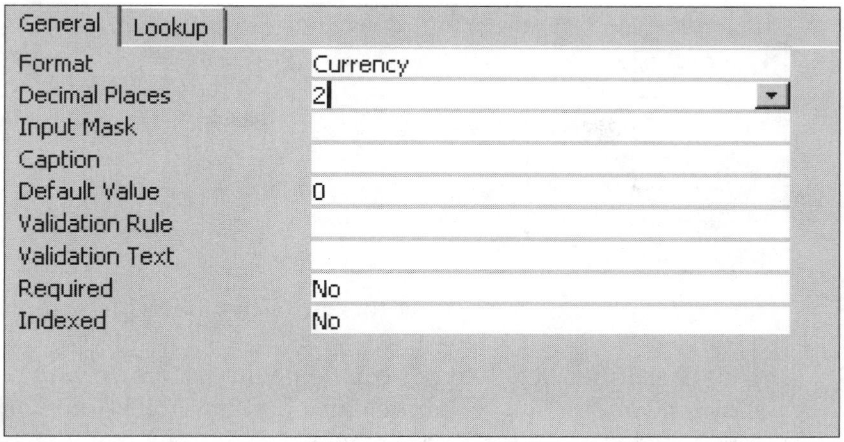

General	Lookup	
Format	Currency	
Decimal Places	2	▼
Input Mask		
Caption		
Default Value	0	
Validation Rule		
Validation Text		
Required	No	
Indexed	No	

FIGURE 8.6

This data type is accurate to four places on the right side of the decimal point and fifteen places to the left. The data in the Table appears with the correct symbol, such as $ or %.

Yes/No Field Type

An interesting data type is the Yes/No type. This type of data is useful when you have a field in your database that keeps track of whether a task is completed, if an item had a particular characteristic, whether a fee has been paid, and the like. [Figure 8.7]

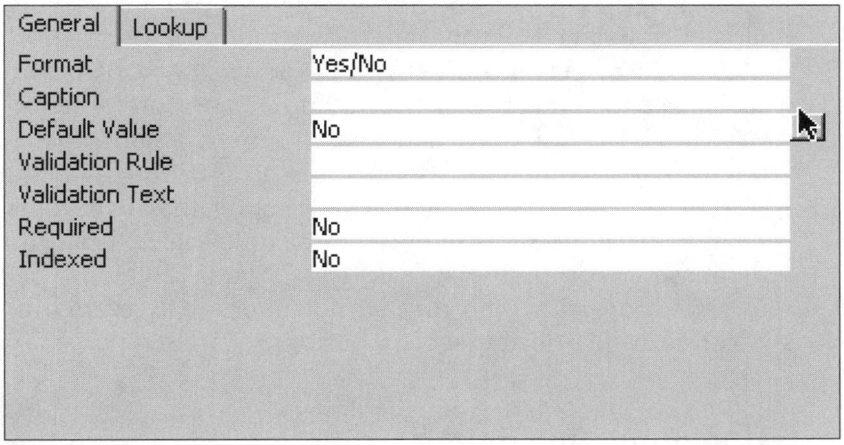

General	Lookup	
Format	Yes/No	
Caption		
Default Value	No	
Validation Rule		
Validation Text		
Required	No	
Indexed	No	

FIGURE 8.7

This is also a good data type in which to set a default value. Choose whichever answer is likely to be the most common for the data in your data table. When you return to the Table view, you see a box in this field with or without a check mark. [Figure 8.8]

FIGURE 8.8

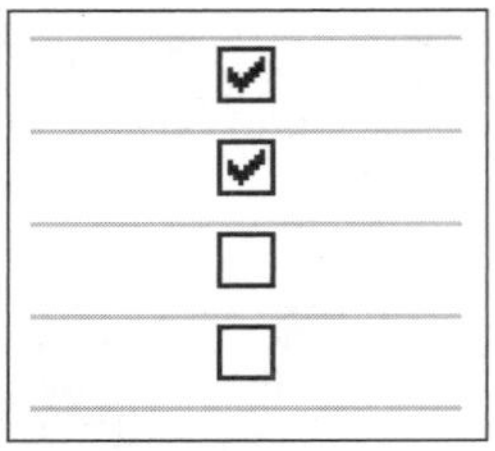

This data type makes it easy to scan a database for completed items, and so on.

These special field types can help you customize your database entries, allowing you the most accurate data entry possible. However, there are other special field types available that you may wish to explore when you become more familiar with *Access*.

CREATING REPORTS

The database created in the preceding chapter is quite small. There is little advantage to putting such a small amount of information into an electronic form. However, learning with small amounts of data is much easier than handling large amounts of data as you start. Of course, databases used in business, by the government, in medicine, in education, and in many other fields generally have a large number of records—frequently tens of thousands with each record made up of a large number of fields.

Access is a powerful database program that would be used to maintain large corporate databases. It has an incredible number of powerful features—many far beyond the scope of this book. If you are working with extremely large sets of data, you will want to learn some of the more advanced features of *Access*. However, for education purposes, this book provides you with the tools needed to meet most of your immediate requirements.

You have designed a database and entered data into it. You have learned to locate records that satisfy particular criteria. You understand the relationship between the field data type and the way the field can be used. Now, you need to learn the steps required to include selected information from your database in printed material. The organization and display of entries intended for use within printed documents are referred to as reports and *Access* provide a flexible set of tools for preparing reports.

Understanding Reports

Before learning how to create reports, take a moment to think about the concept of looking at database information in a variety of ways. Imagine a very small database with two fields in each record and a total of three records. The first field is the Name field. The second field is the Color field. Each record is written on a small card. [Figure 8.9]

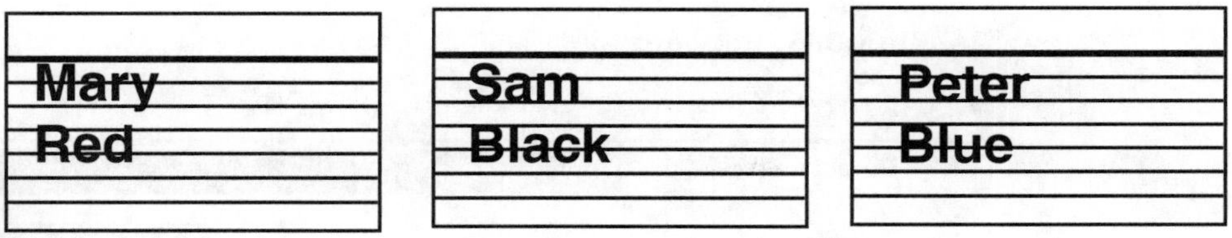

FIGURE 8.9

| Mary | Sam | Peter |
| Red | Black | Blue |

Clearly, we can rearrange the cards. If we stack them with just the name showing, the color name entries become "invisible" if we hold a blank card on the top one. [Figure 8.10]

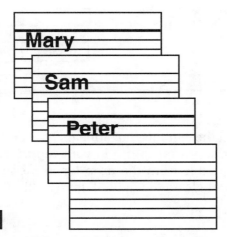

FIGURE 8.10

If you saw the cards arranged like this, you would have no reason to think that there were color words on the cards in addition to names. Similarly, when information in an electronic database is put into a new report, some of the data may not be visible—but the information is still there. As you begin to learn about database reports, keep this simple example in mind.

Creating a New Report

As you have seen earlier, much of your work begins in the Database window. The window has your work to this point organized and easily accessible. You have used many of the tools provided to work with your database to this point. For your first report, you need to create this type of database object from within the database window.

1. In the database window, click on Reports, found in the list on the left side of the window.
2. Click on the New button, found in the set of buttons available along the top of the Database window. [Figure 8.11]

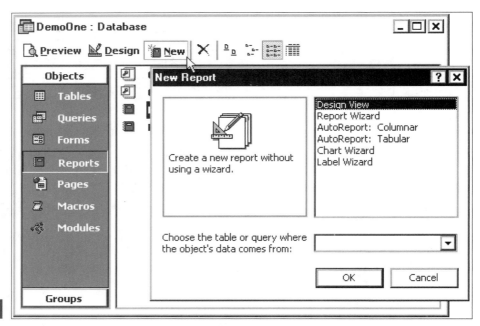

FIGURE 8.11

3. Choose Design View in the window that appears.
4. Choose the table that you want to use in your report by entering the name or selecting the table from the drop-down menu made visible using the disclosure triangle on the right. [Figure 8.12]

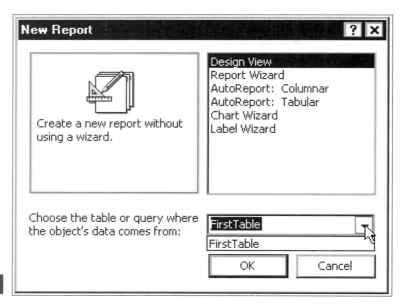

FIGURE 8.12

5. Finally, click OK.
   You see a screen that looks fairly complicated. In addition to the report window, two palettes appear—the toolbox and the list of fields in your chosen table. [Figure 8.13]

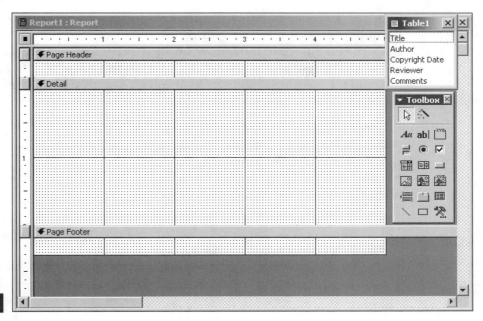

FIGURE 8.13

Before you proceed, be sure to save this report by using the floppy disk icon on the toolbar and be sure to give your report a meaningful name.

Technical Note: You may have noticed that options in the Database window include Create report in Design view. This option is avoided in our example because it does not allow you to control the data type for your fields. The same Report window appears, as does the Toolbox, but you are not connected to a particular table for selecting the fields you need for your report.

Now you are ready to begin customizing your report. To begin, click on one of your field names in the Table box that lists the fields in your selected table and drag the field name to the Detail part of the report window. Notice that if you cannot see all your fields, the Table box can be resized using the click and drag option normally used for resizing windows. [Figure 8.14]

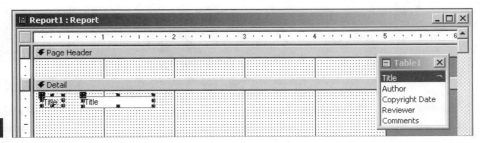

FIGURE 8.14

You will see two boxes, both with visible selection handles. The one on the left is a label that is the name of the field. The box on the right represents the data in your table. Wherever the right box is placed, the data in your database will appear. The selection handles allow you to work with a particular object for modifying the box and formatting the contents.

If you now go to the **File** menu and choose **Print Preview** you can see the way your report will appear if you print it. You will also find a Print Preview button on the *Access* toolbar. Once you have activated this option, it is available on the **View** menu. [Figure 8.15]

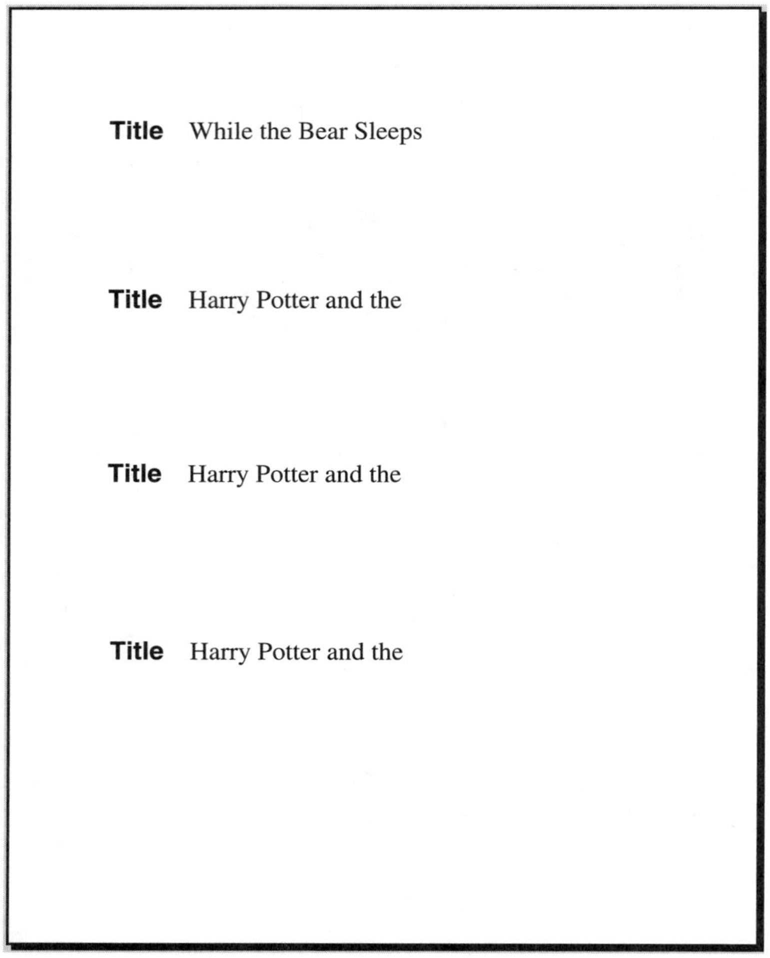

Title   While the Bear Sleeps

Title   Harry Potter and the

Title   Harry Potter and the

Title   Harry Potter and the

FIGURE 8.15

Note that when you move the pointer over the document, the Zoom icon appears. If you click on the Print Preview it enlarges so you can see more detail. Clicking again drops it back down in size. When you enlarge the preview, notice that the titles are incomplete and cannot be read.

You can solve the problem of the titles being cut off by enlarging the box that contains the data. Make sure the selection handles are visible on the text box containing the title data, then click and drag a handle to resize the container. [Figure 8.16]

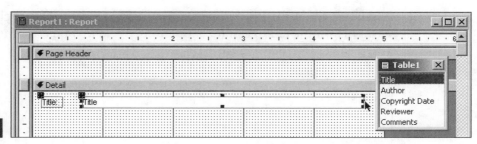

FIGURE 8.16

Again, check the Print Preview to be sure you have included enough space for all of the titles in your database.

When you look at the Print Preview, you see a great deal of white space between each of the titles and the list taking up most of the page. This problem is solved by moving the Page Footer bar up. Move the pointer over the bar that says Page Footer and wait for the special double arrow icon to appear. Then click and drag the bar closer to the title boxes. Go back to the Print Preview to verify that the list of titles is now much easier to read. [Figure 8.17]

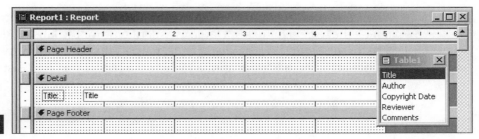

FIGURE 8.17

You can also increase the communication impact of your report by modifying the type size and style in both the label box and the data box. Work with one box at a time and after you have the selection handles visible, make your choices from the standard text formatting menus. In our example, we have applied a serif typeface to the titles and a sans serif typeface to the label. In addition, the label has been enlarged and a bold style applied. It was necessary to resize the label box to allow the modified text to fit. [Figure 8.18]

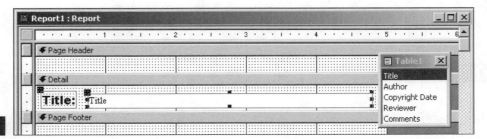

FIGURE 8.18

When you check the Print Preview, you see that the entries are closer together. With this simple change of text appearance and text positioning, the report is much easier to read. [Figure 8.19]

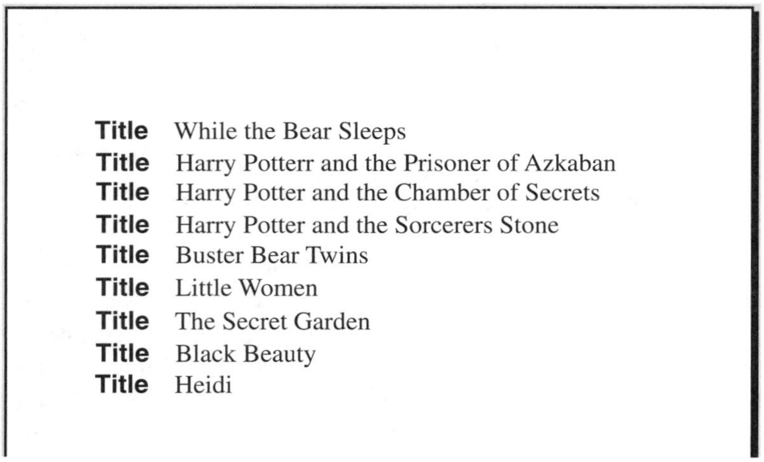

Title   While the Bear Sleeps
Title   Harry Potterr and the Prisoner of Azkaban
Title   Harry Potter and the Chamber of Secrets
Title   Harry Potter and the Sorcerers Stone
Title   Buster Bear Twins
Title   Little Women
Title   The Secret Garden
Title   Black Beauty
Title   Heidi

FIGURE 8.19

When you enlarge the preview, you easily see the distinction between data and label—the reason for using a large sans serif type for the label and a smaller serif type for the data. These choices create a report that is greatly improved from the default settings that were applied when the report was first displayed. [Figure 8.20]

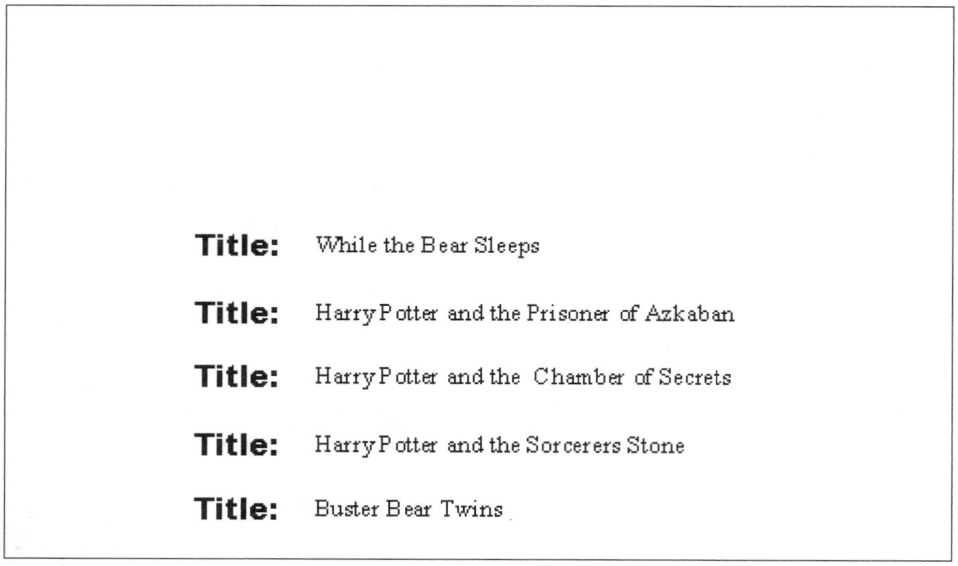

Title: While the Bear Sleeps

Title: Harry Potter and the Prisoner of Azkaban

Title: Harry Potter and the Chamber of Secrets

Title: Harry Potter and the Sorcerers Stone

Title: Buster Bear Twins

FIGURE 8.20

Once you have the detailed content of your database report formatted the way you want, you may want to add a header or a footer. Remember that headers and footers get added to each page in the report. To create our title, we used the toolbox to add a Label box object and a Line object to the Page Header. [Figure 8.21]

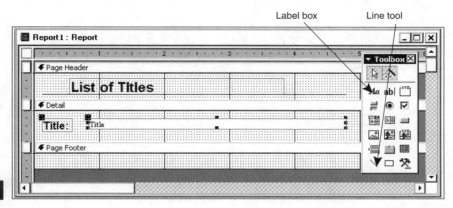

FIGURE 8.21

If you check Print Preview, you see the header at the top of the page, followed by a page of data. The line in the header gives the report a polished appearance and helps the reader identify the report's subject. [Figure 8.22]

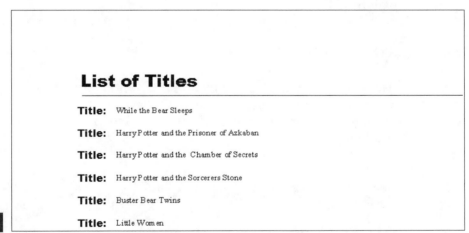

FIGURE 8.22

You can also add color to your reports. The Font/Fore button on the Formatting toolbar changes the color of the text in the selected text box. The Fill/Back button changes the color of the background. [Figure 8.23]

FIGURE 8.23

Be careful not to overdo the use of color. Use it to enhance communication.

You can also add images to your database reports. Click on the Image icon in the toolbox and move your cursor to the place where you want an image. *Access* opens a dialog box you can use to find an image on your hard drive. [Figure 8.24]

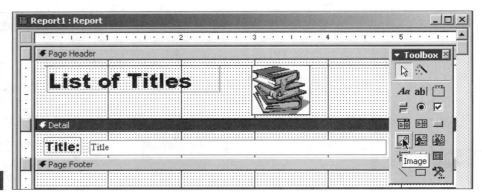

FIGURE 8.24

Be sure you use images carefully. In our example, the image is part of the header and will appear only once on the page. If you put an image in the Detail part of your report, the image will appear with *every* entry in your database.

SOME STANDARD REPORT TYPES

There are many tools available in *Access* for creating reports. In this section we will examine several of these tools. Save any reports you have created. In the database window, click on Reports and then click on New. Select Columnar Report. [Figure 8.25]

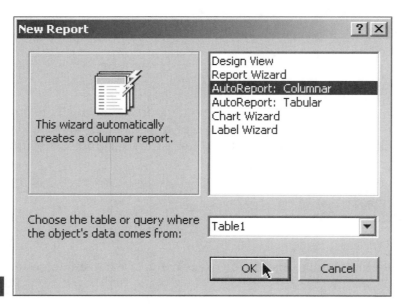

FIGURE 8.25

Access automatically creates a report with each field name and associated data on a separate line. Built-in formatting of text is automatically applied. [Figure 8.26]

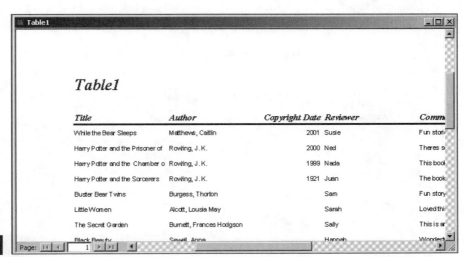

FIGURE 8.26

Go back to the database window and this time create a report with the Tabular option. This time the data appears one record per line and each column of data is automatically headed with the labels at the top. [Figure 8.27]

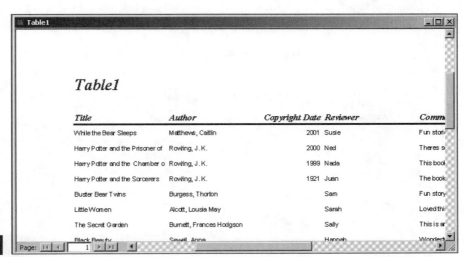

FIGURE 8.27

These two report layouts use all of the fields in your database to create the table. Many times you want a report with fewer fields.

Take the time to examine the two tables you have created using the special built-in options. The formatting choices do not necessarily produce a document formatted to maximize the communication with your reader. You are aware that large amounts of text are much easier to read when they appear in serif type. In addition, the text is not necessarily placed for the most impact. While these options are convenient in many ways, with just a bit of practice you will find that the original approach leaving you in charge of the decisions may in fact be better for creating reports.

You can create similar preset reports with the Report Wizard. You gain the advantage of some control because the Report Wizard immediately asks you to select the fields you want to use. [Figure 8.28]

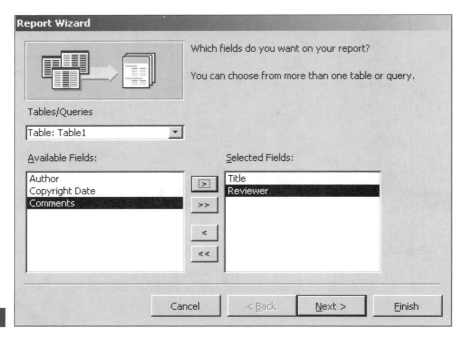

FIGURE 8.28

You can also have your data sorted. [Figure 8.29]

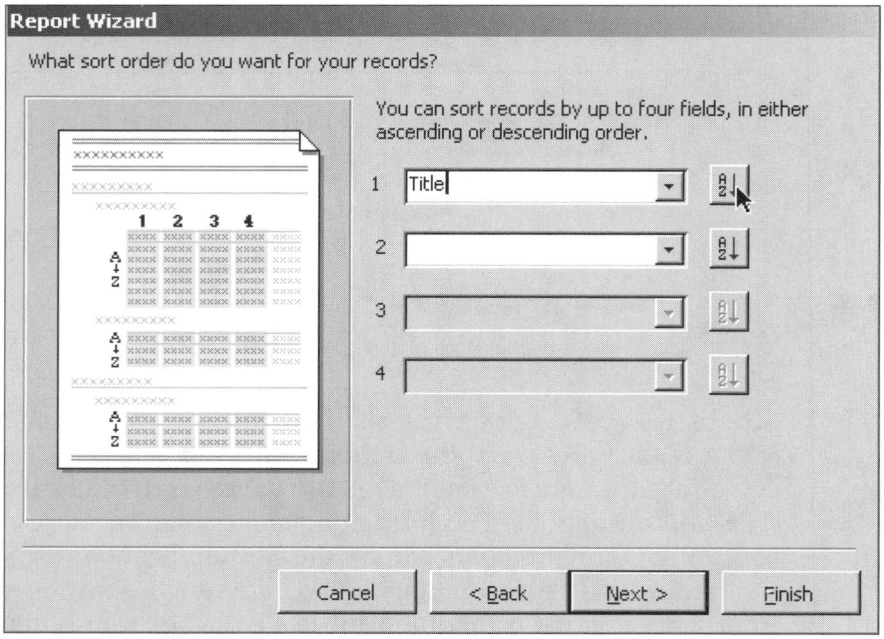

FIGURE 8.29

You can also specify the kind of report you want to use. [Figure 8.30]

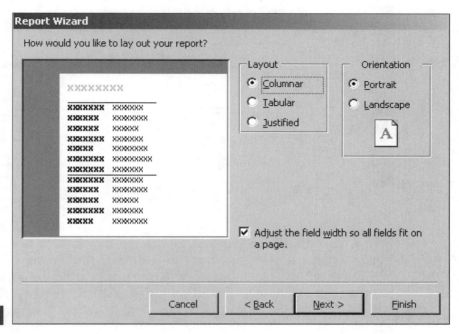

Then you can choose from several styles for your report. [Figure 8.31]

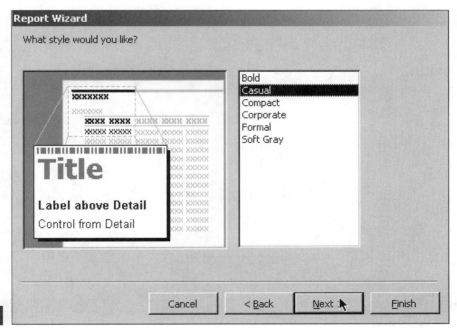

You can also add the title of your choice as well as make other changes in the layout. [Figure 8.32]

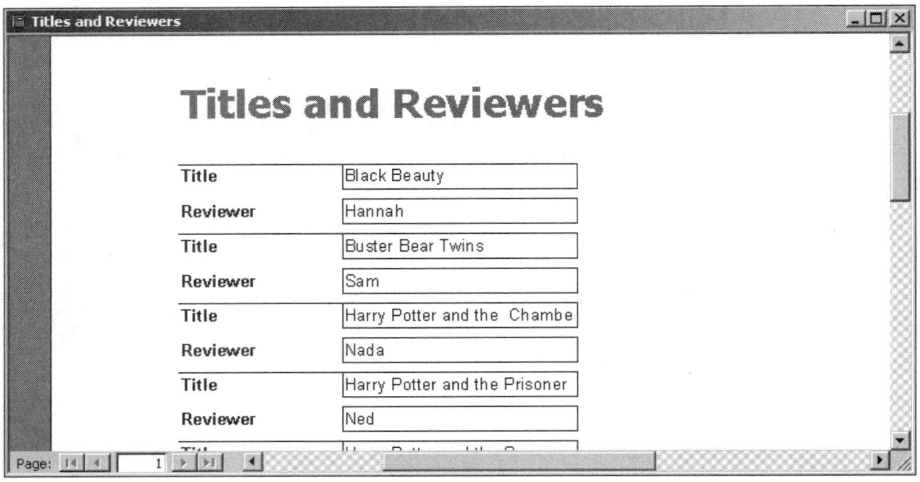

FIGURE 8.32

While you are encouraged to develop the skills to produce your own report layouts, there is one built-in version that offers an extremely useful tool. *Access* offers you a built-in option to produce labels. The Labels Wizard is a tremendous time-saver and simplifies an extremely complex report layout. There are many uses in your classroom for labels. You put labels on storage boxes and drawers, or use them for dividing students into small groups. Once you become comfortable with creating labels, you will find many uses for them.

When you open the Label Wizard, you see a screen in which you choose the kind of labels you want to use. [Figure 8.33]

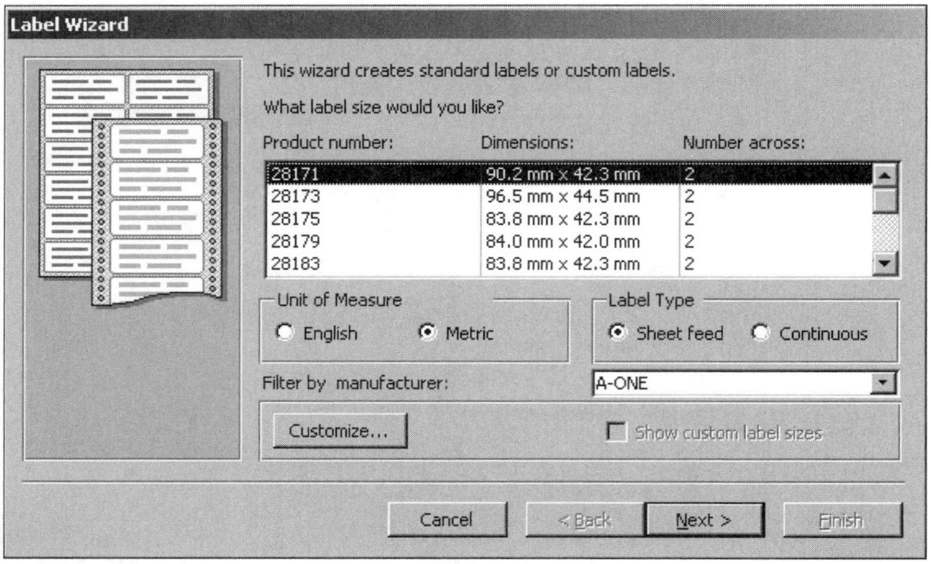

FIGURE 8.33

You can purchase sheets of labels for use with your printer; the numbers on the left refer to the kind of labels you have. Look on the package of labels you plan to use to find a product number that appears in the list. *Access* can then set up your page so that the text will appear at the correct position on the page to match the cuts on the label sheets you have decided to use.

USING MAIL MERGE

You probably find some junk mail each time you check your mailbox. Much of this mail appears to be personalized. It often includes a letter that is addressed specifically to you. Computerized databases are used to create large, apparently personal mailings. *Office* allows you to combine a word processing document with a database to create your own "mass mailings."

The process of combining a database document with a word processing document is called **Mail Merge.** You might, for example, create a letter to parents that tells parents the books that their child has read.

Open *Word*. With the word processing document containing your letter open, select **Mail Merge** from the **Tools** menu. You will see a dialog box that helps you set up the mail merge. First, select the word processing document that you want to use. Notice that you can create a new one or use one that is already available. This means you will want to make a habit of saving your documents if their content is something you may want to use another time. Once you have the *Word* document open, you are ready to choose a database. [Figure 8.34]

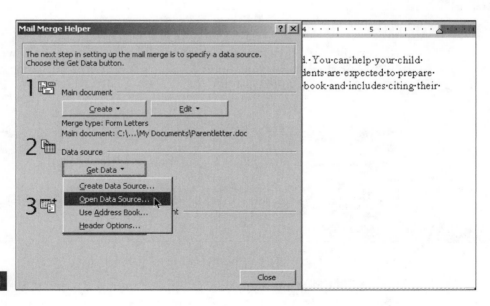

FIGURE 8.34

When you locate the database you want to use, select the Table or Query that you wish to use to merge into your *Word* document. [Figure 8.35]

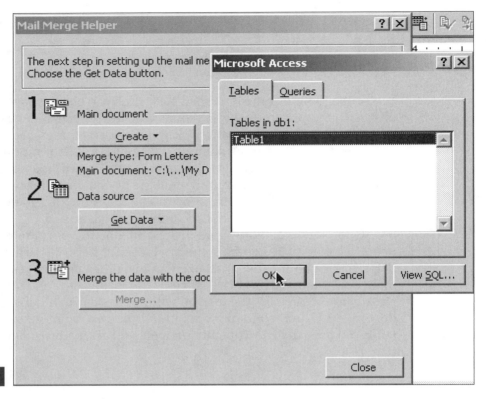

Assuming you are working with a new *Word* document, you will be asked to edit your document. You need to insert the fields you want to use in your *Word* document. [Figure 8.36]

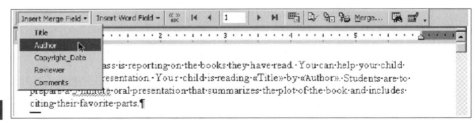

Notice that the field names appear on a drop-down menu. When you choose a field name, that field name appears in your document at the location of the cursor with double angle brackets around it, as shown in the second line of our document.

Now you are ready to create a merged document. *Office* automatically creates one document for each record in your database. [Figure 8.37]

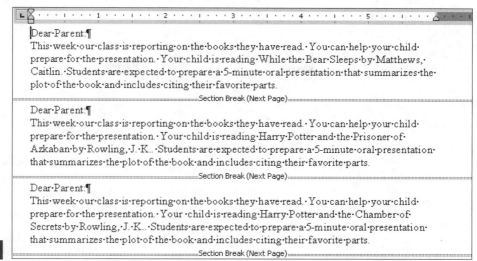

Dear·Parent:¶

This·week·our·class·is·reporting·on·the·books·they·have·read.·You·can·help·your·child· prepare·for·the·presentation.·Your·child·is·reading·While·the·Bear·Sleeps·by·Matthews,· Caitlin.·Students·are·expected·to·prepare·a·5-minute·oral·presentation·that·summarizes·the· plot·of·the·book·and·includes·citing·their·favorite·parts.

══════════Section Break (Next Page)══════════

Dear·Parent:¶

This·week·our·class·is·reporting·on·the·books·they·have·read.·You·can·help·your·child· prepare·for·the·presentation.·Your·child·is·reading·Harry·Potter·and·the·Prisoner·of· Azkaban·by·Rowling,·J.·K..·Students·are·expected·to·prepare·a·5-minute·oral·presentation· that·summarizes·the·plot·of·the·book·and·includes·citing·their·favorite·parts.

══════════Section Break (Next Page)══════════

Dear·Parent:¶

This·week·our·class·is·reporting·on·the·books·they·have·read.·You·can·help·your·child· prepare·for·the·presentation.·Your·child·is·reading·Harry·Potter·and·the·Chamber·of· Secrets·by·Rowling,·J.·K..·Students·are·expected·to·prepare·a·5-minute·oral·presentation· that·summarizes·the·plot·of·the·book·and·includes·citing·their·favorite·parts.

══════════Section Break (Next Page)══════════

FIGURE 8.37

When you have checked to be sure the merge is working correctly, you can save and then print your document.

SUMMARY AND TIPS

Remember that report formats—layouts—are saved with the data file and are quite small compared to the actual data in the database. Thus, adding many reports to your database is not a problem. At all times, you need just the one database file that you have added to your backup files.

If you consider once more the NETS guidelines developed by ISTE, you will realize that understanding and using reports in *Access* gives you great flexibility in communicating your ideas to others. Knowing how to customize a report from within a database to share just the information that is required for each purpose ensures that your message is easily received. Customizing the layout to publish your message rather than relying on the default settings of the software also increases your level of communication.

You may be new to the concept of electronic databases, but the more practice you have, the more skilled you will become. Never underestimate the value of planning what your database is to be used for, how the data will be entered, and the field names to be given to the data entry categories. Careful choices as you begin will pay big dividends as you use the database to complete the tasks you had in mind when you began.

Stop and reflect on your growth and progress with the National Educational Technology Standards. For those of you using *Access,* you have had several new skills added to your long list of achievements. If you are using a Macintosh version of *Office,* you can use a different piece of software to develop these same skills. As you consider how well you can interact with large collections of data, you will realize that you have met new goals on the list of standards, moving you ever closer to being a power computer user.

Sample Document Formatting

This Is a Centered Title

This is body text. Body text makes up the majority of any document and is in a serif typeface. Lorem ipsum dolor sit amet, consectetuer adipiscing elit, sed diam nonummy nibh euismod tincidunt ut laoreet dolore magna aliquam erat volutpat. Ut wisi enim ad minim veniam, quis nostrud exerci tation ullamcorper suscipit lobortis nisl ut aliquip ex ea commodo consequat.

This is paragraph spacing with no indent. Lorem ipsum dolor sit amet, consectetuer adipiscing elit, sed diam nonummy nibh euismod tincidunt ut laoreet dolore magna aliquam erat volutpat. Ut wisi enim ad minim veniam, quis nostrud exerci tation ullamcorper suscipit lobortis nisl ut aliquip ex ea commodo consequat.

This Is a Side Heading

> **This is a block indent.** Used, for example, if you quote a large portion of text from a book you may want to use a block indent. Lorem ipsum dolor sit amet, consectetuer adipiscing elit, sed diam nonummy nibh euismod tincidunt ut laoreet dolore magna aliquam erat volutpat.

Some Uses of Hanging Indent

The following two examples are the most common situations where the hanging-indent format should be used.

This Is a Bulleted List

- Nam liber tempor cum soluta nobis eleifend option congue nihil imperdiet doming id quod mazim placerat facer possim assum.

- Ut wisi enim ad minim veniam, quis nostrud exerci tation ullamcorper suscipit lobortis nisl ut aliquip ex ea commodo consequat.

This Is a Numbered List

1. Duis autem vel eum iriure dolor in hendrerit in vulputate velit esse molestie consequat, vel illum dolore eu feugiat nulla facilisis at vero eros et

2. Lorem ipsum dolor sit amet, consectetuer adipiscing elit, sed diam nonummy nibh euismod tincidunt ut laoreet dolore magna aliquam erat volutpat.

Other Examples of Special Formatting

This is centered text. Ut wisi enim ad minim veniam, quis nostrud exerci tation ullamcorper suscipit lobortis nisl ut aliquip ex ea commodo consequat. Duis autem vel eum iriure dolor in hendrerit in vulputate.

Use Side Heads

Organize your document into sections to help the reader easily follow the contents of your document. Ut wisi enim ad minim veniam, quis nostrud exerci tation ullamcorper suscipit lobortis nisl ut aliquip ex ea commodo consequat. Duis autem vel eum iriure dolor in hendrerit in vulputate. Ut wisi enim ad minim veniam, quis nostrud exerci tation ullamcorper suscipit lobortis nisl ut aliquip ex ea commodo consequat. Duis autem vel eum iriure dolor in hendrerit in vulputate.

INDEX